Colección Támesis
SERIE A: MONOGRAFÍAS, 249

DIAMELA ELTIT
READING THE MOTHER

The Chilean author Diamela Eltit, whose work spans the periods of the Pinochet dictatorship (1973–90) and the Transition to Democracy (1990–), is one of the most innovative and challenging writers in contemporary Latin America. This book focuses on the representation of motherhood in Eltit's first six novels and, through a chronological series of close readings, argues that the maternal body and mother–child relations are crucial for an understanding of the critical challenge posed by Eltit's narrative *oeuvre*, too frequently dismissed as 'hermetic'. An analysis of the novels' structure and language reveals how Eltit seeks to reconfigure the foundations of symbolic structures and so incorporate the mother as a subject. Although the study draws on a feminist psycho-analytic framework to explore Eltit's continuous disarticulation of key concepts that emanate from the West, specifically in relation to the formation of gender and sexuality, the work of the major Chilean cultural theorist Nelly Richard is also used to situate Eltit's work within the political and cultural context of Chile.

MARY GREEN lectures in Hispanic Studies at Swansea University.

MARY GREEN

DIAMELA ELTIT
READING THE MOTHER

TAMESIS

First published 2007 by Tamesis, Woodbridge

ISBN 978–1–85566–155–4

Tamesis is an imprint of Boydell & Brewer Ltd
PO Box 9, Woodbridge, Suffolk IP12 3DF, UK
and of Boydell & Brewer Inc.
668 Mt Hope Avenue, Rochester, NY 14620, USA
website: www.boydellandbrewer.com

A CIP catalogue record for this book is available
from the British Library

This publication is printed on acid-free paper

Typeset by Carnegie Book Production, Lancaster
Printed in Great Britain by Biddles Ltd, King's Lynn

CONTENTS

In memory of my grandmothers,
Elizabeth Murphy and Martha Mary Green;
and my dear friend Jane Thomas

ACKNOWLEDGEMENTS

First and foremost, my profound thanks to Catherine Davies. Her incisive advice, unfailing commitment and encouragement have been invaluable. My thanks also for the advice and guidance offered by Catherine Boyle, John Perivolaris and the readers of this book. Its limitations, however, are my responsibility.

This book could not have been completed without the support of the AHRC and the Universities of Manchester and Stirling. I am also grateful for the efficiency and attention to detail of Ellie Ferguson and all the staff at Tamesis. Both the author and publishers would like to thank the School of Arts, Swansea University, for assistance with the production costs of this volume.

Diamela Eltit has been exceedingly generous in giving of her time and thoughts since we first met during my research trip to Chile in 2000. I would also like to acknowledge the dialogue offered during this trip by Marina Arrate, Soledad Bianchi, Eugenia Brito, Nadia Prado, Nelly Richard, Lotty Rosenfeld and Malú Urriola.

Many thanks are due to George Cartlidge for his unflagging patience and good humour, and to Sharni Holdom and Sharon Bolton for their enduring friendships.

Finally, a big thank you to all my family, but particularly to my parents, for their gracious and generous love and support over many years.

INTRODUCTION

Motherhood in the Chilean Context

This book examines the representation of motherhood in the narrative fiction of the contemporary Chilean author Diamela Eltit (1949–). Through a close reading of Eltit's first six novels, my aim is to show that the terrain of the maternal body and mother–child relations are crucial to an understanding of her narrative *oeuvre*, which passionately scrutinizes and rearticulates symbolic representations of motherhood, sexuality and gender. All of the relationships portrayed in Eltit's novels stem from their intersection with the mother, or the maternal figure, but although motherhood is fundamental to Eltit's narrative, it remains a largely unexplored area of her work to date. I argue that Eltit portrays official discourses of motherhood as the material and symbolic basis for woman's oppression and, as such, her novels urgently demand that attention be drawn to the violence inflicted on the maternal figure by existing masculinist structures, which prevent woman's self-representation and oppressively regulate her desire.[1]

Through the language and structure of her novels, Eltit foregrounds the corpus of signification as emerging from the specificity of the maternal body. She privileges a form of writing that seeks to recuperate the rhythms of the primal relationship to the mother, the libidinal impulses of the maternal body and the pulsations of the maternal unconscious, in this way allowing for the expression of the mother's concealed *jouissance* and a return to a pre-verbal moment of origin that is virtually inaccessible to language and memory. Also noteworthy is the recurring analogy between literary creation and procreation in Eltit's novels, which self-consciously expose the underlying conditions of their narrative production.

A variety of theoretical frameworks exist which seek to challenge dominant representations of motherhood and mother–child relations. In the field of object relations, for example, Nancy Chodorow explores the way in which the desire to mother is reproduced in girls through the structure of the mother–daughter relationship.[2] However, the stress placed by Eltit on the unconscious organization

---

[1] By masculinist I refer to an ideology justifying, promoting or advocating male domination.

[2] Nancy Chodorow, *The Reproduction of Mothering: Psychoanalysis and the Sociology of Gender* (Berkeley: University of California Press, 1978).

of Chilean society; her emphasis on the repression of the maternal body in symbolic representations; and her aim to bring the desire of and for the mother into signifying practice lead me to draw on a predominately psychoanalytic framework throughout this study. The work of Luce Irigaray and Julia Kristeva is aptly suited to my reading of motherhood in Eltit's narrative, since both theorists strive to reconfigure the foundations of symbolic structures to incorporate the mother as a subject, and not just the matrix from which the child develops a subjectivity, and both locate the origins of sexual difference in the child's relation to the mother; these two points are also emphasized by Eltit throughout her *oeuvre*. The challenge posed by Irigaray and, to a lesser extent, Kristeva to the Freudian and Lacanian institutions of psychoanalysis is also of relevance, since Eltit continuously disarticulates key concepts which emanate from Western master narratives, specifically in relation to the formation of gender and social structures.[3] However, before outlining my argument and approach in further detail, it is useful to sketch the trajectory of Eltit's literary and non-fictional work and to place it against the political, literary and cultural context of her homeland, Chile, since the interplay between text and context is crucial to any reading of her novels.

Unlike better-known Chilean authors, such as Isabel Allende and Ariel Dorfman, Eltit remained in Chile during the Pinochet dictatorship (1973–90), and her work spans that period and the Transition to Democracy (from 1990).[4] Eltit published three novels in Chile during the dictatorship: *Lumpérica* (1983); *Por la patria* (1986); and *El cuarto mundo* (1988).[5] During the Transition, she has published another four novels: *Vaca sagrada* (1991); *Los vigilantes* (1994); *Los trabajadores de la muerte* (1998); and *Mano de obra* (2002).[6] The latter was published too late to be included in this study, which closes with a reading of *Los trabajadores de la muerte*. *Mano de obra* (set in a supermarket) tends to privilege an examination of the effects of globalization in the workplace, although the repression of feminine subjectivity continues to be an important aspect of the novel.

In addition to her novels, Eltit has published one short story, 'Consagradas',

---

[3] That Eltit is familiar with the ideas of key Western theorists (not solely Freud and Lacan) is made abundantly evident throughout her published interviews. See, for example, *Conversaciones con Diamela Eltit*, ed. by Leonidas Morales T. (Santiago: Cuarto Propio, 1998), pp. 109–16.

[4] A plebiscite in 1988 signalled the end of the Pinochet dictatorship. The period of the democratic Transition began in March 1990 when Patricio Aylwin was inaugurated as President, but whether the Transition has now come to an end is a point that is continually debated by critics in Chile and beyond. Aylwin assumed the presidency as the leader of an alliance of centre-left political parties, the Concertación de partidos políticos (known as the 'Concertación'), which has been in power since 1990.

[5] *Lumpérica* (Santiago: Ornitorrinco, 1983); *Por la patria* (Santiago: Ornitorrinco, 1986); and *El cuarto mundo* (Santiago: Planeta, 1988). Unless otherwise indicated, I refer to the first edition of Eltit's novels throughout.

[6] *Vaca sagrada* (Buenos Aires: Planeta, 1991); *Los vigilantes* (Santiago: Sudamericana, 1994); *Los trabajadores de la muerte* (Santiago: Seix Barral, 1998); and *Mano de obra* (Santiago: Seix Barral, 2002).

included in a collection of short stories by Chilean women writers which takes as its point of departure the mother–daughter relationship.[7] She has also moved beyond narrative fiction to publish three texts that disrupt traditional literary categories: *El padre mío* (1989), the transcript of the delirious monologue of a male tramp with a prologue by Eltit; the photo essay *El infarto del alma* (1994), published in collaboration with the Chilean photographer Paz Errázuriz, which visually and textually documents love in a psychiatric hospital in rural Chile; and *Puño y letra* (2005), a text that interweaves documentary and fiction, and which focuses on the trial of fellow Chilean Enrique Arancibia Clavel in Buenos Aires in 2000.[8] In collaboration with the visual artist Lotty Rosenfeld, Eltit has also published a chronicle of the suffragist movement in Chile.[9] In addition to these broadly literary texts, Eltit produced her own performance and video art during the dictatorship and collaborated in an artistic collective, further details of which are given in the following section of this chapter. She has written film scripts and continues to collaborate with Rosenfeld on audio-visual projects. Eltit has also published numerous critical essays, a good selection of which can be found in the edited volume *Emergencias* (2000).[10] In 1987, she co-organized the Congreso Internacional de Literatura Femenina Latinoamericana, a cultural landmark in Chile, and from 1990 to 1994, with the re-establishment of democracy, she acted as the Chilean Cultural Attaché in Mexico City.[11] Eltit currently works as a Professor of Spanish-American literature in Santiago and as a visiting professor in numerous universities in the United States. As can be seen from the above, Eltit is a cultural activist in the broadest sense and her work constantly challenges the status quo.

The institutions of motherhood and the family were of huge symbolic importance during the periods of dictatorship and redemocratization in Chile. The Pinochet dictatorship came to power on 11 September 1973 after the brutal overthrow of the Socialist President, Salvador Allende. The military initiated a campaign of terror immediately after the coup, which resulted in the disappearance of those people connected with Allende's Popular Unity government. Death, disappearance, exile and torture ensued from the systemized repression of bodies

[7] 'Consagradas', in *Salidas de madre*, with foreword by Alejandra Rojas (Santiago: Planeta, 1996). Bernadita Llanos is the only critic to have examined Eltit's short story to date, which she refers to in her reading of *El cuarto mundo*. Llanos, 'Pasiones maternales y carnales en la narrativa de Eltit', in *Letras y proclamas: la estética literaria de Diamela Eltit*, ed. by Bernadita Llanos M. (Santiago: Cuarto Propio/Denison University, 2006), pp. 103–41.

[8] *El padre mío* (Santiago: Francisco Zegers, 1989); *El infarto del alma* (Santiago: Francisco Zegers, 1994); and *Puño y letra* (Santiago: Seix Barral, 2005). Arancibia Clavel was charged and found guilty of participating in the murder of the Chilean army general Carlos Prats and his wife in Buenos Aires in 1974.

[9] *Crónica del sufragio femenino en Chile* (Santiago: SERNAM, 1994).

[10] *Emergencias: escritos sobre literatura, arte y política*, ed. with prologue by Leonidas Morales T. (Santiago: Planeta/Ariel, 2000).

[11] The proceedings of the congress were subsequently published as *Escribir en los bordes*, ed. by Carmen Berenguer *et al.* (Santiago: Cuarto Propio, 1990).

sanctioned by the military. Simultaneously, the military mobilized the concept of the patriarchal nuclear family in its programme to reinstate the 'patria', at the expense of the radical political reforms initiated by Allende. The military junta sought to unite the ideological nucleus of the family through the glorification of woman as wife and mother, and thus through the veneration of the essentialist figure of woman as reproducer and nurturer. Indeed, Pinochet appealed directly to women shortly after the coup, declaring woman to be 'la gran defensora y la gran transmisora de los valores espirituales', and emphasizing the importance for the ongoing reconstruction of Chile of the active participation of women in their maternal role: 'La formación de las nuevas generaciones está en las manos de las madres.'[12] Motherhood was lauded in the Catholic-inflected military discourse and woman exalted as the vehicle for the perpetuation of the moral values of the nation, but always within a concept of nation controlled by the father. As Giselle Munizaga explains: 'Las mujeres dan a luz a la patria y la entregan a las fuerzas armadas para que cuiden de ella como un padre protector, procurando su crecimiento fuerte y sano, su grandeza futura.'[13]

'La patria' (the fatherland) is a feminine noun in Spanish, but as Munizaga demonstrates, the concept of nationhood invoked by the military is that of patriarchy, in which the feminine gender is occluded and the maternal role appropriated and controlled by the paternal figure. The position of women, even as mothers, was thus overwritten in Chilean nationalist discourse and the maternal ethic prescribed in Pinochet's discourse, to use Diana Taylor's turn of phrase, was 'merely the projection of the masculinist version of maternity – patriarchy in drag'.[14] The symbolic importance of motherhood in the military's gendered political discourse was, ultimately, subordinated to the demands of the state, since mothers were responsible for the reproduction of authorized concepts of gender, sexuality and nationhood within a patriarchal family structure. Mary Beth Tierney-Tello makes the important point that while the term 'madre patria' is best translated as 'motherland', it 'also carries within it the sense of fatherland (*patria*)', and is thus, I would add, a term that indicates a collusion on the part of mothers in official narratives of nation, a point that does not escape Eltit's attention.[15]

The experience of dictatorship circumscribed the process of subject-formation while also heightening the experience of motherhood, since the connection and separation that mark the relationship to the mother were brutally intensified within those families which were subject to state repression. While women of

---

[12] Augusto Pinochet Ugarte, *Mensaje a la mujer chilena: texto del discurso* (Santiago: Editorial Nacional Gabriela Mistral, 1976), p. 9.

[13] Giselle Munizaga, *El discurso público de Pinochet: un análisis semiológico* (Santiago: CESOC/CENECA, 1988), p. 86.

[14] Diana Taylor, *Disappearing Acts: Spectacles of Gender and Nationalism in Argentina's Dirty War* (Durham and London: Duke University Press, 1997), p. 77.

[15] Mary Beth Tierney-Tello, *Allegories of Transgression and Transformation: Experimental Fiction by Women Writing Under Dictatorship* (New York: State University of New York Press, 1996), p. 114.

the upper and middle classes (generally supportive of the dictatorship) were endowed, as mothers, with monumental cultural and political significations, military abuses forced women of the popular classes (generally opposed to the dictatorship) to confront the destruction of their families. These women, also wives and mothers, who saw male family members killed, imprisoned or disappeared, now had to provide for their families. Women were thus forced either to defend the 'patria' from dissolution through the fulfilment of a self-sacrificing maternal role or assume familial authority when male relatives were no longer present. The latter led to a brusque overhaul of traditional gender roles and, as Eltit has noted, these women subsequently entered the public domain, often for the first time, to campaign against authoritarianism.[16] One of their most enduring strategies was to march through the streets in silence, carrying photographs of their missing relatives, a course of action initiated by the influential movement of the Madres de la Plaza de Mayo in Argentina.

As noted by the Chilean cultural critic Nelly Richard, the public protests of women in Chile transgressed the traditional link between mother and home, and disrupted the order that the military aimed to instil through the imposition of anachronistic social roles.[17] Indeed, the Chilean sociologist Julieta Kirkwood affirms that the analogy drawn between authoritarian and patriarchal violence was an important aspect of the political mobilization of women at this time, which resulted in gender issues being thrust to the fore of women's activism and inserted into the political debates surrounding the run-up to the Transition.[18] Women thus campaigned for the end of the dictatorship with the following feminist slogan: 'Democracia en el país y en la casa'.

Although the feminist movements established during the dictatorship were fundamental to the success of the political campaign for redemocratization, Raquel Olea states that feminist aims were soon curtailed during the Transition: 'el discurso feminista es un deseo político que nunca estuvo en la voluntad de los sectores concertados para instalar la democracia en el país'.[19] Richard explains that the militancy of women's movements dissolved during the Transition primarily because feminist activists were dispersed and institutionalized through their incorporation into governmental bodies such as SERNAM (Servicio Nacional de la Mujer).[20] The critical analysis of gender

---

[16] Mary Green, 'Dialogue with Diamela Eltit', *Feminist Review. Latin America: History, War and Independence*, 79 (2005), 164–71 (p. 167).

[17] Nelly Richard, *Residuos y metáforas: ensayos de crítica cultural sobre el Chile de la Transición* (Santiago: Cuarto Propio, 1998), p. 201. Richard has forged an internationally recognized position as a cutting-edge theorist in Latin America. She is an essayist who has published widely on a variety of subjects, such as postmodernism, gender and memory, as they apply to Latin America and specifically Chile.

[18] Julieta Kirkwood, *Ser política en Chile: los nudos de la sabiduría feminista*, 2nd edn (Santiago: Cuarto Propio, 1990), p. 38.

[19] Raquel Olea, 'La redemocratización; mujer, feminismo y política', *Revista de crítica cultural*, 5 (1992), 30–2 (p. 30).

[20] Nelly Richard, 'La problemática del feminismo en los años de la transición en Chile', <www.globalcult.org.ve/pub/Clacso2/richard.pdf> 227–39 (p. 230).

thus became subordinated to the normalizing process of what many critics, such as Richard, have termed the 'politics of consensus' practised by the Concertación governments.[21] According to Richard, the Concertación aimed to create a shared experience of identification with the construct of the family, hoping that this, in turn, would efface the memory of a violent past and unify an extremely polarized and traumatized populace.[22] She also points to the complicity between the values espoused by the Concertación and the dogma of the Catholic Church, which reveres the maternal figure as the moral pillar of the family. The Church, states Richard, garnered much of its political power during the Transition from its defence of human rights during the dictatorship, and Catholic beliefs have become so influential that they form the basis of what she terms 'una fuerte política normativizadora que censura sexualidades, cuerpos e identidades'.[23] Those bodies and sexualities that fall outside traditional family structures are marginalized, and this, argues Richard, allows a dominant masculine culture to remain intact. I would also add that the insistence on the family as the centrepiece for social unification places an immense imposition on women, many of whom are still campaigning for justice, fighting precisely against the 'whitewashing' of the past that has been deployed by the Concertación governments in order to present Chile as exemplary in the way in which it has reverted to democracy.[24]

Gendered identities in post-dictatorship society have thus been officially constituted by what Richard terms 'la vocación materna y paterna de roles programados por un ideal trascendente de valores universales'.[25] It is no surprise then, she observes, that the polemical eruption of gender into national debate in 1995 should have so profoundly antagonized those (mostly male) senators who, in alliance with the Church, sustain that '"el esencial de la mujer es ser madre"'.[26] The inclusion of the term 'gender' in the documentation which outlined Chile's official position in the Fourth International Women's Conference in Beijing exposed the antagonistic ideological positions previously occluded by the Concertación governments in the interests of political stability. According to Richard, the concept of gender was viewed so suspiciously because of its uncertain (Western) origins and its potential to undermine the 'natural' categories of sexual difference that linked woman to motherhood and the family.[27]

Kemy Oyarzún draws a direct parallel between the attempts by the Chilean

---

[21] Chile reverted to democracy following a series of pacts and negotiations between the Concertación leadership and the outgoing military. The Concertación governments were, from the very start, restricted by the 1980 constitution and by certain economic and judicial binding laws, leading to what critics have referred to as a consensual style of politics.

[22] *Residuos y metáforas*, pp. 200–1.

[23] *Residuos y metáforas*, p. 204.

[24] I borrow the term 'whitewashing' ('el blanqueo') from Tomás Moulian, who examines the important topic of memory in post-dictatorship Chile. See *Chile actual: anatomía de un mito*, 19th edn (Santiago: LOM/Arcis, 1998).

[25] *Residuos y metáforas*, p. 205.

[26] *Residuos y metáforas*, p. 207.

[27] 'La problemática del feminismo', p. 233.

Senate to stifle a discourse that sought to contest traditional categories of gender and the brutal closure of meaning previously enacted by the military. In both instances, she argues, traditional gender roles are championed as the basis of Chilean–ness, and she points to the contradictory position of celebrating the social progress that is supposedly inherent to neo-liberal values while at the same time sustaining archaic gender roles.[28] Indeed, Richard notes that it is precisely to counter the threat to traditional social values which globalization brings in its wake that political parties, especially the right wing, emphasize the importance of the family and woman's role as mother.[29]

Consequently, the cultural power of motherhood in Chilean society has been mobilized for such diverse ends in the recent past that it has resulted in what Richard describes as 'la relación mujer-patria que extremara una polaridad de valores contrarios'.[30] With the arrest of Pinochet in London in 1998, women again took to the streets either in protest at, or in support of, his detention. Supporting his arrest were those women who were still campaigning for justice; those protesting at his detention were predominately from affluent social sectors, and their strident fury has been linked by Richard to the public outrage of the right-wing female militants who took to the streets during the final weeks of the Allende government, banging pots and pans in protest at the lack of staple goods.[31] In both cases, argues Richard, these bourgeois women justified their appropriation of the public sphere in terms of their defence of the nation. Moreover, she states, it is specifically woman in her 'natural' maternal role that has been called upon in political situations of 'crisis' such as these to safeguard national values.[32]

As can be seen from the above, official discourses of motherhood in recent Chilean history have been scripted to uphold and transmit a diverse range of social and symbolic norms and values. They have also served as a powerful means to subject women, and, as such, they are clearly identified by Eltit as lying at the heart of women's social and psychological subordination. Throughout her novels, Eltit probes the charged symbolism of the patriarchal version of the maternal function in Chile to destabilize and dismantle dominant definitions of motherhood, sexuality and gender.[33] As Bernadita Llanos observes, the maternal figure in Eltit's narrative is located 'en posiciones de sujeto que

---

[28] Kemy Oyarzún, 'Estudios de género: saberes, políticas, dominios', *Revista de crítica cultural*, 12 (1996), 24–9 (p. 28). The neo-liberal policies referred to here were introduced in the mid-1970s by a group of young Chilean economists known as the 'Chicago boys' because of their affiliation with the economist Professor Milton Friedman at the University of Chicago.

[29] 'La problemática del feminismo', p. 232.

[30] *Residuos y metáforas*, p. 200.

[31] Nelly Richard, 'Reescrituras, sobreimpresiones: las protestas de mujeres en la calle', *Revista de crítica cultural*, 18 (1999), 17–20 (p. 18).

[32] 'Reescrituras, sobreimpresiones', p. 18.

[33] I use the terms 'maternal function' and, later, 'paternal function' to refer to a symbolic function of maternity and paternity, respectively.

exceden o desmienten la ideología de la maternidad patriarcal'.[34] Eltit's novels highlight aspects of motherhood repressed by official representations, such as maternal desire, in order to explode maternal stereotypes and illustrate that gender roles are neither essential nor natural, but culturally and historically grounded. Motherhood is wrested away from the control of patriarchal institutions that aim to subordinate it to an agenda of violence and bloodshed or of whitewashing the past and propagating consumerism. Eltit draws on the transgressive aspect of motherhood that, paradoxically, emerged among the popular classes during the dictatorship to depict resistance to authoritarianism in gendered terms through the challenge to linguistic, cultural and social norms that the maternal figure can and will defiantly enact. However, I argue that maternal transgression becomes progressively debilitated in her novels, which reflects the dissolution of the militancy of women's activism since 1990.

Eltit's novels consistently posit a concept of motherhood that is not reduced to the functions of reproduction and nurturing, and they thus attempt to open up a space for woman's self-expression beyond her maternal role. However, Eltit also illustrates that this is impossible within the patriarchal family structures continuously imposed on Chilean society, since they confine the mother in a space that allows no room for her self-fulfilment as a woman. The boundary between family and nation is shattered in Eltit's novels so that, like motherhood, the family is shown to be an institution manipulated for political gain.

Throughout her *oeuvre*, Eltit tirelessly explores and rearticulates patterns of desire within the family, portraying traditional family relations as dysfunctional and damaging for men and women alike. In contrast to the continual emphasis placed on the family sphere as the bastion of moral and sexual order in official discourses, the family home is rewritten in her novels as a space of crisis, traversed by sexual and linguistic aberrations. However, it is important to note that the family sphere depicted by Eltit is never that of the abstract, bourgeois family appealed to by the State, but is always shaped by social and economic marginalization.

Eltit foregrounds the complexity and ambiguity inherent in the maternal role, but she avoids idealizing the mother or the symbiotic completeness of mother–child relations *in utero* and during infancy. Threatening alternatives are frequently developed to counter traditional passive images of the maternal role and female sexuality, such as the monstrosity of the mother or the fearsome portrayal of maternal rage, which foreground the mother's feelings of destructiveness towards the child. Importantly, Eltit does not depict the mother as an innocent victim of authoritarian or patriarchal law; the mother is often shown to be complicit in their propagation, a point that becomes progressively apparent in her novels published during the Transition, which offer disturbing and thought-provoking reading.

While challenging the dominant discourses of her country through the reconfiguration of motherhood, Eltit also defies the maternal legacy of her

---

[34] Llanos, in *Letras y proclamas* (see Llanos), p. 112.

literary predecessor, Gabriela Mistral (1889–1957). Mistral embodied the enduring myth of bountiful and benign motherhood in Chile, and her maternal image was subsequently appropriated by the Pinochet dictatorship for its purposes of national reconstruction, manipulating her representation to such an extent that she came to be viewed, as Eltit comments, as 'una especie de útero que ha parido hijos para la patria'.[35] It is, of course, ironic that Mistral never gave birth but still came to be projected, as Sylvia Molloy points out, as 'spiritual mother and teacher of Latin America'.[36] However, Licia Fiol-Matta argues that motherhood was a construction manipulated by the poet and her critics to occlude her lesbianism, and has profoundly influenced the sentimental celebration of the maternal in her work.[37] Conversely, Eltit is a mother whose writing seeks to allow a maternal voice and subjectivity to emerge which will not be appropriated and recodified by hegemonic discourses.

Importantly, however, although the public role adopted by Mistral has greatly influenced cultural representations of motherhood in Chile, another side to Mistral's relationship to the maternal can be found in a number of her poems, in which the representation of the mother and of mother–daughter relations dramatically subverts the maternal stereotypes associated with her public persona. While it is beyond the remit of this book to explore Mistral's poetry in detail, it is worth pointing to her portrayal of the transgressive desire between mother and daughter; the metaphor of the mother tongue; and the cruelty, madness and monstrosity associated with the mother in several of her poems.[38] Such an audacious and disturbing representation of motherhood and mother–daughter relations can also be found in Eltit's novels, suggesting a recuperation on Eltit's part of aspects of the maternal in Mistral's poetry which have been largely overlooked until recently.

From Dictatorship to Democracy: The Literary and Cultural Context

The military coup led to the death, disappearance, imprisonment or exodus of a large number of Chilean artists and intellectuals, but after the initial repression the military appeared to allow the reduced cultural sphere a certain amount of leeway. The major threat was perceived as coming from armed extremist groups, such as the MIR (Movimiento Izquierdo Revolucionario), and the most

---

[35] Juan Andrés Piña, *Conversaciones con la narrativa chilena* (Santiago: Los Andes, 1991), p. 253.

[36] *Women's Writing in Latin America: An Anthology*, ed. by Sara Castro-Klarén, Sylvia Molloy and Beatriz Sarlo (Boulder: Westview Press, 1991), p. 116. Mistral did adopt a son, Juan Miguel Godoy, whom she called Yin-Yin.

[37] Licia Fiol-Matta, *A Queer Mother For the Nation: The State and Gabriela Mistral* (Minneapolis and London: University of Minnesota Press, 2002), p. 15.

[38] See, for example, 'La otra', in *Lagar* (1938). Molloy offers a brief but incisive challenge to established and sentimentalized interpretations of motherhood in Mistral's poetry in her reading of the poems 'La fuga' and 'Electra en la niebla'. Castro-Klarén, Molloy and Sarlo, p. 113.

draconian cultural repression was focused on those creative forms, such as street theatre and folklore, which were associated with the Popular Unity government. So, in the late 1970s clandestine opposition to the military began to re-emerge in the cultural sphere through the promotion of an art of direct political commitment, primarily testimonial literature and protest song. However, a movement of artists, writers and intellectuals also emerged at this time which broke away from the cultural organizations of left-wing parties. Termed the *escena de avanzada* (neo-avant-garde) by its most important theoretician, Nelly Richard, this vanguard movement encompassed a broad spectrum of literary and artistic practices which focused on unconventional acts of political protest.[39]

According to Richard, the practices of the *avanzada* sought to subvert univocal, militaristic discourse through linguistic plurivalency and ambiguity.[40] The *avanzada* also resisted the compartmentalization of their work through the use of various technical registers, an act described by Eltit as 'committing incest', and which is itself a prevalent attribute of her writing.[41] Eltit's first novel, *Lumpérica*, formed part of the production of the *avanzada*, but she was also a founder of one of the leading groups of this artistic and cultural vanguard, collaborating with two visual artists, a poet and a sociologist to form the interdisciplinary group CADA (Colectivo de Acciones de Arte).[42] Between 1979 and 1982 CADA produced a series of artistic actions which, Eltit explains, aimed to intervene directly in the public sphere in order to reoccupy the city, the worst site of military repression.[43]

The relationship of the *avanzada* with established left-wing parties was problematic, since the *avanzada*, Richard explains, rejected popular cultural forms and opposed the thinking that art should respond solely as a dimension of the organized political struggle.[44] Existing outside party structures, and carrying out artistic practices openly rather than clandestinely, the *avanzada* – in their use of multimedia technology, such as the video camera – were viewed with suspicion by left-wing parties, which linked the emphasis of the *avanzada* on the new to the progressive economic discourse of the military and its attempts to eliminate all traces of the past. Richard describes how the left-wing press summarily condemned the work of the *avanzada* as 'elite' and 'self-referential', itself a form of censorship upheld by exiled Chilean artists and

---

[39] Richard most fully explores the counter-institutional art forms elaborated within Chile during the dictatorship in her bilingual text *Margins and Institutions: Art in Chile since 1973*, ed. by Paul Foss and Paul Taylor (Melbourne: Art and Text, 1986).

[40] *Margins and Institutions*, p. 12.

[41] Eugenia Brito, 'Desde la mujer a la androginia', *Pluma y pincel* (1985), 42–5 (p. 43).

[42] The other co-founders and members of CADA were: the sociologist Fernando Balcells; the visual artists Juan Castillo and Lotty Rosenfeld; and the poet Raúl Zurita.

[43] Robert Neustadt, *CADA DIA: la creación de un arte social* (Santiago: Cuarto Propio, 2001), p. 93.

[44] *Margins and Institutions*, p. 14.

writers through their support of a cultural ban on Chile.[45] Similar criticisms were directed towards the post-coup literary production of what Eugenia Brito terms the *nueva escena*, which emerged parallel to the *avanzada* and includes the early narrative fiction of Eltit along with the work of several poets.[46] Brito, however, questions the insistence on the continuation of pre-military cultural forms, arguing that such an insistence merely reduced art to political propaganda.[47]

Direct political opposition was no longer an alternative in a context of repression and censorship, and so the *avanzada* aimed to intervene in the public sphere through their emphasis on the body and their experimentation with what Richard describes as a speech which resides in the fissure or gap; a strategy also emphasized in the literary production of the *nueva escena*, which Brito describes as speaking from 'los huecos, las perforaciones, los hiatos'.[48] While Richard links the uncodified discourse of the *avanzada* to the evasion of censorship, she also asserts that self-censorship was often more restrictive than censorship itself: while the arbitrary nature of censorship affected the mode of communication, self-censorship penetrated the very fabric of meaning.[49] Censorship at this time also operated on a more subtle level. Manuscripts, for example, could be published if not overtly denunciatory, but as books they were prevented from receiving widespread critical attention. Universities and the media were controlled by the military and its supporters, and so emerging literary and artistic productions received limited critical analysis. As Brito states: 'el público [...] carente de medios alternativos, escuelas, revistas, universidades que aportaran criterios de comprensión hacia los nuevos productos artísticos, simplemente los ignoró.'[50] So, while artists and writers still felt vulnerable during the period of dictatorship, Eltit has stated that she began to realize that the military, in her terms, 'no me iban a matar a mí: iban a matar a mi libro'.[51]

Three of the novels studied here were published during the Transition, a period that has posed a new set of problems for writers and artists in Chile. Although the military's culture of fear may have evaporated since 1990, Eltit has commented on the uncomfortable position in which she, as an author, has found herself since the end of the dictatorship. Firstly, because of the manner in which popular subjects, who consistently populate Eltit's narrative, have come to be categorized by the Concertación governments solely as consumers or criminals; and secondly, because of the reduction of the field of culture to what Eltit describes as 'una masividad [...] una cultura del espectáculo [...]

[45] *Margins and Institutions*, p. 21.

[46] Eugenia Brito, *Campos minados: literatura post-golpe en Chile*, 2nd edn (Santiago: Cuarto Propio, 1994).

[47] *Campos minados*, p. 115.

[48] Richard, *Margins and Institutions*, p. 18, pp. 71–2; and Brito, *Campos minados*, p. 14.

[49] *Margins and Institutions*, p. 26, p. 30.

[50] *Campos minados*, p. 115.

[51] Interview with the author, 7 September 2000, Santiago, Chile.

una cultura también desechable que se consume acríticamente'.[52] Richard makes a similar point when she argues that cultural discourse in post-dictatorship society must now confront three factors that stifle debate: 'masividad', 'monumentalidad' and 'pluralismo'.[53] In other words, she refers to the dominance of a mass cultural production that seeks to erase discursive ambiguity and confrontation, reflecting the consensual style of politics and market-orientated economy of the Transition.

Olea argues that the embrace of market values that characterizes the Transition has depoliticized marginal identities and spaces, since the potential for social and political agency previously located in the margins has been appropriated for the purposes of widespread consumerism, which in turn is complicit with official political discourse.[54] Objects of mass consumption, states Olea, become a fetish of mass desire, and any critical analysis is subsumed by what Richard describes as a passive consumption of transparent meanings which eschew any literary complexity.[55] Olea also highlights how 'el tema mujer' has been appropriated as a means to guarantee mass sales of a variety of cultural forms, a point that has not escaped Eltit's attention in relation to the recent boom in women's writing. However, Eltit refuses to criticize directly the work of bestselling Chilean female authors, such as Allende and Marcela Serrano, arguing that 'Lo que buscaría el sistema sería poner a las mujeres en competencia y dejar abierto y protegido el espacio literario para lo masculino.'[56] Eltit does, however, clearly distinguish between their narrative projects and her own. Indeed, Eltit's resistance to the social expectation that writing by women should fit neatly into predetermined genres and themes has led her consistently to reject the concept of women's writing. This, she argues, is merely a ploy by publishing houses to achieve vast sales, and results only in essentializing 'woman' and ghettoizing female authors and their female readers.[57]

The repercussions for a younger generation of female authors in Chile who buck social expectations of what constitutes women's writing are made disturbingly apparent in a press review by Javier Edwards of *Escenarios de guerra* (2000), the first novel by the young Chilean author Andrea Jeftanovic.[58] Jeftanovic, we learn in the first line, 'es otra de las hijas de Diamela Eltit, la

[52] Michael J. Lazzara, *Diamela Eltit: Conversaciones en Princeton*, PLAS Cuadernos, 5 (Program in Latin American Studies, Princeton University, 2002), p. 55, p. 60.

[53] Nelly Richard, *Masculino/femenino: prácticas de la diferencia y cultura democrática* (Santiago: Francisco Zegers, 1993), pp. 13–14.

[54] Raquel Olea, 'La mujer, un tema social de mercado', *Revista de crítica cultural*, 14 (1997), 74–5 (p. 74).

[55] Nelly Richard, 'Feminismo, experiencia y representación', *Revista Iberoamericana*, 62 (1996), 733–44 (p. 743).

[56] Julio Ortega, 'Resistencia y sujeto femenino: entrevista con Diamela Eltit', *La Torre*, 14 (1990), 229–41 (p. 237).

[57] See her comments in Claudia Posadas, 'Un territorio de zozobra: entrevista con Diamela Eltit', <www.ucm.es/info/especulo/numero25/eltit.html> [no page numbers].

[58] Javier Edwards Renard, 'Memorias de la sangre', *El Mercurio*, 16 September 2000, section Revista del Libro, p. 3.

menor de todas, la que ha aprendido de hermanas, primas y tías, porque la familia es grande y sigue creciendo'. Strikingly, Edwards thrusts Eltit into the role of matriarch in a family structure from which male members are absent, fulfilling her maternal role by inculcating in her female 'progeny' a 'maniacal' language that Edwards locates in Jeftanovic's novel. Edwards thus alienates Eltit and her female literary 'brood' from any meaningful literary dialogue outside of their 'delirious' feminine circle. The lack of distinction between the narrative production of Jeftanovic (and, implicitly, of certain other female authors of her generation) and that of Eltit, as well as the emphasis placed on Jeftanovic's 'familial' relation to Eltit, rather than a serious analysis of the literary merit of her novel, flagrantly discredits Jeftanovic's work by denying her an autonomous authorial position. Indeed, Edwards concludes that Eltit's 'daughters' will be able to construct an autonomous authorial stance only through the repression of their 'mother'. He thus disturbingly endorses the formation of a feminine subjectivity which is founded on the absence and silence of the mother and the daughter's identification with the father – a replica of the Oedipal construction of subjectivity which is contested by Eltit throughout her novels, as we shall see.

From Authoritarianism to the Market: Reading and Writing Strategies of Resistance

Eltit has stated that the act of writing during dictatorship constituted what she terms 'Mi resistencia política secreta. Cuando se vive en un entorno que se derrumba, construir un libro puede ser quizás uno de los escasos gestos de sobrevivencia.'[59] The experimental style of Eltit's early novels can also be read as a very specific means to defy military censorship. Indeed, Eltit has commented that 'Cuando mi libertad – no lo digo en el sentido literal, sino en toda su amplitud simbólica – estaba amenazada, pues yo me tomé la libertad de escribir con libertad.'[60] However, the experimentalism of her early novels can also be linked to the effect of self-censorship, induced by fear, which accompanied the writing process at a time during which, as Eltit explains, 'Lo importante empezó a radicar más que en "lo dicho", en "lo no dicho", o bien en las zonas fluctuantes y ambiguas que permitían la censura y la autocensura.'[61] Although Eltit believed her first novel, *Lumpérica*, to be so politically subversive that it would be refused approval for publication, she has also humorously commented that it was probably one of the manuscripts most rapidly dispatched by the censors, presumably because it baffled those who attempted to read it.[62]

Richard has read the rupture of linguistic and syntactical norms in Eltit's early narrative in two ways. Firstly, she links the reader's immediate sense of

---

[59] 'Errante, errática', in *Una poética de literatura menor: la narrativa de Diamela Eltit*, ed. by Juan Carlos Lértora (Santiago: Cuarto Propio, 1993), pp. 17–25 (p. 19).
[60] Eltit, in *Una poética de literatura menor* (see Lértora), p. 18.
[61] Posadas [no page numbers].
[62] Morales, *Conversaciones*, pp. 148–9.

discomfort and disorientation to the crisis of intelligibility in post-coup Chilean society, which from one day to the next lost all sense of cultural, social and political references.[63] Secondly, she argues that the rhetorical and syntactical violence effected by Eltit has as its aim the subversion of dominant military discourse. By unravelling any fixed relationship between sign and signified, and so opening up meaning within the text, Eltit's narrative undermined the military's command over interpretation.[64] Eltit thus employs a deconstructive stance in her writing, in the sense that she dismantles the structures of meaning surrounding the symbols which underpin military legitimacy, symbols such as 'mother' and 'family', so that they are unveiled as an artifice manipulated for political gain. As Donetta Hines observes in relation to *El cuarto mundo*, the text 'deconstructs aesthetically what it proposes to deconstruct politically', a point that I would extend to Eltit's *oeuvre* more generally.[65] In short, Eltit uses fiction to undermine the fictions used to uphold the discourse of political power.

Juan Carlos Lértora states that it is the emphasis on semantics that makes Eltit's novels so singular in post-coup Chilean literature, since he argues that the narrative of this period tends to privilege the level of the signified and stops short of claiming any collaboration from the reader.[66] Eltit's linguistic act of sabotage does, indeed, require active collaboration from the reader, who must grapple with a ramifying polyphony of meaning; the elimination of a linear plot, character identification and unity; the rupture of language; and the inclusion of alliteration, neologisms and non-grammatical constructions. Eltit has made clear her desire for a complicit reader of her texts, stating that 'The part of me that writes is neither comfortable nor resigned and does not want readers who aren't partners in a dialogue, accomplices in a certain disconformity.'[67] The description given of her desired reader closely corresponds to Wolfgang Iser's construct of the 'implied reader', who must actively participate in the construction of meaning through the process of reading by filling in the blanks on the page.[68] The act of reading is therefore supremely important to the success of Eltit's narrative project, and is a point to which I will return.

Eltit has described her first novel, *Lumpérica*, as 'el gesto de una ruptura [...] una novela gestual [...] porque lo que señala es su clausura con la linealidad monolítica de una tradición narrativa'.[69] She has stated that her aim in writing

---

[63] Nelly Richard, 'Tres funciones de escritura: desconstrucción, simulación, hibridación', in *Una poética de literatura menor* (see Lértora), pp. 37–51 (p. 42); and *Margins and Institutions*, p. 17.

[64] Richard, in *Una poética de literatura menor* (see Lértora), p. 38.

[65] Donetta Hines, '"Woman" and Chile: in Transition', *Letras femeninas*, 28 (2002), 60–76 (p. 73).

[66] Juan Carlos Lértora, 'Presentación', in *Una poética de literatura menor*, pp. 11–15 (p. 11).

[67] 'Writing and Resisting', trans. by Alfred MacAdam, *Review: Latin American Literature and Arts*, 49 (1994), 19.

[68] Wolfgang Iser, *The Act of Reading: A Theory of Aesthetic Response* (London: Routledge & Kegan Paul, 1978), p. 34.

[69] Brito, 'Desde la mujer a la androginia', p. 42.

this novel was doubly political: to challenge the literary models institutionalized in Chile, which she viewed as limiting and utilitarian in their use of language, while elucidating her contingent political position. Looking back on the early period of her writing, Eltit has made clear that she did not perceive literature as a means to effect a change in the political structure of her society, but that her pursuit of a more radical form of writing was linked to her firm belief in the political, indeed 'revolutionary', potential inherent in the renovation of literary structures.[70] Eltit's novels may thus be considered political in the sense put forward by Kristeva, whose view of revolutionary poetic language is described by Elizabeth Grosz as follows: 'If the text's literariness consists in its estrangement from conventions [...] its effects are political. They question prevailing representational norms, norms which also regulate the subject's libidinal economy. If literature has the capacity to estrange, shock and force re-evaluations, this cannot but have political effects.'[71] Kristeva champions poetic language because it allows the maternal semiotic to erupt into the symbolic function of language by rupturing traditional structures of grammar and syntax, and she describes its revolutionary potential in terms of its 'acceptance of the symbolic law together with a transgression of the law for the purpose of renovating the law'.[72] In a reflection of Kristeva's position, Eltit emphasizes that the politics of her writing lie in her textual practice and that it is the language in which a novel is written, rather than the message it communicates, which generates a political strategy of protest or resistance. As she states: 'Writing a novel is not innocent: The deployment of linguistic materials evinces a political meaning, by which I mean a politics of writing.'[73]

Kristeva bases her theory of revolutionary language on avant-garde literature, and the radically innovative and challenging quality of Eltit's *oeuvre*, especially her first two novels, would certainly place it in the realm of the Chilean avant-garde, a point that has been acknowledged by Chilean literary critics.[74] Correspondences between Eltit's literary experimentalism and the aesthetic, social and political preoccupations of the historical avant-garde can also be identified. However, as Susan Rubin Suleiman points out, the historical

---

[70] Robert Neustadt, 'Interrogando los signos: conversando con Diamela Eltit', *Inti: revista de literatura hispanoamericana*, 46–7 (1997), 293–305 (p. 304).

[71] Elizabeth Grosz, *Sexual Subversions: Three French Feminists* (St Leonards: Allen & Unwin, 1989), p. 54.

[72] Julia Kristeva, *Revolution in Poetic Language*, trans. by Margaret Waller with introduction by Leon S. Roudiez (New York: Columbia University Press, 1984), p. 101. Briefly, for Kristeva the use of the term 'symbolic' correlates to the definition it acquires in Lacanian psychoanalysis, while the semiotic represents that which is forbidden by paternal law, since it is associated with the child's pre-Oedipal bodily drives, affects and relation to the maternal body.

[73] 'Writing and Resisting', p. 19.

[74] See, for example, Rodrigo Cánovas, *Novela chilena, nuevas generaciones: el abordaje de los huérfanos* (Santiago: Universidad Católica de Chile, 1997), p. 60. Artaud and Joyce are two of the male avant-garde authors central to Kristeva's essays on poetic language and they have also been frequently cited by Eltit as a central influence on her own writing. See, for example, Morales, *Conversaciones*, p. 29.

avant-garde did not question gender categories nor did they provide a voice for women, an important point that distances Eltit's literary production from their work.[75] In more general terms, Rubin Suleiman's critique reflects Jean Franco's assertion that what distinguished the Chilean neo-avant-garde from the traditional left was the former's transgression of established gender categories.[76]

Although I have referred to the experimentalism and innovation of Eltit's early narrative production, I do not intend to suggest that she aims to effect an absolute rupture with the Chilean literary heritage. It is important to note that, rather than being radically experimental, Eltit perceives her writing as reworking existing linguistic structures: 'Yo no me siento "experimentando" con el lenguaje, sino "usando" lo que está ahí: he estado trabajando con algo que está disponible para mí.'[77] Indeed, it is worth bearing in mind, as Philip Swanson notes, that the Latin American 'new' novel in the 1960s was also marked by its formal experimentalism and a rejection of 'the premises and formal structures of conventional realism'.[78] In the Chilean context, Eltit's reclamation of disturbing aspects of the maternal in Mistral's poetry has already been mentioned. I would also point out that the ludic word games and syntactical fragmentation that are so central to Eltit's early novels also characterize the avant-garde poetry of Vicente Huidobro and Pablo Neruda. However, although poetry assumes a privileged position in the Chilean literary canon, it is primarily aspects of the novelistic tradition in Chile that recur in Eltit's *oeuvre*, such as the transgressive and grotesque representations of women that appear in the short stories of Marta Brunet and in José Donoso's *El obsceno pájaro de la noche* (1970).[79] The unstable narrative voice that is so central to Donoso's novel is also to be found in Eltit's novels, and the inversion of gender categories that underpins Donoso's *El lugar sin límites* (1966) can also be located in *Por la patria* and *El cuarto mundo*.[80]

Further similarities with Eltit's literary predecessors could be made here, such

---

[75] Susan Rubin Suleiman, *Subversive Intent: Gender, Politics and the Avant-Garde* (Cambridge, MA: Harvard University Press, 1990), p. xv.

[76] Jean Franco, *Critical Passions: Selected Essays*, ed. with introduction by Mary Louise Pratt and Kathleen Newman (Durham and London: Duke University Press, 1999), p. 117.

[77] Ana María Larraín, 'El trabajo es la vida y mi vida', *El Mercurio*, 21 May 1989, section Revista del Libro, pp. 1–5 (p. 5).

[78] Philip Swanson, *The New Novel in Latin America: Politics and Popular Culture after the Boom* (Manchester: Manchester University Press, 1995), p. 2. Swanson also questions the extent to which the term 'new novel' is applicable to Latin American fiction published during the 1960s. Swanson, pp. 1–18.

[79] See Eltit's own comments on Donoso's 'viejas chillonas' as a source for the army of mothers portrayed in *Por la patria* in Morales, *Conversaciones*, p. 39.

[80] For a more detailed analysis of the correspondences between Eltit's narrative and that of previous generations of Chilean authors, specifically Bombal, Brunet and Donoso, see Rubí Carreño, 'Eltit y su red local/global de citas: rescates del fundo y del supermercado', in *Letras y proclamas* (see Llanos), pp. 143–71. See also the excellent overview of twentieth-century Chilean narrative offered by Leonidas Morales, which culminates in a brief analysis of *Lumpérica*. Leonidas Morales T., *Novela chilena contemporánea: José Donoso y Diamela Eltit* (Santiago: Cuarto Propio, 2004), pp. 17–51.

as the primacy given by Eltit to the unconscious, specifically dreams, and unful-filled female desire, which were also explored by María Luisa Bombal in the 1930s, but my point is that Eltit does acknowledge and radically rework innovative themes and narrative strategies previously incorporated into Chilean literature. Brito, however, has highlighted the rupture between Eltit's narrative and the realist tradition that has characterized Chilean literature, and I would also point to the interdisciplinary trait of Eltit's *oeuvre*, which consistently draws on various genres, as a strategy that most notably marks a departure from the novelistic tradition in Chile.[81] Notably, the Spanish word 'género' refers to both 'gender' and 'genre'. So, while Eltit's novels seek to challenge and unsettle traditional gender categories, they do so from within a narrative structure that resists literary compartmentalization, allowing Eltit to overcome her initial perception of the narrative genre as monolithic and asphyxiating through the renovation of literary models and the construction of a non-traditional narrative model that suits her overall aesthetic project.

It is through the marginal languages, spaces and cultures inscribed in Eltit's novels that we, as readers, are granted an insight into the construction of the hegemonic power formation in Chilean society and the possibility for social and cultural change to be found in marginal structures. Eltit has made reference to the influence of the rich vein of marginality that exists throughout twentieth-century Chilean literature, examples of which include the novels of José Donoso, Carlos Droguett and Manuel Rojas, all of whom approach the theme of marginality by re-enforcing the belligerent energy and paradoxes of indigent communities.[82] Having been brought up in such impoverished neighbourhoods herself, Eltit consistently rejects a romanticized portrayal of marginality, stating that her aim is to restore 'la estética que pertenece y moviliza esos espacios'.[83] In other words, she seeks to confer narrative stature on voices traditionally silenced by official discourses and distorted by narratives of redemption, often by committing what she has referred to as acts of linguistic 'incest' (see p. 10); in other words, by fusing marginal voices with discourses traditionally associated with high culture or religion, such as the baroque or mysticism.[84] For her part, Brito has argued that Eltit's *oeuvre* posits 'un afán de poetizar y politizar el habla de las minorías oprimidas'.[85] In Spivak's terms, then, her purpose is to allow the subaltern to speak.

Marginality is thus an important theme in Eltit's *oeuvre* and she has described

---

[81] Eugenia Brito, 'Utopía y quiebres en la narrativa de Diamela Eltit', in *Letras y proclamas* (see Llanos), pp. 19–32 (p. 19). Eltit has, in interviews, frequently made reference to the multiple sources that have influenced her writing. Such sources come from a range of disciplines; from across the centuries; and from both the Western and Latin American context.

[82] See, for example, Walescka Pino-Ojeda, *Sobre castas y puentes: conversaciones con Elena Poniatowska, Rosario Ferré y Diamela Eltit* (Santiago: Cuarto Propio, 2000), p. 141.

[83] Ortega, 'Resistencia y sujeto femenino', p. 232.

[84] See Eltit's comments in Lazzara, pp. 34–5; and Morales, *Conversaciones*, pp. 34–5.

[85] Brito, in *Letras y proclamas* (see Llanos), p. 23.

her interest in the marginal lumpen as residing in the manner in which they
act as the negative, unconscious reflection of society, so constituting an often
distorted image of what she terms 'the most repressed and elided psychic zones
[of society]'.[86] Tierney-Tello observes that Eltit 'writes what lies on the margins
of culture, not by making this sphere coherent and hence manageable but by
inscribing the periphery in all its heteroglossic chaos'.[87] Eltit's novels are
traversed by the violence, transgression, psychosis and disintegration of the
underbelly of Chilean society, and it is through a consistent focus on the psychic
structures of social marginality that they make visible the bodily tics and
traumas which map unconscious desires and fears, in a challenge to consciousness
as the informing principle of meaning. In her novels, the reader is left alone
to reconstruct events as far as possible through a linguistic confrontation with
a series of abject subjects whom Djelal Kadir describes as banefully
foregrounding 'an obverse alterity whose aberrant existence gives normalcy its
normality'.[88]

Marginality, for Eltit, takes place not only at a material or economic level,
but also at a symbolic level, and it is here that she locates all those who are
marginalized in her society in terms of the feminine. As she explains:

> If, at the symbolic level, the feminine is that which is oppressed by the central
> power, it seems legitimate to extend that category to include all those groups
> which share their condition, since the condition of abandonment – be it at
> the symbolic or material level – is not unique to the social and biological
> body of women.[89]

So, Eltit perceives the feminine as a position defined by its relation to the
centralized power structure, and thus as mobile and provisional. By forging a
link between the condition of the socially dispossessed and woman, Eltit
ruptures the link between sex and gender, but I would argue that she does not
do so uncritically. Eltit always foregrounds the tensions inherent in gender
categories and never fails to address the disturbing repression of woman in
both dominant (masculine) and marginalized (feminine) discourses in Chile.

Let me now return to the act of reading Eltit's novels. Both Idelber Avelar
and Ronald Christ have referred to *Lumpérica* as 'writerly', in the sense given
to this concept by Roland Barthes, who classifies as writerly those texts that
self-consciously violate normal reading conventions to make readers aware that
they are artistic fabrications.[90] I would extend the reference of 'writerly' to all

---

[86] 'Writing and Resisting', p. 19.

[87] Tierney-Tello, p. 96.

[88] Djelal Kadir, *The Other Writing: Postcolonial Essays in Latin America's Writing
Culture* (W. Lafayette: Purdue University Press, 1993), p. 182.

[89] 'On Literary Creation', trans. by Michael Buzan and Guillermo García-Corales, in *The
Novel in the Americas*, ed. by Raymond L. Williams (Niwot: The University Press of
Colorado, 1992), pp. 143–50 (p. 149).

[90] Idelber Avelar, *The Untimely Present: Postdictatorial Latin American Fiction and the
Task of Mourning* (Durham and London: Duke University Press, 1999), p. 173; Ronald

of Eltit's novels, since they clearly signpost their own reflexivity as a comment on the narrative process and as a means to undercut any effect of transparency. The publication of Eltit's third novel, *El cuarto mundo* (1988), has led critics to comment upon the increasing linearity and accessibility of her novels from this point on, a shift possibly influenced by the 1988 plebiscite and the advent of democracy, although it is also worth pointing to Eltit's reflections on how critics' descriptions of her first two novels as 'unintelligible' began to affect her writing from *El cuarto mundo* on.[91] However, while Eltit's novels post-1988 are undoubtedly more readable ('lisible') in linguistic and structural terms, they retain their complexity and audacity on a semantic and thematic level. As such, they continue to inscribe the 'writerly' qualities that encourage readers to collaborate in the production, rather than the consumption, of each novel, in this way actively resisting the commodification of literature endorsed by market forces in contemporary Chile.

Although the Barthesian concept of the writerly text is useful in locating Eltit's narrative, the labels of hermetic, obscure and difficult which are consistently tagged onto her work, even by readers with a wide knowledge of literary and cultural traditions, cannot be fully explained by Barthes's concept. Eltit's novels are fascinating and endlessly provocative, and strive to achieve a creative relationship between reader and text. This is not to deny that her novels are also complex, demanding and disconcerting, and the reader is often rebuffed in his/her attempts to interpret the text fully, a point that has not been warmly welcomed by some readers and critics. The contradictions, silences and absences that puncture Eltit's narrative lead me to draw on the terms 'marginal' or 'minority', in the sense given by Doris Sommer, to address the question of why Eltit poses such a challenging writing.

Sommer draws on a range of texts, mostly from Latin America, to illustrate how their 'minority' or 'marginality' resides in the limits that they pose to the reader's textual intimacy and access. As she warns: 'they can sting readers who feel entitled to know everything as they approach a text [...] Readers who are bent on understanding may neglect another kind of engagement, one that would make respect a reading requirement.'[92] Sommer shifts the purposeful incomprehensibility of these marginal or minority texts away from elitist or esoteric restrictions to argue that our reading engagement should be structured in terms of 'an ethical distance from the object of desire [...] confessed ignorance [...] cautious approaches'.[93] Although Eltit's novels are not included in Sommer's study, the paradigm shift that they demand and the troublesome

---

Christ, 'Extravag(r)ant and Un/erring Spirit', in Diamela Eltit, *E. Luminata*, trans. with afterword by Ronald Christ (Santa Fe: Lumen, 1997), pp. 205–34 (p. 220); and Ronald Barthes, *S/Z: An Essay*, trans. by Richard Miller (New York: Hill & Wang, 1974), pp. 3–11.

[91] See, for example, her comments in Morales, *Conversaciones*, pp. 179–84.

[92] Doris Sommer, *Proceed with Caution, When Engaged with Minority Writing in the Americas* (Cambridge, MA: Harvard University Press, 1999), p. ix.

[93] Sommer, p. 31.

slipperiness towards interpretation that they posit correspond to the withholding of anticipated intimacy that marks the texts examined by Sommer. In an attempt to challenge the reductive labels that have been unhelpfully branded on Eltit's literary production, I would thus suggest, like Sommer, that respect be a reading requirement of her novels, since a level of affect and meaning resides in Eltit's narrative that is simply inaccessible to many readers. Eltit's novels seek to resist mastery by inscribing an epistemological and ethical difference in their very structure that many readers cannot know, and to claim that we do would result in the appropriation and subsumption of alterity.

All of the texts examined by Sommer foreclose a passing sentimental attachment to the otherness that they portray, a point also pertinent to Eltit's novels and which can be read as an important element in her strategy to resist the passive consumption of literature that is so prevalent in market-driven Chile. Indeed, Franco perceives Eltit's narrative as posing a challenge to market forces by putting into writing 'something that is refractory to commodities, to comfortable signs'.[94] Eltit refuses to write novels that provide instant intelligibility and entertainment, and deliberately avoids the conventional and transparent use of language and plot employed in formulaic, bestselling fiction. She has expressed her belief that there are dominant forms of writing that the market expects, legitimates and promotes, which leads to the exclusion of other types of writing. She states that the censorial power of market forces in Chile is such that in many ways it surpasses even military censorship: 'Así que el mercado neo-liberal está más eficaz en silenciar los textos, digamos, marginales que la dictadura en cierta manera.'[95] Interestingly, though, Eltit does not perceive her own writing as silenced by market forces. Indeed, she has made reference to the peripheral position which she occupies in relation to the rampant commercialization of literature in Chile as one that is deliberately assumed on her part: 'Soy la única que se mantiene fuera pudiendo estar dentro, porque hay gente que no puede estar dentro, está fuera, porque no puede aceder.'[96] Deliberately assuming such a position can be read as a means to protect her integrity as an author, since it undoubtedly allows Eltit to maintain a critical distance from the economic and political structures that are continually challenged in her novels.

The Critical Reception

The many accusations of 'difficult', 'hermetic' and 'cryptic' that have been levelled by reviewers in Chile and beyond at Eltit's work have been directly countered by Eltit through her assertion that the problem lies not in her style

---

[94] Franco, p. 205.
[95] Carmen L. Oquendo, 'Yo nunca querría ser una vaca sagrada: entrevista con Diamela Eltit', *Nómada: creación, teoría, crítica*, 2 (1995), 113–17 (p. 116); and Neustadt, 'Interrogando los signos', p. 305.
[96] Pino-Ojeda, p. 144.

of writing, but in the domestication of certain modes of reading dictated by powerful, international publishing houses, especially since redemocratization.[97] Agata Gligo has foregrounded the gendered nature of the resistance to Eltit's literary project in Chile by suggesting that Eltit's innovative practice would perhaps have received a wider acceptance if it had come from 'alguna "mano masculina"', a point which reflects Eleonora Cróquer Pedrón's assessment that such criticisms 'parecen censurar que una mujer *no escriba como debería hacerlo una mujer*'.[98] Eltit herself has commented that the reiterated refrain of 'no se entiende', which could be perceived as complimentary when applied to the work of male authors, in her case has become simply a determinant and discriminatory slogan, and the frequent descriptions of her, as an author, as 'muy intelectual', far from being flattering, have served only to alienate many potential readers from her work.[99]

Nevertheless, there is a growing body of critical readings of Eltit's work which indicate the richness of her novels and the manifold interpretations that they invite.[100] Surprisingly, however, only two book-length studies have been published to date. Sylvia Tafra examines rites of passage and sacrifice in Eltit's first three novels, linking them to the search for identity and the foundation of a new social and sexual order, and Gisela Norat includes Eltit's novelistic and non-fictional body of work in her collection of essays, which takes as its starting point the theme of marginalities.[101] Three edited collections of critical readings have also been published, as well as a number of articles and book chapters which examine Eltit's narrative production.[102] The themes analysed in the critical readings referred to here are multiple, and include the relation between language, gender and power; aesthetics and neo-liberalism; performance and deconstruction; and the representation of the female body. All are framed

[97] Eltit, in *The Novel in the Americas* (see Williams), p. 145.

[98] Agata Gligo in interview with Guillermo Blanco, 'Las mujeres se interrogan', *Hoy*, 10–16 August 1987, pp. 49–50 (p. 49); and Eleonora Cróquer Pedrón, *El gesto de Antígona o la escritura como responsabilidad (Clarice Lispector, Diamela Eltit y Carmen Boullosa)* (Santiago: Cuarto Propio, 2000), p. 23. Emphasis hers.

[99] Eltit, in *Una poética de literatura menor* (see Lértora), pp. 23–4.

[100] Gwen Kirkpatrick offers a good overview of critical readings of Eltit's literary production. See 'El "hambre de ciudad" de Diamela Eltit: forjando un lenguaje del sur', in *Letras y proclamas* (see Llanos), pp. 33–68 (pp. 46–65).

[101] Publication details are as follows: Sylvia Tafra, *Diamela Eltit: el rito de pasaje como estrategia textual* (Santiago: RIL, 1998); and Gisela Norat, *Marginalities: Diamela Eltit and the Subversion of Mainstream Literature in Chile* (Newark: University of Delaware Press, 2002).

[102] Details of the edited collections are: *Una poética de literatura menor: la narrativa de Diamela Eltit*, ed. by Lértora; *Creación y resistencia: la narrativa de Diamela Eltit, 1983–1998*, Serie Monográfica *Nomadías*, ed. by María Inés Lagos (Santiago: Universidad de Chile/Cuarto Propio, 2000); and *Letras y proclamas: la estética literaria de Diamela Eltit*, ed. by Llanos. Several critical readings of Eltit's narrative, as well as an article by Eltit herself, are also included in *Revista Casa de las Américas*, 230 (2003), 108–41. These readings formed part of the proceedings of a symposium organized by the Casa de las Américas in La Habana in 2002 to mark the 'Semana de Autora' dedicated to Eltit.

by a variety of theoretical approaches. Their thematic and theoretical diversity leads me to include a brief overview at the beginning of each chapter of this book, prior to my own reading of Eltit's novels.

Brito and Richard, who have consistently engaged with Eltit's literary production, are two critics to have foregrounded the mother as the central figure around which Eltit's writing turns. Brito locates the emphasis on the maternal within the literary practice of the *nueva escena* more generally and foregrounds their aim of recuperating an elided zone that is based on 'un duelo de la tierra-madre: la matriz generadora del lenguaje, violada, tomada, reducida a la calidad de fantasma'.[103] For her part, Richard states that 'D. Eltit sabe mejor que nadie (lo ha practicado en sus novelas) que la escritura surge de un duelo amoroso – de una lucha de amor y muerte – con el cuerpo de la madre.'[104] Richard does not aim to explore in detail the relation between the maternal body and language in Eltit's *oeuvre*, but she has incisively pointed to the importance of the following points, which are addressed in this book: the mother–child separation as the origin of language (Chapters 2, 3 and 5); the unquenched orality that marks the child's separation from the mother (Chapter 2); the eroticized return to the mother through the repressed semiotic element of language (Chapters 1, 2 and 3); and the link between the maternal body and the materiality and corporality of language (Chapters 1, 2, 3 and 5). The following themes, not referred to by Richard, are also prominent in Eltit's narrative and are examined here: the relationships among women as mothers and daughters (Chapters 2, 3 and 4); aspects of specifically female experience, such as menstruation and childbirth (Chapters 3, 4 and 6); explorations of maternal desire (Chapters 1, 2, 3 and 6); the mother–son relationship (Chapters 3, 5 and 6); and the portrayal of motherhood as a source of cultural as well as biological creativity (Chapters 1, 2 and 3). Although Richard does not seek to offer a theoretical discourse of maternity, her work is nonetheless extremely important for locating Eltit's narrative within the specific cultural and political context of contemporary Chile and will be referred to throughout this study.

Franco describes Richard's work on gender as stemming from the notion of the feminine in 'French feminism' [sic] as the site of marginality and dispersion.[105] This, argues Franco, allows Richard to make the peripheral and the feminine 'the privileged site of insubordination'.[106] The work of Irigaray

---

[103] *Campos minados*, p. 11. Julio Ortega also points to the centrality of the repression of the mother and the mother–child relationship in Eltit's novels. See 'Diamela Eltit y el imaginario de la virtualidad', in *Una poética de literatura menor* (see Lértora), pp. 53–81 (p. 71).

[104] Richard, 'Síntoma y arabescos', *Revista de crítica cultural*, 10 (1995), 59–60 (p. 60).

[105] Franco, p. 118. 'French Feminism' is a label that has been tagged onto the work of Irigaray and Kristeva, along with that of Hélène Cixous. Although these critics reside in France and write in French, none of them is actually French. In turn, Richard is referred to, and positions herself, as a Chilean cultural critic, but she is originally French. She has, however, lived in Chile since 1970 and her work is written in Spanish.

[106] Franco, p. 118.

and Kristeva has clearly influenced Richard's analysis of gender in the Chilean context, a point acknowledged by Richard through her commendation of the challenge that their work poses to phallocentric, psychoanalytic theory:

> la primera de reformulación de un inconsciente sexualmente *diferenciado* en su estructura por repolarización materna del deseo (es la propuesta de Luce Irigaray), y la segunda teorización de un sujeto cuya dinámica transemiótica logre pulverizar las fronteras de una subjetividad dividida entre habla y pulsiones (es la propuesta de Julia Kristeva).[107]

Although Richard initially concurs with Irigaray's assertion that sexual difference is fundamental to any analysis of identity, in her later work she clearly becomes irritated by the insistence of local feminist criticism on the importance of 'experience' and 'corporality'.[108] She now begins to foreground the need to move beyond sexual difference in any analysis of gender, emphasizing the potential of perceiving of the feminine as a series of plural and mobile subject positions. She also dismisses Irigaray (and Cixous) for their emphasis on the link between feminine writing and woman's corporeal experience, and for their defence of an autonomous culture of women, positing instead the (Kristevan) construction of 'una subjetividad en proceso y movimiento'; a subjectivity that is heterogeneous and traversed by internal contradictions.[109]

The ongoing dialogue between Eltit and Richard, who have worked closely alongside each other for over thirty years, is traced throughout this study. Both can be seen to correspond closely in their conception of the feminine as the site of resistance and insubordination, and as a shifting position rather than a fixed identity, which emerges from a play of signs and facilitates the analysis of signifying and discursive practices. They also overlap in perceiving a heterogeneous, transgressive feminine writing that emerges from the interplay of the Kristevan semiotic and symbolic functions of language.[110] However, while Eltit and Richard both observe the usefulness of Kristeva's theory of discharging a linguistic substratum of semiotic drives to subvert hegemonic masculine discourse, they can also be seen to challenge her assertion that woman's recuperation of the repressed maternal semiotic element of language mostly results in psychosis or even death.[111] Indeed, Richard argues that women are better predisposed than men to unleash the transgressive force of the semiotic, and she points to Eltit's narrative to exemplify the explosive rupture of language, subjectivity and representation that make possible the textual construction of what she terms 'lo femenino como diferencia y *diferenciación* activas: [...] la

---

[107] *La estratificación de los márgenes: sobre arte, cultura y política/s* (Santiago: Francisco Zegers, 1989), p. 64; emphasis hers.

[108] 'Feminismo, experiencia y representación', p. 738.

[109] 'Feminismo, experiencia y representación', p. 742.

[110] See Kristeva, *Revolution in Poetic Language*, pp. 68–71.

[111] Julia Kristeva, 'Talking about *Polylogue*', in *Feminist Literary Theory: A Reader*, ed. by Mary Eagleton, 2nd edn (Oxford: Blackwell, 1996), pp. 301–3 (p. 303).

posición crítica que consiste en interrogar los mecanismos de constitución del sentido y de la identidad.'[112]

Nevertheless, it is important to note that there are differences as well as similarities between Eltit and Richard, resulting in a productive tension between their work. While Richard progressively moves away from woman's corporeal experience, Eltit never loses sight of the specificity of the female body. The continual emphasis placed by her novels on the terrain of the body has been recognized by many critics, such as Olea, who argues that the locus of the female body operates in Eltit's narrative 'como espacio de contención, de depósito de experiencias: sexuales, sociales y culturales'.[113] As stated, my focus throughout is specifically on the maternal body, which is consistently foregrounded by Eltit to expose and disarticulate the symbolic conflation of woman and mother that violently debases women in Chilean society. Eltit's emphasis on the maternal makes evident her acknowledgement that the hierarchy of sexual difference is a reality in her society and must be addressed, a stance which distances her from Richard and moves her closer to the position taken by Irigaray in the Western context.

A chronological approach is taken to Eltit's novels in order to trace the development and transformations of the maternal figure and the child's relation to the mother, as well as the recurring maternal images and themes. In the next chapter, the relation between language, vision and the maternal body in *Lumpérica* is examined. My reading of *Por la patria* (Chapter 2) hinges on the deconstruction of the Oedipal narrative and the primacy granted to the mother–daughter bond as a means to contest authoritarian repression. In Chapter 3, the construction of gender and the representation of motherhood are examined in *El cuarto mundo*. A reading of *Vaca sagrada* in terms of Kristeva's theory of abjection is offered in Chapter 4, but in Chapter 5, I draw predominately on the poststructuralist work of Michel Foucault, specifically in relation to power and surveillance, to examine *Los vigilantes*. In Chapter 6, my reading focuses on the challenge posed by Eltit to the Freudian myth of origins in the last of her novels to be included here, *Los trabajadores de la muerte*.

My aim throughout is not to subordinate Eltit's narrative to any one theory, nor to privilege the theoretical text over the literary text, but rather to draw on the key theoretical positions outlined above to examine the complex structures of analysis that are formulated by Eltit in her novels. It is important to note that Eltit always responds to the lived social and political experiences of Chile, and as such her novels offer a fertile and exemplary path for understanding contemporary Chilean cultural identities and literary production.

---

[112] 'Feminismo, experiencia y representación', p. 743; emphasis hers.
[113] Raquel Olea, 'El cuerpo-mujer. Un recorte de lectura en la narrativa de Diamela Eltit', in *Una poética de literatura menor* (see Lértora), pp. 83–95 (p. 86).

1

Language, Vision and Feminine Subjectivity in *Lumpérica*

The Visual Arts and Writing

Lumpérica was originally published in 1983 by the small Chilean publishing house Ornitorrinco.[1] The period during which Eltit wrote *Lumpérica* (1976–83) marked the time of her involvement with CADA (Colectivo de Acciones de Arte), and it is this novel which is most influenced by Eltit's artistic and political activism, both in CADA and through her concurrent elaboration of individual video-performances. Indeed, Richard has described *Lumpérica* as more of a performance than a novel because of its appropriation of other, non-literary techniques, a point also made by Robert Neustadt.[2]

In an interview given in 1985, Eltit states that she does not compartmentalize her visual and literary practices, which illustrates that her creative writing at this time responded to and extended the concerns posed in her performative work.[3] The front cover of the first edition of the novel portrays a video-still of the projection of Eltit's face onto walls opposite a brothel, in and around which she carried out her individual performance, 'Maipú', in 1983.[4] Part of this performance consisted of reading an unpublished excerpt of *Lumpérica* inside the brothel, the aim of which, Eltit has stated, was momentarily to replace the daily flow of sexual exchange for one of cultural exchange.[5] The audience for this reading consisted of the resident prostitutes; the men, women and children of the impoverished neighbourhood; and a small group of Eltit's artistic collaborators. *Lumpérica*, viewed by critics as the most hermetic of Eltit's novels,

---

[1] The second (1991) and third (1998) editions of the novel were published in Chile by Seix Barral. The novel has been translated into English and French.

[2] Richard, in *Una poética de literatura menor* (see Lértora), p. 44; and Robert Neustadt, *(Con)Fusing Signs and Postmodern Positions. Spanish American Performance, Experimental Writing and the Critique of Political Confusion* (New York and London: Garland, 1999), p. xix, p. 32. This tendency towards performance in Eltit's *oeuvre* is perceived more broadly by Mabel Moraña in 'Diamela Eltit: el espejo roto', *Inti: revista de literatura hispano-americana*, 55–6 (2002), 161–4 (p. 164).

[3] Brito, 'Desde la mujer a la androginia', p. 43.

[4] For further details of 'Maipú', see Richard, *Margins and Institutions*, pp. 65–73.

[5] Piña, p. 234.

was thus read to a mainly uneducated yet extremely respectful audience, whose reaction Eltit has described as one of 'astonishment'.[6]

Reading *Lumpérica* in a brothel, thus breaking all formal, literary protocols, can be seen as an instance of Eltit's questioning of the 'domestication' of the novel in Chile. Yet this reading also constituted a personal quest for Eltit, as she has commented: 'yo necesitaba otra experiencia en vivo [...] con el libro [...] necesitaba acercarme a ciertas cosas que eran marginal, al cuerpo "otro" [...] ese "otro" que yo buscaba conformar literariamente [...] después lo saldé teóricamente.'[7] Perhaps the most striking example of Eltit's aim to approach the material reality of the corpus of the marginal 'other' that forms the fulcrum of her literary work is her video-performance 'El beso', in which she kisses a nonplussed and filthy male vagrant in an attempt to deconstruct the Hollywood kiss.[8]

Eltit has referred to the influence of Severo Sarduy's *Cobra* (1972) on the writing of her novel, commenting that what she perceived as its 'audacity' gave her the courage to bring to fruition her own audacious literary project.[9] Surprisingly, though, Eltit has stated that it was only through a retrospective reading of the novel that she became aware of its 'extravagant' nature: 'Ni siquiera sospeché que *Lumpérica* era una novela extravagante [...] Yo pensaba que era un hacer literario normal, totalmente normal, y me di cuenta que era anómalo [...] y que esta ambigüedad que yo trabajaba producía algunos problemas [...] el punto de lugar, género, cambio de escritura, cambio de narrador.'[10] Eltit has also commented on her aversion to the act of naming at the time of writing the novel, stating that she considered as reductive the use of anything but an oblique name for the protagonist, L.Iluminada.[11] Since the novel was intended as a metaphor for Chile under dictatorship, endowing the character with a commonplace name would, in Eltit's view, have blurred this metaphor. The originality of the protagonist's name also reflects the innovative narrative context in which she appears and, like the title of the novel, is a neologism. Eltit has explained that through the title, her aim was to create an immediate link to the lumpen portrayed in the novel.[12] Several critics have read the title as a pun on the words 'América' and 'lumpen', and I would also add that the term 'perica' is used in Chile to refer to young girls, usually of the lower classes, and carries with it sexual connotations.

Lumpérica is, essentially, a novel that stages a minimal scenario, revolving around a claustrophobic thematic structure that hinges on the three unities of Greek tragedy: one character (L.Iluminada), one space (a public plaza) and a

---

[6] Author's interview with Eltit, 7 September 2000, Santiago.

[7] Author's interview with Eltit, 7 September 2000, Santiago.

[8] Details of this performance were given in an interview with the author, 7 September 2000, Santiago.

[9] Morales, *Conversaciones*, p. 37.

[10] Morales, *Conversaciones*, pp. 79–80.

[11] Morales, *Conversaciones*, pp. 56–7.

[12] Morales, *Conversaciones*, pp. 57–8, pp. 72–3.

defined length of time (one night). The most immediate impact of the novel lies in its radically experimental character. There is no plot in the traditional sense, only the reinterpretation of the same scene from different perspectives and related in diverse narrative styles. These include the rather functional commentary offered in parts of the first chapter; the transcription of an interrogation scene in the second and seventh chapters; and the intense imagery and rhythm of the third chapter and parts of the fourth and sixth chapters. Visual, cinematographic and autobiographical codes are also inscribed in the novel, which tirelessly pushes at the boundaries of the novelistic genre to produce explosive theatricality, lyricism and a raw, emotional energy that maps the darkest internal and physical landscapes of violation, power, and individual and communal collapse.

The novel consists of ten chapters, each clearly marked numerically and some carrying titles. The first chapter sets up the plaza as a stage, a literary and visual artifice that is occupied centrally by L.Iluminada under the spotlight of 'el luminoso', a flashing neon advertising hoarding elevated on the top of a building. L.Iluminada assumes her place at the highly symbolic, yet empty, centre of the plaza in which would normally be found a statue commemorating some founding father of the nation. The scene that is repeatedly exposed to view is the nightly congregation of L.Iluminada and the 'pálidos', the colourless, androgynous, homeless beings who restlessly roam the city during the day and take up their positions in the plaza at night. The novel is traversed by metalepsis, and the lack of any explanatory narrative or authorial voice to guide the disorientated reader through the terrifying, fragmented images of a society blown apart by violence forces him/her to confront the series of images of variable clarity alone. The time frame condenses: a scene that began in the early evening jumps abruptly to dawn, and the gaps, in both temporal and textual terms, produce more questions that must be addressed. It is thus the reader who is responsible for making sense of this writerly novel – not an easy task when its structure and language almost buckle under the weight of the textual and physical violence unleashed.

In spite of the very constricted cultural sphere, the publication of *Lumpérica* in 1983 did lead to a handful of reviews in the Chilean press, most of which were cautiously positive, if rather unsure of what the novel was actually about. Ana María Foxley states that *Lumpérica* and *Por la patria* were, perhaps, more talked about than actually read within Chile when first published, and Brito has described the reaction to *Lumpérica* as dual: fascination on the one hand and horror on the other, expressed through descriptions which relate to the novel's 'oscuridad' and 'cripticismo'.[13] The review of *Lumpérica* by the highly

---

[13] Ana María Foxley, 'Diamela Eltit: me interesa todo aquello que esté a contrapelo del poder', *La Época*, 20 November 1988, section Literatura y Libros, pp. 4–5 (p. 4); and Brito, *Campos minados*, p. 115. The horror and fascination provoked by the novel, as described by Brito, is strikingly similar to Kristeva's description of the subject's reaction to the abject, placing the novel in the realm of abject literature, a point that will be discussed again in my reading of *Vaca sagrada* (see Chapter 4).

influential Ignacio Valente appeared in the right-wing and morally conservative daily newspaper *El Mercurio*, and sets in place the irritated and baffled tone that continues to underlie press reviews of Eltit's work in Chile and stamps the labels of 'cryptic' and 'hermetic' onto her literary production.[14]

Critical readings of the novel to date indicate that many of the central themes of Eltit's narrative production have their origins in *Lumpérica*. Several critics place the novel within the realm of the postmodern, because of its metaliterary comments and textual self-awareness, while the possibilities offered for the (self-) representation of fragmented subjects are sketched by Eva Klein.[15] The fundamental theme of power relations as experienced from a position of marginality, which recurs throughout Eltit's *oeuvre*, is analysed by Guillermo García Corales, and Djelal Kadir eloquently assesses the connection forged by Eltit between literary vocation and social commitment.[16]

Kadir's reading can be usefully explored alongside those of Idelber Avelar and Kate Jenckes. While Avelar argues that the novel, albeit fleetingly, portrays a utopian affirmation through prosopopoeic communion, Jenckes challenges this argument and assesses how the figuration of community is represented 'precisely in and through writing itself'.[17] In turn, the crisis of representation and community are brought together by Julio Ortega, who argues that in the novel 'se busca poner en crisis la misma representación, radicalizar el emblema de la plaza, vaciada de su razón comunitaria'.[18]

Not surprisingly, it is the centrality of the female body which has formed the focus of most readings of the novel to date, such as that of Sara Castro-Klarén, who lucidly analyses the link between the female body and language.[19] For her part, María Inés Lagos offers a useful theoretical-cultural framework from which to read the fragmented and marginal female body in the novel, and Raquel Olea provides a more general overview of the social-political implications of the sexual and textual bodies foregrounded throughout Eltit's narrative.[20] Brito also examines the significance of the female protagonist, but

[14] Ignacio Valente, 'Diamela Eltit: una novela experimental', *El Mercurio*, 25 March 1984, section E, p. 3.

[15] For an analysis of the postmodern elements of the novel, see, for example, Neustadt, *(Con)Fusing Signs*, pp. 25–76; Julio Ortega, 'Diamela Eltit y el imaginario de la virtualidad', in *Una poética de literatura menor* (see Lértora), pp. 53–81; and Raymond Leslie Williams, 'Women Writing in the Americas: New Projects of the 1980s', in *The Novel in the Americas* (see Williams), pp. 119–31. See also Eva Klein, 'La (auto) representación en ruinas: *Lumpérica*, de Diamela Eltit', *Revista Casa de las Américas*, 230 (2003), 130–5.

[16] Guillermo García Corales, 'La desconstrucción del poder en *Lumpérica*', in *Una poética de literatura menor* (see Lértora), pp. 111–25; and Kadir, pp. 179–92.

[17] Avelar, pp. 164–78; and Kate Jenckes, 'The Work of Literature and the Unworking of Community or Writing in Eltit's *Lumpérica*', *The New Centennial Review*, 3:1 (2003), 67–80 (p. 68).

[18] Ortega, in *Una poética de literatura menor* (see Lértora), p. 58.

[19] Sara Castro-Klarén, 'Escritura y cuerpo en *Lumpérica*', in *Una poética de literatura menor* (see Lértora), pp. 97–110.

[20] María Inés Lagos, 'Reflexiones sobre la representación del sujeto en dos textos de Diamela Eltit: *Lumpérica* y *El cuarto mundo*', in *Una poética de literatura menor* (see

her aim is to illustrate how the novel seeks to recover the most elided zones of Chilean culture: 'lo marginal, lo indígena, lo femenino'.[21]

The aim of my reading is to examine the tension between prevailing representational norms and textual strategies of subjectivity in the novel, in order to illustrate how the semiotic terrain of the maternal body is visually and textually represented as the repressed foundation of social and linguistic structures. The third section of this chapter is framed by Kristeva's theory of the heterogeneous nature of language and seeks to explore how the novel insistently foregrounds the linguistic process that constitutes signification. The way in which the novel recuperates the occluded semiotic foundation of symbolic processes is examined in order to illustrate how the dynamic interaction of the symbolic and the semiotic functions of language are represented and put into practice on the page of the text. Irigaray's double-edged critique of the specular relationship and the symbolic occlusion of the maternal body frames the fourth section of this chapter, which traces the emergence and subsequent subjugation of a new representation of feminine subjectivity. In the next section, my aim is to discuss briefly the use of the field of light and vision in the novel, an important narrative strategy employed by Eltit which impacts on the subsequent readings offered here.[22]

The Visual Realm

Eltit has stated that the image which formed the backdrop to the writing of *Lumpérica* was that of a phantasmagoric, nocturnal plaza, illuminated and yet empty, which she glimpsed in Santiago during the hours of curfew, leading her to describe the novel as '*la* novela del toque de queda'.[23] Emphasis is placed throughout the novel on the artificial nature of the fictional public square, and what strikes the reader from the very start are the various references to poses, roles, scenes, spectacle, theatricality and film, which place the scenario firmly within the realm of visual performance and representation. However, like the nocturnal plaza viewed by Eltit, the empty benches in the fictional plaza highlight the lack of spectators, and it is the reader who takes on this role,

Lértora), pp. 127–40; and Olea, *Lengua víbora. Producciones de lo femenino en la escritura de mujeres chilenas* (Santiago: Cuarto Propio, 1998), pp. 47–82. See also the reading by Alice Nelson, who aligns corporeal and textual resistance in the novel, and that of Gisela Norat, who examines the sexual subversions that underlie the female protagonist's autonomy. Nelson, *Political Bodies: Gender, History, and the Struggle for Narrative Power in Recent Chilean Literature* (Lewisburg: Bucknell University Press, 2002), pp. 157–69; and Norat, pp. 29–49.

[21] *Campos minados*, p. 113.

[22] Avelar also points to the importance of light 'and the whole semantic web of vision', and Ronald Christ reflects on how he translated the novel's title 'to make it coincide with the English sound of the informing *illuminate*'. See Avelar, p. 169; and Christ, in *E. Luminata* (see Eltit), p. 214; emphasis his.

[23] Lazzara, p. 31; emphasis in the original. Piña, p. 235.

observing L.Iluminada as she performs for the 'pálidos' and the 'luminoso', and the 'pálidos' as they, in turn, perform for L.Iluminada. The plaza exists in a self-contained state, where every element achieves a visibility that is seemingly witnessed solely by the reader, as dazzling light pours forth from the 'luminoso' into the abandoned and lustreless city that is Santiago de Chile.

The use of the field of vision is of notable impact in the novel, which explains its enthusiastic reception by visual artists in Chile when first published.[24] The pages of the novel are frequently used by Eltit as a stage, scenario or canvas, which beckon the reader into a realm of violent spectacle where reading is transformed into watching as a series of projected images fleet by. Only rarely does colour cut into view, as in the final chapter, when the blood-red letters thrown out by the 'luminoso' seep down the grey woollen dress of L.Iluminada as she is swathed in its light. Visual texture is important and formal techniques of the visual arts are thoughtfully judged throughout, influencing the mood and composition of the images that emerge. The 'pálidos', for example, are staged in 'una distribución casi bella' (p. 7), their movements seemingly choreographed to constitute a visual complement to L.Iluminada as they watch her from the edges of the plaza. Eltit plays with the visual sensations of the reader and writing itself is referred to in the novel as 'un zoom' (p. 91), the zoom-lens being a device on a camera that picks up on what the unaided eye would have missed. The reader's view is magnified to focus on the most minute gestures made by L.Iluminada, from the crossing and uncrossing of her legs to the sweep of her hand. This technique is employed to greatest effect at the beginning of the fifth chapter: 'Desde lejos es una sábana extendida sobre el pasto, desde cerca es una mujer abierta, desde más lejos es pasto, más allá no es nada' (p. 91).[25]

The dynamics of light and darkness, and the delineation of foreground and background are drawn on prominently throughout, epitomized by the black-and-white photograph of Eltit that nestles within the novel at the beginning of the eighth chapter. Visibility is of primary concern as L.Iluminada searches insatiably for the light, the two sources of which are the street-lamps that border the plaza and the 'luminoso', the latter offering the most powerful and penetrating beam. The scenes portrayed are arranged so that their points of emphasis coincide with the beam of the 'luminoso', with light and darkness seemingly deployed to produce a chiaroscuro vision in an alarming *trompe d'oeil* world. The harsh glare of the 'luminoso' endows the wracked body of L.Iluminada, and at times the bodies of the recessive 'pálidos', with visual prominence. Their gestures and actions would be invisible without the beam of the 'luminoso'; this, in turn, would be meaningless without L.Iluminada, as we learn in the final chapter: 'ella tan sólo era la que, subyagada, había recibido

---

[24] My thanks to Eugenia Brito for pointing this out to me.

[25] See the importance given by Eltit to her own bodily gestures in her performative work in her article 'Socavada de sed', *Ruptura*, 6 (1982), no page numbers. Excerpts of this article appear in the novel, highlighting the fluidity of Eltit's narrative and performative work at this time.

el mensaje, no del producto sino del luminoso mismo, de su existencia como tal' (p. 190), a point to which I will return.

The continuous play of light and darkness leaves the reader to grapple with what lies beyond the beam of the 'luminoso', since it 'blinds' the reader to that which is lost in the play of shadows. An important reference is made in the first chapter to the 'parpadeos del luminoso' (p. 13). If the 'luminoso' blinks, then there is a split second in which darkness fleetingly encompasses the square and the 'luminoso' loses sight of what is taking place beneath it. A tension is thus set up between what is made visible and what is occluded in the visual realm. It is the textual body, the page of the text, which offers an unblinking stare at that which is elided from view on the 'stage' of the text when the 'luminoso' is switched off, thus challenging the dualism of light and darkness, and offering a glimpse of darkness made visible.

The use of cinematographic codes in the first chapter of the novel makes evident from the start the narrative strategy of forcing the reader to question representational norms. Throughout the chapter, the reader is drawn into a complicated web of looks as L.Iluminada gazes at the 'luminoso', the 'pálidos' gaze at L.Iluminada, and all, in turn, are watched by a nameless male spectator ('ése') and a disembodied male eye that films the unfolding spectacle in the plaza. The reader is slowly made aware that his/her gaze is controlled by the focus of the camera and the male gaze, shifting his/her attention towards the structures of representation. Cinema, as Laura Mulvey has argued, is an advanced representation system that 'poses questions of the ways the unconscious (formed by the dominant order) structures ways of seeing and pleasure in looking'.[26] The reader is led to question who is directing our gaze, and our attention is thus drawn to the male gaze that frames the violent and sexual representation of the female body. The novel thus demands an alternative interpretative strategy, forcing the reader to question the relationship between power/violence and prevailing representational norms through the act of reading and his/her relationship to language and vision.

The Textual Construction of Subjectivity

Kristeva argues that the speaking subject emerges from the heterogeneous elements of the signifying process: the symbolic and the semiotic. For Kristeva, the semiotic is located in the period prior to the Lacanian mirror stage and the acquisition of language, in a maternal space which she terms the semiotic *chora*. Concurring with Lacan that the end result of the 'archaic stages' that precede the mirror stage is 'the grasping of the image by the child', she concedes that the process prior to the mirror stage can be called 'imaginary',

[26] Laura Mulvey, *Visual and Other Pleasures* (London: Macmillan, 1989), p. 29. An essay co-authored by Eltit and Rosenfeld, published in 1982, illustrates Eltit's awareness of many of the precepts that inform feminist film theory. See 'Un filme subterráneo', *Ruptura*, 6 (1982), p. 10.

'but not in the specular sense of the word, because it passes through voice, taste, skin and so on, all the senses, yet doesn't necessarily mobilize sight'.[27] Kristeva thus theorizes the 'imaginary' process in terms of what she describes as 'the *semiotic* variety of meaning', as opposed to 'the *symbolic* variety of meaning', which conceives of the image as 'coherent' and 'full', and produces a verbal sign that she describes as referring to 'objects which are total and not split'.[28] In contrast, Kristeva links the semiotic variety of meaning to the crisis of representation in modern art, especially visual representation, the fragmented images of which are founded on what she describes as 'a sort of elaboration of this narcissistic and prenarcissistic dynamic, where the figure is not yet constituted as one, as a coherent figure, where hearing, skin, taste and so on enter into account'.[29] It is precisely the semiotic variety of meaning discussed here by Kristeva that I wish to unearth in my reading of the novel, in order to examine how Eltit makes visible the heterogeneous nature of signifying practice.

In the tenth chapter the novel closes as a now nameless woman, easily identified through the description of her body and movements as L.Iluminada, sits alone on a wooden bench in the plaza at dusk, watching the city's inhabitants hurry home before darkness falls. Although visibility becomes steadily poorer, it is only in this final chapter that any indication of life beyond the nightmarish plaza comes into view. Suddenly, the lights in the now abandoned plaza are switched on, just as darkness descends. As the disembodied third-person narrative voice informs us: 'La perspectiva cambia con la luz encendida' (p. 186). The nameless woman, seated directly below the beam of a street-lamp, is now illuminated as the focal point of visibility. However, in contrast to previous chapters, she no longer constitutes the spectacle in the plaza that was illuminated by the 'luminoso' and 'watched' by the 'pálidos' and the reader. It is now the 'luminoso' that provides the spectacle, which, in turn, is watched by L.Iluminada, marking her as the subject, rather than the object, of the gaze: 'todo ese espectáculo era para ella [...] Alguien había montado esa costosa tramoya en la ciudad, como don para sí; con escritura y colores, con colores y movimientos, cálculos ingenieriles, trabajo manual, permisos [...] activados por baterías, la sometieran a ella' (pp. 190–1).

Although previously subjugated to the blinding beam of the 'luminoso', the woman is now able to glimpse beyond the superficial meanings of the advertising slogans thrown out, which are themselves indications of the military's relentless imposition of neo-liberal market values in Chile. She can now clearly perceive the metal and wooden scaffolding that provides the support for this spectacle of light, an analogy for what appears to be her insight into the mechanics of official discourse, with the reference to 'permisos' and 'baterías' hinting at the underlying source of military authority responsible for this costly

---

[27] 'Julia Kristeva in Conversation with Rosalind Coward', in *The Portable Kristeva*, ed. by Kelly Oliver (New York: Columbia University Press, 1997), pp. 331–40 (p. 333).

[28] *The Portable Kristeva*, p. 334; emphasis hers.

[29] *The Portable Kristeva*, p. 334.

artifice. The following sentence not only reveals how L.Iluminada achieves interpretative power, but also takes on a didactic quality, providing a key to the reading of Eltit's fiction: 'Lo había logrado uniendo las letras más distantes; las encendidas y las apagadas, los cruces de ambas, los signos que se construían en el medio, los aparentes vacíos, el intercambio entre mensaje y mensaje' (pp. 191–2). Signification is thus portrayed as arising from the interaction of that which is visible and that which is elided from view. In Kristeva's terms, signification emerges from the tension between the symbolic (that which can be fully represented in language) and the repressed drives of the semiotic, which erupt into signification through the gaps ('los aparentes vacíos') in language.[30]

Similarly to Richard, who has emphasized the need for feminist (and cultural) criticism to deconstruct hegemonic discourse in order to reveal the processes of signification, Eltit also stresses the importance of a theoretical analysis of dominant signifying and discursive practices as a means to open up a space for discourses of contestation.[31] In her novel, the woman is now able to form a specular relationship that is based on an understanding of the structures and interplay of signifying practice rather than on the repression of the maternal body, which forms the basis of the critique of the Lacanian mirror stage by Irigaray and Kristeva.[32] As night turns towards dawn and the power of illumination of the 'luminoso' reaches its peak, the third-person narrator declares that a moment of intensity has arrived and a new cycle is about to begin. L.Iluminada opens the brown paper bag that she had previously clutched on her knees and takes out a hand-held mirror, which she holds up to her face, fully illuminated by the street-lamp above her:

> Miró su rostro largamente, incluso ensayó una sonrisa. Pasó repetidamente su mano por la cara. Alejó y acercó el espejo. Se miró desde todos los ángulos posibles [...]
> Se levantó enseguida caminando hacia el centro. Se volvió a exponer al luminoso. Miró su cara en el espejo mucho más diluida y cruzada frágilmente por las luces. (p. 194)

Her incessantly appliquéd face, which had been hidden from view throughout the novel, is here reflected in the mirror through a series of visual rehearsals that signify the woman's emergence from the 'archaic stages' of the imaginary. Although she does assume a specular relationship, the 'grasping of the image'

---

[30] Meaning as residing within the fissures or gaps of discourse (following Barthes and proponents of deconstruction) is also a point made by Richard in relation to the *escena de avanzada* and by Brito in relation to the *nueva escena*, discussed in the Introduction.

[31] Richard, *Masculino/femenino*, p. 11.

[32] See, for example, Luce Irigaray, *Speculum of the Other Woman*, trans. by Gillian C. Gill (Ithaca: Cornell University Press, 1985), pp. 144–6; and Julia Kristeva, *Desire in Language: A Semiotic Approach to Literature and Art*, ed. by Leon S. Roudiez and trans. by Thomas Gora, Alice Jardine and Leon S. Roudiez (New York: Columbia University Press, 1980), pp. 281–3.

in the mirror is partial. Her reflection becomes fainter and fissured when she stands below the beam of the 'luminoso', which suggests that she will never be a coherent, full and visible whole, representable within the symbolic variety of meaning. She thus emerges as a fragmented subject who lacks the unity of symbolic identity; in Kristeva's terms, a 'subject-in-process'.[33] However, her subsequent act of cutting her hair in the centre of the plaza below the beam of the 'luminoso', using the mirror to fashion her image, portrays a viable attempt at self-representation, a point also made by Brito, who observes that the woman's act of cutting indicates her movement towards 'la búsqueda de su propia liberación'.[34] Notably, this process of cutting no longer involves the erasure of the female body from the screen of representation (a point to which I will return) nor self-wounding, as it did throughout the previous chapters.

It is at this point, using the hand-held mirror, that the woman is able to reflect back the image of the 'luminoso': 'Se miró levantando e inclinando el espejo. Por un momento se reflejó en él el luminoso y hasta un pedazo de rama de árbol' (p. 194). In Irigaray's terms, without a backcloth (woman), symbolic processes would falter, since the male subject 'can sustain himself only by bouncing back off some objectiveness, some objective'.[35] The female body is thus no longer reduced to the object that reflects back the image of the 'luminoso' (see pp. 40–1), but distorts his representational power by turning discourse back on itself, so disarticulating its structure and presuppositions.

The similarity of narrative style and pace between the final chapter and much of the first chapter of the novel suggests that they be read in conjunction. And yet, it is seemingly impossible to determine the order in which they should be read. The opening line of the novel makes reference to a previous period of time when the face of L.Iluminada shone in natural daylight, but while various references are made to the artificiality of the light in the nocturnal plaza, natural light seeps into the novel only in the closing line. Any attempt to determine the chronological order is disrupted, as the novel resists any notion of closure by turning back on itself and emerging solely as the sum of its fractured parts, rather than a coherent whole. In Kristeva's terms, then, it is a text that is continually in process.

Similarly, the image that emerges in the first chapter of the novel of the body of L.Iluminada as it is lit up by the 'luminoso' is also one of fragmented parts: 'el rostro a pedazos [...] sus labios entreabiertos y sus piernas extendidas sobre el pasto' (p. 7). The portrayal of the physiological body as simply the truncated sum of its corporeal parts reflects the disjointed composition of the textual body, referred to above. This corporeal fragmentation also works against the all-seeing, masterful gaze, just as the textual body refutes any notion of a totalizing narrative. The novel can thus be seen to privilege the semiotic variety of meaning, as put forward by Kristeva.

[33] *Desire in Language*, p. 135.
[34] *Campos minados*, p. 124.
[35] *Speculum*, p. 133.

Composed of four 'scenes', the first chapter follows the different poses of L.Iluminada within the plaza and immediately unfolds into a spectacle of violence: the repeated enactment of a disconcerting, nocturnal baptismal ceremony.[36] The 'luminoso' flashes on and off in a rhythmical manner, imitating the functioning of a clock, and the insidious cold takes on qualities usually associated with time: 'Porque el frío en esta plaza es el tiempo que se ha marcado para suponerse un nombre propio, donado por el letrero que se encendará y se apagará, rítmico y ritual, en el proceso que en definitiva les dará la vida: su identificación ciudadana' (p. 7).[37] The function of the 'luminoso' is thus made clear: it will name those exposed beneath it, the act of naming being associated with the violent inscription of the name of L.Iluminada and of all her possible aliases onto her flesh by the 'luminoso', as she convulses and bangs her head against the cement floor of the plaza: 'Le ratifica el nombre en dos colores paralelos, el luminoso ampliado sobre el cuerpo escribe L. Iluminada y rítmicamente va pasando la cantidad posible de apodos' (p. 8). Richard has referred to the use of aliases during the dictatorship to disguise dangerous identities, and the bodily inscription can here be read as a form of political branding that aims to contain all identities within a circumscribed meaning, but it is specifically the branding of the female body which is highlighted by Eltit.[38]

This violent writing on the body is later briefly repeated with the 'pálidos', but they never assume an individual identity or name; they huddle together in a starving herd, and their sexually unmarked bodies stand in stark contrast to the visible female morphology of the body of L.Iluminada. Richard has argued that violent state intervention during the dictatorship resulted in a 'feminization' or symbolic castration of its male victims, which produced a duality in Chilean society: masculinity was appropriated as the exclusive prerogative of the military and those who opposed them were categorized as feminine, abject, degenerate and castrated.[39] In Richard's terms, then, the 'pálidos' represent the abject and castrated oppressed underclass, and the porous quality of their flesh when exposed to the beam of the 'luminoso' emphasizes their position within the category of the feminine.

The nocturnal naming ceremony can be associated with the order of naming carried out in the paternal Symbolic, in which reference, meaning and enunciation are made possible only when the child is marked with the father's name as his exclusive property. The 'luminoso' can thus be seen as the representative

---

[36] Baptism is the quintessential act of nomination and, in Christian terms, signifies entry into the 'enlightenment' of Christianity. For a reading of the novel in terms of a rite of initiation, see Tafra, pp. 33–52.

[37] Irigaray links 'proper names' to the establishment of ownership and appropriation that she perceives in the connected systems of capitalism and patriarchy. See *This Sex Which is Not One*, trans. by Catherine Porter with Carolyn Burke (Ithaca: Cornell University Press, 1985), p. 134.

[38] *Residuos y metáforas*, p. 64.

[39] *Masculino/femenino*, p. 65.

of patriarchal law, but imposing the father's name in such barbaric and unrelenting terms that the presence of an imaginary father who might facilitate the child's entry into the Symbolic through a discourse of love, as put forward by Kristeva, is brutally discounted.[40] I read the first chapter of the novel as a fictional depiction of an enforced descent to the pre-linguistic, 'archaic stages' prior to the mirror stage, wherein identity is savagely reconstituted within the context of authoritarian society.[41] The ferocious naming ceremony not only forcibly constitutes a new form of identity but also annihilates any traces of a previous sense of self, wringing from the body of L.Iluminada any self-identity that she may have had, as made evident after the first baptismal ceremony when reference is made, paradoxically, to L.Iluminada having lost 'el nombre propio' (p. 8). An indication is also given of the obliteration of memory, 'la borradura del pasado' (p. 21), which corresponds to Richard's argument that an abrupt and severe mutilation of the immediate past was effected in post-coup Chilean society in order to inaugurate a new beginning.[42]

Although torture is not mentioned once in this chapter, the naming carried out is portrayed as an unnatural and tortuous ceremony during which bodies are reduced to flesh, upon which an identity is physically inscribed. Such brutal corporeal inscription reflects the violent methods enacted by the military to shape the social body and also corresponds to the triangular formation of the practice of torture as described by Diana Taylor in relation to the acts carried out during the Dirty War in Argentina: the military leaders who manipulated discourse constituted 'author-ity'; the torturers functioned as the instrument of inscription; and the victim was exposed as 'the producible/expendable body-text'.[43] The 'luminoso' may thus be read as the instrument of torture; its supporting structure as the 'author-ity' that produces and manipulates discourse; and the bodies of L.Iluminada and the 'pálidos' as 'the producible/expendable body-text', which in Eltit's novel is depicted in particularly gendered terms. The triangular formation of torture as elucidated by Taylor usefully maps onto the triangular structure of the nuclear family, the structure within which identity is constituted in patriarchy, but which here becomes aligned with the state-sanctioned violence of torture. Authoritarianism and patriarchy are thus conflated, and the violence that lies at the heart of both is made shockingly evident.

What has so far been absent from the naming ceremony made visible here is the maternal body, the pivotal role of which has been emphasized by Kristeva in the semiotic realm. The 'luminoso' is portrayed as appropriating the maternal

[40] Julia Kristeva, Tales of Love, trans. by Leon S. Roudiez (New York: Columbia University Press, 1987), pp. 46–8. Elizabeth Grosz describes the 'imaginary father' as 'the forerunner of the sign and, more generally, of the symbolic order', not to be confused with the biological father or 'with any concrete empirical male subject'. Grosz, p. 88.

[41] In Por la patria, Eltit depicts an enforced return to the pre-Oedipal stage in the context of a female concentration camp (see Chapter 2).

[42] Nelly Richard, La insubordinación de los signos (Santiago: Cuarto Propio, 1994), pp. 13–36.

[43] Taylor, p. 152.

function, giving life to L.Iluminada and the 'pálidos' within the containing chamber of the plaza: 'Incubados de nuevo, la tecnología les da vida' (p. 17). The locus of the semiotic, the maternal *chora*, is overwritten by the harshly visible male acts of penetration effected by the beam of the 'luminoso', and it is only when visibility is obscured – when the beam of the 'luminoso' is switched off – that the reader is able to perceive the corporeal interaction with the maternal body, the repression of which is made so evident in the textual body:

1.3   Aún en la noche – a oscuras – vuelven a la plaza y por eso:

1.   Vuelven los pálidos a la plaza para permanecer allí con el cuerpo distendido, apoyados con sus espaldas en los árboles.

   árboles – césped – luz eléctrica – cemento
   ramas y cables que trasladan luz a los faroles
   faroles que también iluminan los bancos
   y mi cara de madona mirando su cara de madona. (p. 23)

Occurring as a series of ten points in the third section of the first chapter, the unidentified first-person female narrative voice underlying each of these points gives expression first to the mirror gaze with the archetypal mother, the Madonna, and then to a series of progressively intimate physical acts with the maternal body: 'y mis labios de madona sorben su pecho de madona con ansias' (p. 24). A seemingly paradoxical connection is made in the seventh of these points between infertility and the maternal body, but this is no less inconceivable than the connection between virginity and motherhood that encapsulates the figure of the Madonna in Catholic discourse.[44]

In her essay 'Stabat Mater', Kristeva argues that the Virgin Mother is a symbolic mother, controlled by the paternal law that represses the maternal semiotic and erases from representation the mother's *jouissance* in the primal scene through the biblical assertion of an immaculate conception.[45] For Kristeva, any expression of the semiotic nature of the maternal body – the mother's pain and *jouissance* – is a challenge to the Catholic discourse of the Virgin Mary, which she perceives as the only, and wholly inadequate, discourse of motherhood available to women. In Eltit's novel, the visual occlusion of the relationship with the mother on the 'stage' of the text signifies its repression within the norms of representation, but here the primacy of vision is challenged in favour of a diffuse, tactile, erotic pleasure unveiled and experienced only in the textual body. The potential of the semiotic variety of meaning to make manifest the prohibited desire of and for the mother is thus highlighted, in a direct challenge to paternal law.

---

[44] The paradoxical juxtaposition of infertility and motherhood is further developed by Eltit in *Por la patria* (see Chapter 2).

[45] *Tales of Love*, pp. 234–63 (pp. 248–53).

In the tenth point, the subversion of the Catholic discourse that projects the Virgin Mother as pure and stripped of sexual desire culminates in a depiction of a female act of cunnilingus ('y mis manos de madona abren sus piernas de madona y la lamen' (p. 25)), which not only portrays the maternal figure as a sexual being but also undermines the idea that there is one natural form of sexuality: that of reproductive heterosexuality. The desire for the mother and the mother's own desire are here merged and made explicit, as the mirror gaze with the mother unravels into a primarily sensual experience, which corresponds to the predominately non-specular relationship located by Kristeva in the imaginary.

The second section of the sixth chapter of the novel reflects Kristeva's argument that 'Our discourse – all discourse – moves with and against the chora in the sense that it simultaneously depends upon and refuses it.'[46] The disjointed typography in this section of the novel makes visible the topology of language as underpinned by the bodily drives and affects of the semiotic. Entitled in bold capitals 'LOS GRAFITIS DE LA PLAZA', writings are posited here that are variously described as a folly, fiction, seduction, evasion or mockery, amongst others. Each writing in this series occupies one full page of the text and all follow the same typographical format. The first of this series makes reference to the unrepresentability of the foundations of writing and the social order, as follows (see next page):

---

[46] *Revolution in Poetic Language*, p. 26.

La escritura como proclama.

Santiago de Chile que apareció de modo
mentiroso y con erratas le han quitado
construcciones y es por eso que los
pálidos lo acosan como a usted que se creía
protegido [...]
Pero sin embargo ésos tematizan sobre otras
fundaciones que es imposible comprender
a cabalidad, porque los lugares en que se
proponen vienen de lo más primario, de la
desinteligencia del que no conoce el
cemento nada más que en una de sus partes.

Escribió:
Como la más rajada de las madonas le presté mi cuerpo tirada en la
plaza para que me lo lamiera. (p. 111)

What appears on the top of the page, and is most visible to the reader, is a meditation on the building of the city. At the bottom of the page, easily overlooked in a hurried reading of the novel, the foundation of discourse and the social order is shown to be the maternal space of the semiotic, implied by reference to the archetypal mother. The profane and sexual terms that imbue this space once again challenge the purity associated with the Madonna in Catholic discourse by graphically delineating the semiotic nature of the maternal body. Throughout this series of writings, the maternal body is portrayed as tormented, drenched, stained and soiled, continually unpeeling and blossoming through acts of *jouissance*. It is, then, through textual representation that Eltit again highlights how social and signifying structures depend upon and yet strive to repress the maternal semiotic.

On the very last page of the sixth chapter, the novel again takes on a didactic quality by pointing to the space from which a feminine subjectivity may emerge. Positioned in the very centre of an otherwise blank page are the following words:

Escribió:
iluminada entera, encendida. (p. 124)

The language inscribed by the unidentified female figure is located precisely in the space that had previously scarred the text; the space that marks the gap between the realms of symbolic processes (grammar and logical discourse) and the semiotic (displacement, condensation, alliterations, vocal and gestural rhythms). The threshold of the realms of the symbolic and the semiotic, defined by Kristeva as 'the thetic', is thus depicted as the space from which a language may be inscribed that gives voice to woman's luminous subjectivity and shimmering desire.[47] In short, the page visually represents Kristeva's argument that the speaking subject emerges from the heterogeneous process of signifying practice.

Woman's Specular Relationship

The spectacle in the plaza presented in the first chapter of the novel is, essentially, a representation of the workings of the symbolic organization of society, based on a subject-object relationship. It is the 'luminoso', as male subject, that savagely takes possession of the female object, L.Iluminada, controlling and inscribing the female body by repeatedly naming her during the tortuous baptismal process. L.Iluminada, in turn, is portrayed as a corporeal screen upon which the images projected by the 'luminoso' will be violently imprinted:

Y ella misma, que ha tomado su lugar, se va lentamente hasta su imagen y se pone bajo él para imprimirse.

[47] *Revolution in Poetic Language*, pp. 43–5.

Sus ropas grises reciben los tonos del luminoso. Le sirven de tela para su proyección. (p. 26)

As noted above, the final chapter of the novel portrays the now nameless woman as turning back the image of the 'luminoso' using the hand-held mirror, but here the body of L.Iluminada acts as the screen upon which the dynamics of power are written by reflecting the image of the 'luminoso'. In Irigaray's terms, the 'luminoso' projects 'a something to absorb, to take, to see, to possess', while the body of L.Iluminada presents 'a patch of ground to stand upon, a mirror to catch his reflection'.[48] The body of L.Iluminada is thus portrayed as the backcloth of representation, or the tain of the mirror, but the erasure of the female body from the screen of representation is disturbingly exposed throughout the first chapter of the novel. The 'comentarios', 'indicaciones' and 'errores' that conclude the first, second and fourth scenes describe the kinesics of the previous performances by L.Iluminada and the 'pálidos'. It is here that the nameless male 'ésos' who direct the visual action in the plaza are shown to correct and modify the filmic proofs, since they overwrite the representation of the female body through a process of editorial cutting. At the end of the first scene an unnamed male figure, referred to only as 'ése', is superimposed onto the screen of representation. He usurps the central role of L.Iluminada, as the poses and gestures previously enacted by her are now subtly transferred to this unidentified male body. At the end of the second scene, the scream produced by L.Iluminada is dubbed and it is now her aural representation that is upstaged: 'Volverlo a repetir [...] para que se vaya transformando lentamente – por tecnología – desde el timbre femenino a distintos gritos masculinos' (p. 19). Male authority or censorship thus determines what is seen or heard, occluding the violence inflicted on the female body in the plaza from future viewers of the film. It is only in the textual body that this violence is uncovered to the reader.

The second chapter of the novel, the first of two interrogation scenes, again foregrounds the invisibility of the female body in the cultural imaginary. The typography of this chapter changes so that it visually represents a typewritten transcript of an interrogation, which centres on the daily use of the public plaza. The daytime plaza is described by the interrogated male subject as a place where the most intimate of human relationships are played out in the most public of spaces. It is also portrayed as a site where the threat of 'contamination' from marginal sectors of society, such as vagrants and beggars (who can be seen to represent the 'pálidos'), is paramount. However, even they, we learn from the interrogated subject, are granted 'la propiedad que les otorga el lugar público' (p. 43). It is only during rainy days and at night, he states, that the plaza remains empty, the very times in which the novel makes visible L. Iluminada's presence there.

In the first chapter of the novel, reciprocal witnessing is shown to be at the

---

[48] *Speculum*, p. 134.

heart of the relationship between L.Iluminada and the 'pálidos': 'Si los pálidos
que obtuvieron nuevo nombre ciudadano prescindieran de L.Iluminada perderían
su soporte, es decir, quizás nadie pregonaría ese hecho' (p. 13). The 'pálidos'
are similarly described in terms of reliable witnesses to the actions of L.
Iluminada: 'Se ha dicho que ellos tienen los ojos prendidos a otros paisajes,
pero ella [...] les va borrando esa imagen; por su cara dañada ella es la que
sin duda los rige' (p. 16). However, what I wish to uncover here is how the
relationship of reciprocity between the 'pálidos' and L.Iluminada falters when
she attempts to gain self-representation. It is the fifth chapter of the novel that
portrays the disturbing shift in their relationship, uncovered in narrative rather
than visual terms: 'Situación ahora no fílmica sino narrativa, ambigua, errada'
(p. 91).

In *Speculum of the Other Woman*, Irigaray argues that woman functions as
the blindspot within the logic of patriarchal culture, and for this reason she
seeks out the blindspots, or excess, of discourse, which underlie discourse but
are disavowed. Like Irigaray, Eltit's strategy can be seen to shed light on the
blindspot of discourse. In her novel, the 'pálidos' appear only halfway through
the fifth chapter, the 'luminoso' is switched off, and it is immediately made
clear that a different perspective is being offered to the reader, who is left alone
with L.Iluminada, as it were, to read her: 'Es una imagen completamente
distinta para el que la lee' (p. 91). As such, she is given existence only by the
reader, whose new narrative perspective forces him/her to perceive L.Iluminada
in relation to her function within the text, which is that of a linguistic sign
imprinted onto the page: 'Está a punto de perder su aparataje, ella no era un
adorno para la plaza sino a la inversa: la plaza era su página, sólo eso'
(p. 92).

Reference is made later in the chapter to the multiple poses or representations of femininity that L.Iluminada can and will enact through mimesis when
situated beneath the spotlight, which reflects Irigaray's argument that language
and female identity, as they currently exist, are accessible to women only
through mimicry.[49] But in the absence of the 'luminoso', the onus is on the
reader to read in such a way that allows for the textual inscription of feminine
subjectivity to develop and emerge from beneath prescribed feminine roles. As
Ortega argues, what we are witnessing in the novel is the birth of a female
subject, the origin of which is 'la plaza/página, es decir la escritura'.[50] So, if
the reader, and not the spotlight, controls the focus on her, the text, a different
story has the potential to emerge: 'Si el foco, si el foco se apagara, la trama
empezaría realmente' (p. 101).

The linguistic foundations of this other, feminine text are described as 'las
matrices listas ya para la reproducción' (p. 93). The matrix of discourse,
associated by Irigaray with the maternal womb, is thus firmly located as the

---

[49] *This Sex Which is Not One*, p. 76.
[50] Ortega, in *Una poética de literatura menor* (see Lértora), p. 63.

origin of language and the act of procreation is linked to literary creation, a point that is made again by Eltit in more dramatic terms in *El cuarto mundo* (see Chapter 3).[51] The female body is no longer reduced to supporting male-dominated systems of representation but achieves self-representation through the materiality of language, represented in the text through the woman's inter-weaving of the woollen threads of her grey dress. The inference that a fragile sense of self is unfolding on the page is made evident through the image of an infant who delights in its reflection in the mirror: 'Reaparece la mujer que duerme o quiere dormir, pero no es así: es el placer de extenderse jugando con el deleite de su propia imagen. Infantil tendida es ésta' (p. 91). There are, however, no objects in the plaza with which to form a specular relationship: 'Sin reflectores de ninguna especie, ensaya' (p. 93). So, not only does the blossoming self-representation of woman emerge through a non-specular process that does not subject the maternal body to subtending the imaginary stage, it also stems from woman's tactile relationship with her own body, moving the female body away from its previous position as object of masculine discourse so that it becomes, in Irigaray's terms, 'the object of a female subjec-tivity experiencing and identifying itself'.[52]

Against the backdrop of the nocturnal, rain-soaked plaza, L.Iluminada rubs her legs against the grass and other external elements, and fantasizes about rubbing against the bodies of the absent 'pálidos'. Her sexuality is described in terms of 'un refrote', and does not solicit male penetration or a voyeuristic male gaze but is auto-erotic, thus privileging the dispersed pleasure experienced through sensations of movement and touch, which surface in language through the semiotic variety of meaning. The emphasis placed on touch, fluidity and physical rubbing reflects the corporeal experiences that Kristeva locates within the imaginary, but also closely corresponds to the characteristics of a feminine style of writing advocated by Irigaray: 'This "style" does not privilege sight [...] It is always fluid, without neglecting the characteristics of fluids that are difficult to idealize: those rubbings between two infinitely near neighbours that create a dynamic.'[53] Similarly to Irigaray, Eltit attempts to symbolize an emerging subjectivity that encompasses female specificity and sexuality through the prominent inscription of the morphology of the female body in the text. Importantly, the first-person narrative voice that gives expression to the delicate sense of self unfurling on the page foregrounds its emergence from the corporeal interaction with, rather than separation from, the maternal body:

> Si yo misma presté mis piernas vacías, púbicas, vellosas, mis pobres piernas lapidadas y así me saltó mi verdadero nombre propio al montar ese vello púbico en las nalgas, llamándome la luz, que era tan pesada sobre su cabeza

---

[51] Irigaray, *Speculum*, p. 18.

[52] Luce Irigaray, *je, tu, nous: Toward a Culture of Difference*, trans. by Alison Martin (New York and London: Routledge, 1993), p. 59.

[53] *This Sex Which is Not One*, p. 79.

que la nominé la madre con sus vellos en mi cadera, al adolorido riñón,
buscando incansablemente el refrote. (p. 95)

In contrast to the first chapter of the novel, the woman now assumes a 'proper
name', in pleasurable rather than savagely violent terms. Her subjectivity can
be seen to issue from the 'refrote' that gives expression to the desire of and
for the mother, which places the mother, not the father, as the origin of the
constitution of the female subject.

However, when the rain ceases and the 'pálidos' arrive in the plaza, the
woman's attempt to gain self-representation is curtailed, a curtailment depicted
in terms of her sterility, thus once again linking linguistic production with
procreation: 'Le restan pocas proyecciones lanzada al borde de la esterilidad'
(p. 102). That the 'pálidos' assume the narrative and visual order and authority
that was previously the domain of the 'luminoso' is made evident upon their
arrival: 'hasta llamar por espectáculo a los pálidos que ordenarán una lectura
posible, corrigiendo algunos textos, sacando otros, manteniendo en apogeo las
baterías, toda esa luz eléctrica que contraria la lluvia' (p. 94). Although previously portrayed as reliable witnesses, their gaze is now indifferent to the
shivering body of the woman who attempts to give voice to her corporeal
pleasure. Although voiceless, the 'pálidos' retain ultimate control of what can
be seen and written in the plaza in the absence of the 'luminoso'. In their
presence, the corporeal visibility of the woman vanishes:

En cambio
Si lumpérico orden el foco iluminase, ella perdería de inmediato su pelada,
su pie, su costilla, su espalda, su hombro, su enfoque entero, todo su trabajo.
(p. 99)

The 'pálidos' are associated in this chapter with words such as 'carteles',
'proclama' and 'manifiesto'; words that align them with the popular masses so
central to Allende's government and subsequently the 'feminized' target of
military repression. Indeed, previous allusions in the novel to demonstrations,
marches and public fervour bring to mind the many rallies that took place in
the Plaza de la Libertad outside the Moneda (government) palace during the
Allende years, which locates the plaza as a receptacle for urban memory. It is,
then, against this political backdrop that the dynamics of power that structure
the relationship between the politically oppressed underclass (the 'pálidos') and
the would-be female subject (L.Iluminada) are made visible, foregrounding the
category of the feminine as a shifting position rather than a fixed identity. In
the absence of the male subject, represented by the 'luminoso', the 'pálidos'
are shown to collude with the masculine 'author-ity' which underpins hegemonic
discourse by seeking to erase the female body from representation.

The struggle for representation between L.Iluminada and the 'pálidos' is
played out through writing. L.Iluminada attempts to inscribe the words 'dónde
vas' with chalk in the centre of the plaza, words which echo the Latin title of

this chapter of the novel, '¿Quo vadis?', and posit an open-ended question with biblical connotations. The 'pálidos' eventually comprehend the woman's 'aggressive' act of writing and obscure her inscription with their bodies: 'Así nada está escrito sobre el suelo, siguen como protagonistas ocupando el cemento. Es evidente que se sienten expulsados hasta los bordes de la plaza como notas al margen' (p. 104). As Nelson notes, the 'pálidos' are ejected from their position as protagonists of the text and 'relegated to the position of footnotes'.[54] Supplanted by the woman who writes, the 'pálidos' first attempt to suppress her writing and then rhythmically erase it. They eventually move into the centre of the plaza, where they reinstate themselves in a narrative position of centrality while simultaneously usurping the woman's authorial position by inscribing the very same words that she had previously written onto the floor with chalk. By the end of the chapter, the attempts by L.Iluminada to attain self-expression are overwritten by the lumpen in order for the voiceless masses to attain a voice. L.Iluminada is again reduced to the position of object as she writhes under the gaze of the 'pálidos', sustaining their discourse with her body as she becomes indistinguishable from their chalk-written words: 'Van hacia los bancos y le dejan el lugar de la lectura y por fin el "dónde vas" es ella misma en el centro de la plaza, bañada en palidez, reseca entera' (p. 106). Her now pallid body, devoid of the fluid that had previously drenched it, is positioned as the tain of the mirror, or the screen of representation, as it reflects back to the 'pálidos' their own pallidity.

The 'pálidos', who arrogate narrative and symbolic order in the absence of the 'luminoso', thus act as a regulating force when the 'luminoso' is switched off, forcing female specificity back into masculine structures and sign systems, and using language as the instrument of a masculine hegemony that seeks to reproduce the world in its image. Woman's access to language and representation is now dependent on their authority, but they wrench authorship from L.Iluminada, relegating her once again to the backcloth of representation. Although representative of a discourse of contestation, the 'pálidos', like the 'luminoso', are also governed by cultural and ideological norms that bury the matrix of discourse, or the maternal womb: 'Circulante material abusado por la extranjería del ojo ajeno a la plaza que no sabrá de los originales estropeados, del abandono de las matrices' (p. 103). Their discourse is thus implicated in the symbolic burial of the mother, or matricide, that Irigaray so compellingly critiques, and which forecloses any space for woman.[55]

By foregrounding the internal powerplays within a supposedly collective discourse of resistance, Eltit illustrates that woman is doubly marginalized and repressed. The difficulty in mobilizing a possible other imaginary that can symbolize female specificity is thus highlighted. However, by seeking out the blindspot of discourse, Eltit does succeed in fleetingly opening up a space

[54] Nelson, p. 166.
[55] See, for example, 'The Bodily Encounter with the Mother', in *The Irigaray Reader*, ed. with introduction by Margaret Whitford (Oxford: Blackwell, 1991), pp. 34–46.

where a feminine sense of self can unfold, and the discerning reader is offered a glimpse of what, in Irigaray's terms, lies behind the specular surface of the female body: 'not the void of nothingness but the dazzle of multifaceted speleology'.[56] Importantly, the sensual pleasure and desire of and for the maternal figure are shown to underlie both this feminine space and the process of signification in the novel, an important point that is taken up and further elaborated by Eltit in her following novel, *Por la patria.*

---

[56] *Speculum*, p. 143.

2

Por la patria: Mother, Family and Nation

Todas íbamos a ser reinas,
De cuatro reinos sobre el mar:
Rosalía con Efigenia
Y Lucila con Soledad.

Gabriela Mistral, 'Todas íbamos a ser reinas'[1]

The Violence of the Oedipal Narrative

Eltit was awarded a Guggenheim Fellowship for Literature in 1985 to complete her second novel, *Por la patria* (1986), the first female author in Chile to have been accorded this prestigious prize.[2] Eltit concedes that *Por la patria* is her most marginal novel if judged in terms of its subdued critical reception and sparse critical readings to date.[3] However, it is this novel, she states, which is the most meaningful to her, as an author: 'si tuviera que decir que soy escritora es porque escribí ese libro'.[4]

While employing staple narrative strategies associated with the boom writers, such as a shifting narrative voice and time frame, Eltit acknowledges the profoundly fractured structure of her novel, which she links to the violent death of her father in 1983.[5] She has spoken publicly of how her subsequent grief dramatically affected the structure of her novel: 'la escritura que realizaba se contaminó por la cercanía del duelo, afectando mi sintaxis en grandes extremos y llegué a escribir la novela más límite que he producido hasta ahora'.[6] This

---

[1] Gabriela Mistral, *Tala* (Buenos Aires: Losada, 1998), p. 93

[2] Throughout this chapter I refer to the second edition of *Por la patria* (Santiago: Cuarto Propio, 1995).

[3] Morales, *Conversaciones*, p. 38.

[4] Ortega, 'Resistencia y sujeto femenino', p. 232.

[5] Morales, *Conversaciones*, p. 40.

[6] 'Experiencia literaria y palabra en duelo', in *Duelo y creatividad*, ed. by Eleonora Casaula, Edmundo Covarrubias and Diamela Eltit (Santiago: Cuarto Propio, 1990), pp. 21–7 (p. 27). Although Eltit does not explicitly explain how her father's death led to the breakdown of coherent syntactical signification, the lack of a father, in psychoanalytic terms, signifies the absence of the phallus and thus the absence of narrative authority. Eltit has also drawn a direct link between the emotional impact of her father's frequent absences throughout her childhood and later years, and the innovative narrative style that she employs, stating that

syntactical rupture was a trigger for unleashing a torrent of language that Eltit found hard to restrain, but which allowed her to identify what she describes as 'la memoria de mi origen y desde allí, las diversas memorias que me habitaban en estado larvario'.[7] The title of the novel, she states, is a coded epitaph to her father and, by extension, an epitaph of solidarity to all those killed or disappeared in Chile through the systematic violence of the military.[8] *Por la patria*, a phrase that echoes the vow taken by soldiers to defend their homeland, and which was ominously repeated by the Chilean military as a justification for their repressive actions, becomes a titular dedication embedded in irony.[9] The loaded implications of the term 'patria' and the destructive operations of those who act in its name are mercilessly exploded by Eltit in a novel whose tone leans more towards that of an elegy for her country (and father/fatherland) than a eulogy.

The novel draws on genres that include epic narrative, Greek tragedy, drama, mysticism and a ludic, baroque wordplay, all of which are interwoven with oral tradition, popular language, myth and the parodied strident, nationalist discourse of the military.[10] As with *Lumpérica*, the most immediate impact lies in its experimental character: the fragmented and disjointed prose; the rupture of language and syntax; diverse and discordant narrative styles and voices; and the unstable narrative voice of Coya, the female protagonist, who constantly lies and negates previous statements. Any coherent plot or timescale falters, and the result is a writerly text in which the exuberance of meaning precludes the possibility of capturing any one truth or reality.

The novel is divided into two sections, but the brief, elliptical paragraphs and sentences work to construct a series of fleeting images rather than chapters, and the typography and page composition vary according to the urgency and emotional impact of the unfolding events. The first section, entitled 'La luz, la luz, la luz, la luz del día', focuses on the events which lead up to and include the military invasion of the young woman Coya's marginal neighbourhood, centering on the focal point of her community: the bar run by her father.[11] Against the backdrop of authoritarian repression, Eltit consistently examines the powerplays at the level of interpersonal relationships within the family and community, merging the domains of family and nation-state. It is Juan, the

---

'yo creo que él no es ajeno, claro, a esto de no hacer una literatura tan "centrista", tan convencional'. Morales, *Conversaciones*, p. 25.

[7] Eltit, in *Duelo y creatividad*, p. 27.

[8] Eltit, in *Duelo y creatividad*, p. 27.

[9] Rodrigo Cánovas also explains the significance of the phrase 'hacerlo por la patria' in Chilean popular culture: 'hacerle el favor (sexual) a la mujer (aunque sea fea) como un acto de reafirmación (masculina)'. 'Apuntes sobre la novela *Por la patria* (1986), de Diamela Eltit', *Acta Literaria*, 15 (1990), 147–60 (p. 159).

[10] Following Bakhtin, Sylvia Tafra also identifies an element of the carnivalesque in the novel. Tafra, p. 55.

[11] The titles of the two sections of the novel again pick up on the opposition between light and darkness, which is prevalent in *Lumpérica* and throughout Eltit's novels (see Chapters 1, 5 and 6).

impotent would-be lover of Coya and 'soplón' (traitor), who sells out his community to the military. Juan's act of betrayal leads to a devastating spiral of violence that results in the death of Coya's father, the disappearance of her mother, and the mass arrest and detention of Coya and her neighbourhood in the concentration camp of Pisagua.[12] As Juan later explains to Coya: 'Lo hice porque me sentí enjuiciado por ti, me pusiste débil y defectuoso' (p. 163). Out of this private drama of emasculated manhood, then, comes the collective tragedy of the repression of an entire community, which indicates that discordant gender relations are at the root of military violence.[13] The shocking collapse of the boundary between private and public spheres exposes military repression as stemming from the need for revenge of a man scorned and humiliated by a woman. While Coya becomes manly in her taunts and postures, in being spoken to and treated in this way Juan becomes unmanned. Neither, therefore, complies with traditional gender roles. Juan's aim is to construct a heterosexual relationship based on male domination and female submission, and he thus abets the military raid to recuperate his virility, reinstate his authority along patriarchal lines and re-establish traditional gender roles.

The second section of the novel, entitled 'Se funde, se opaca, se yergue la épica', rewrites the notion of epic as based on male heroic adventures, exemplified in Chilean literature by Alonso de Ercilla y Zúñiga's *La Araucana*.[14] In Ercilla's epic poem, the celebration of the indigenous Araucanian population for heroically defending their territory from the invading Spaniards has led to a Chilean myth of origins that rests on self-sacrificing male virility and valour, recognized and reinforced by women, which obscures the violent oppression of indigenous communities that continues to this day. In response to Ercilla, Eltit posits an epic of maternal, 'mestiza' marginality, as Coya proclaims at the end of the novel: 'Hay una épica' (p. 291). In Eltit's epic, the virile 'hero' is emasculated, the 'honour' and 'valour' of the warring military collapses into treachery, and race as a discourse of oppression is foregrounded. Coya is portrayed as both victim and relentless antihero, embodying a ferocious female presence that subverts the usual tropes of nationhood by ousting the young male hero and the figure of the woman to be defended.

The second section of the novel develops in the women's concentration camp in which Coya and her female friends and neighbours are incarcerated. The focus here is the complex relationship between Coya and her three close friends: Berta, Flora and Rucia. The women are forced to endure brutal torture,

---

[12] Pisagua was a concentration camp used by the Pinochet regime. It is located in the north of Chile and was the military's most important northern camp.

[13] Isabel Allende also portrays discordant gender relations (a slight to a man's sexual potency) as underlying military repression in Chile in her novel *De amor y de sombra* (1984).

[14] Alonso de Ercilla y Zúñiga was a member of the Spanish royal court who took part in a military offensive against the indigenous Araucanian people in Chile. His epic poem was written in the sixteenth century and grants heroic stature to the Araucanians, a heroism that Chileans still talk about with pride when referring to the Araucanian expulsion of the Spaniards from southern Chile.

interrogation and rape, but it is precisely from within an institution of military power that Coya initiates a process of writing that aims to grant the women a voice that is not silenced or appropriated by the discourse of their torturers.

Although, as Eltit has commented, critical readings of this work are sparse in comparison to those of her other novels, several detailed and incisive readings do exist, such as those by Marina Arrate and Mary-Beth Tierney-Tello.[15] Through the prism of Lacanian psychoanalysis, Arrate focuses on the connection forged between Latin American history and a feminine identity, while Tierney-Tello explores how Eltit challenges patriarchy and authoritarianism through the conflation of the sexual and political realms, and her transgressive linguistic experimentalism. Both critics also highlight the centrality of the mother–daughter relationship in the novel, as do Alice Nelson and Julio Ortega.[16] Indeed, Ortega observes that the novel gives prominence to 'la necesidad de recomenzar desde la madre', an important point that forms the fulcrum of my own reading.[17] For her part, Brito assesses how a feminine identity emerges in the novel, which gives voice to the repressed, indigenous substratum of society and posits a new psychic structure founded on '"lo indio", lo "marginal" y lo "delictual"'.[18] Brito also foregrounds the representation of memory in the novel, an important point which is also considered by Djelal Kadir, who examines the paradoxical centrality of Coya as the female embodiment of history and collective memory.[19]

My reading of the novel hinges on the lethal connection that is shown to exist between the nuclear patriarchal family and authoritarian repression. In the novel, the prescribed formation of kinship and sexuality is shown to correspond to Western Oedipal structures, which in Freudian terms prohibit the transgression of the incest taboo and institute the symbolic repression within the family that pushes children towards the father and heterosexuality, and away from the mother. Eltit has stated that in this novel she wished to recuperate the child's lost, original desire for the mother: 'yo pienso que ese deseo primigenio es también hacia la madre y quise salvar esa pulsión'.[20] Her stress on the need to grant representation to this desire corresponds with the critique of psychoanalysis offered by Irigaray in her essay 'The Bodily Encounter with the Mother', in which Irigaray describes the desire for the mother and the mother's own

[15] Marina Arrate, 'Una novela como radiografía: *Por la patria*' (unpublished master's thesis, Universidad de Concepción, 1992); and Tierney-Tello, pp. 79–127. See especially the final section of Tierney-Tello's reading for an excellent discussion of the subversion embodied in the maternal figure. Tierney-Tello, pp. 109–27.

[16] Nelson, pp. 169–84; and Ortega, in *Una poética de literatura menor* (see Lértora), p. 71. Olga Uribe T. also points to the centrality of the maternal body in the novel. See 'Breves anotaciones sobre las estrategias narrativas en *Lumpérica*, *Por la patria* y *El cuarto mundo* de Diamela Eltit', *Hispanic Journal*, 16 (1995), 21–37 (p. 29).

[17] Ortega, in *Una poética de literatura menor* (see Lértora), p. 71.

[18] *Campos minados*, p. 134. Gisela Norat also focuses on the significance of Coya's symbolical embodiment of the repressed indigenous heritage of Chile. Norat, pp. 85–120.

[19] Kadir, pp. 192–201.

[20] Claudia Donoso, 'Tenemos puesto el espejo para el otro lado', *APSI*, 26 January–8 February 1987, 47–8 (p. 47).

desire as 'forbidden by the law of the father', linking the father's severance of mother and child intimacy to the imposition of his language and law.[21] Interestingly, Eltit has spoken of her familiarity with Irigaray's essay, which she read after writing *Por la patria*, and Irigaray's critique of the repression of mother–child intimacy is also to be found in Eltit's novel through the emphasis placed by Eltit on recuperating the (female) child's desire for the mother.[22]

Irigaray also argues that there is a lack of symbolic representation of the mother–daughter relationship and a maternal genealogy, and her contention is that this results in women's inability to view the mother not only as a mother, but also as a woman, and prevents women from representing their relation to the mother and to origins in their own terms.[23] She thus stresses the transgressive potential of any attempt to symbolize the mother–daughter relationship, arguing that this will destabilize the very foundations of the patriarchal Symbolic order. Irigaray's work is aptly suited to my reading of this novel and frames this chapter.

The first section of my reading focuses on the relationship between Coya and her nameless father, and draws on Freudian paradigms to examine how the classical formation of family relations is unsettled and rewritten at the symbolic level in an attempt to rearticulate the paternal bond of love. However, Eltit illustrates the impossibility of shifting the paternal body away from paternal law and thus endowing the father with cultural and political significations that are other than those imposed on the authoritative paternal figure by Oedipal norms and the masculinist discourse of the military.

The second section of my reading examines the mother–daughter dyad in the novel. I argue that Eltit conflates the psychic violence brought about by the rupture of the mother–daughter bond at the end of the first section of the novel – a violence constitutive of the Symbolic order – with the external, physical violence unleashed during the military raid of Coya's neighbourhood. Military violence, as indicative of widespread state repression in Chile, culminates in the separation of mother and daughter. Coya is herded onto military transport destined for a concentration camp and her mother 'disappears' from the novel, her absence forming an unresolved ellipsis in the text. By lifting the mother–daughter separation out of the realm of the individual and into the realms of the collective and the political, the novel draws a direct parallel between the regulation of sexual desire within the Oedipal family and political repression. In other words, Eltit once again illustrates that patriarchy and authoritarianism are intertwined. The manner in which Eltit aims to represent the mother and the mother–daughter relationship is examined in the third section of my reading. First, though, let me outline the social and political context, and the prominence given in the novel to the discourse of race.

[21] *The Irigaray Reader*, p. 36.
[22] Morales, *Conversaciones*, pp. 80–1.
[23] *The Irigaray Reader*, pp. 39–40.

Described by Eltit as 'mi novela de la dictadura', her chilling and brooding novel was written at a time when social and political unrest in Chile escalated during the period 1983–84 into a series of popular protests brutally quelled by the military.[24] The Pinochet regime declared a state of emergency and sent thousands of troops onto the streets of Santiago and into the peripheral 'poblaciones', where most of the demonstrations were concentrated. Eltit refers to one particular civil protest that resulted in the death of over forty men, women and children in their own homes.[25] She also describes her shock when she learnt that military raids of dispossessed communities were often effected to round up common criminals, even those who had already served their jail sentences, in order to send them to concentration camps such as Pisagua. In a period when no valid institutions were permitted to function, and common criminals were viewed as a political problem, Eltit thus came to view the dividing line between delinquency and politics, and legality and illegality, as muddied: 'Entonces ahí vi que lo político y lo delictual estaban tan cerca, en todos los niveles. Y a mí me parecía, bueno, que el gobierno era delictual, que ellos a su vez ejercían esa falta de límites, digamos, concretamente en sus medidas arbitrarias.'[26]

Unconvinced by traditional political narratives of denunciation, Eltit states that her aim was to challenge the illegal political violence by foregrounding other types of repression.[27] The historical violence of the conquest of the Americas is the most prominent example, and the invasion and usurpation of land, culture, language, race and legal rights that the conquest brought in its wake are echoed in the novel and encapsulated in the name of the protagonist, Coya. As Eltit explains, this name, historically, was given to the wife of an Inca ruler. This wife would also be his sister, and while the Inca could take more than one wife, it was only the male offspring of this sister-wife who were eligible to inherit the title of Inca.[28] The nobility and respect accorded to Coya, the Inca queen, contrast starkly to the social degradation of her namesake in the novel – a sterile, 'mestiza' queen of a devastated shantytown: 'Irrumpí Coya, reina electa y légitima estéril de esos eriales' (p. 161).

It is primarily at a linguistic level that Eltit traces the social repression and decline of indigenous values and nobility, through what she refers to as 'la cercanía lingüística extrema entre Coya y coa'.[29] Coupling the historical name

---

[24] Interview with the author, 1 November 2000, Santiago. The reasons for these public protests included Pinochet's assured victory in the 1980 plebiscite, which sanctioned the constitution formulated by the military and extended Pinochet's presidency until 1989, and the severity of the economic collapse in 1982, which hit the lower classes exceptionally hard.

[25] Ortega, 'Resistencia y sujeto femenino', p. 234.

[26] Morales, *Conversaciones*, p. 63.

[27] Morales, *Conversaciones*, p. 65.

[28] Morales, *Conversaciones*, p. 62, pp. 64–5.

[29] Morales, *Conversaciones*, p. 63. Armando Méndez Carrasco defines the argot of 'coa' as follows: 'Los delincuentes, quizás inconscientemente, crearon el coa como una necesidad social, como un medio de defensa con respecto a las clases organizadas.' *Diccionario coa,*

of Coya to the term 'coa', which refers to the slang spoken by the marginal and criminal sectors of Chilean society, results in a fusion, Coya-Coa, that Eltit describes as follows: 'Coya como la generadora de una estirpe que se va pervirtiendo porque tiene su origen en el incesto, hasta llegar a esa especie de hampa proletaria.'[30] Arrate notes that the emphasis on oral language in the novel challenges 'official' written Spanish, associated with the conquerors and the military. I would also add that by drawing on a criminal argot Eltit deliberately flouts the analogy established by nineteenth-century grammarians, specifically Andrés Bello in the Chilean context, who, as Ivan Jaksic points out, equated defence of standards of language with respect for the law and the state.[31]

The denigration of indigenous cultural norms, specifically incest, are highlighted in the novel through what Eltit terms linguistic 'incest' or 'mestizaje'; that is, the intermingling of high language and slang.[32] Her aim, she states, is twofold: to pervert linguistic norms and grant stature to the popular language of 'coa' by transforming it into a literary language; and to transpose incestuous drives into linguistic structures.[33] Nelson argues that in Eltit's narrative, incest corresponds to 'an aesthetic practice (the frote, fragmentation), [which] disrupts reading by fracturing syntax, exploding recognized codes, mixing-and-matching discursive strategies'.[34] It can also be read as a practice that fuses differential categories, in this case, high/low culture and language. In Kristeva's terms, Eltit's richly poetic language would signify the equivalent of incest for the subject-in-process, because it allows the maternal territory and the repressed, archaic desire for the mother to enter into signification, a point to which I will return.[35]

As Tierney-Tello observes, since the incest taboo is central to the formation of a gender identity and social organization, it is not surprising that Eltit uses

ed. by Armando Méndez Carrasco (Santiago: Nascimento, 1979), p. 7. Many Chileans are unable to decipher 'coa', which is most often heard in the peripheral 'poblaciones' of Santiago, and Eltit herself has commented in interviews on her use of Méndez Carrasco's dictionary to 'translate' parts of her novel into 'coa'.

[30] Donoso, p. 48. The linguistic proximity between Coya-Coa and Coca-Cola (one of the most emblematic brand names of globalization) also affords a critique of the market values imposed by the military. By juxtaposing the name of Coya-Coa, which encapsulates the decline of indigenous culture to present-day social and linguistic marginalization, to the trademark Coca-Cola ('The Real Thing') a link can be drawn between the oppression of the conquest and the degradation and poverty experienced by many in Latin America because of globalization.

[31] Arrate, p. 82; and Ivan Jaksic, *Andrés Bello: Scholarship and Nation-Building in Nineteenth-Century Latin America* (Cambridge: Cambridge University Press, 2001), pp. 152–6.

[32] The etymology of the word 'incest' is the Latin noun *incestus*, which in turn is a derivative of the adjective meaning impure or defiled. *The Oxford Dictionary of English Etymology*, ed. by C. T. Onions (Oxford: Clarendon Press, 1966), p. 468.

[33] Ana María Foxley, 'Diamela Eltit: acoplamiento incestuoso', *Hoy*, 421 (1985), 41. The metaphor of incest is explored further in Eltit's following novel, *El cuarto mundo* (see Chapter 3).

[34] Nelson, p. 184.

[35] *Desire in Language*, p. 136.

incest 'as a key metaphor for enacting a political as well as a sexual transgression'.[36] In addition, Eltit strategically draws on the historical tradition of
incest in indigenous society as a means to highlight what she terms the 'artifi-
cially constructed' nature of sexual taboos.[37] By placing Coya as the female
descendent of a noble, indigenous world legally based on incest, and illustrating
that what was once acceptable is now taboo, Eltit questions the socially contingent
nature of kinship and unveils the fictional nature of the Oedipal family. I do not,
however, intend to suggest that the novel inscribes an endorsement of incestuous
relations, but rather that the implication of incest in the relationship between
Coya and her parents is a means of challenging the structure of family relations.
It is notable that, in contrast to Freud, who recognizes the taboo solely in terms
of the son's incestuous desire for the mother and the daughter's sexual desire
for the father, in Eltit's novel the taboo of incest is primarily associated with
the female child's unrecognized desire for the mother.

As noted in the Introduction, the nuclear family was one of the founding
fictions on which the military constructed its nationalist discourse. It is against
the backdrop of the appropriation of the terms 'family' and 'mother' for authoritarian purposes that Eltit's novel highlights the contradictory manner in which
the military employed these terms. In the novel, the destruction of the family
through state violence undermines the sanctity of 'mother' and 'family' that
the military had publicly sought to champion. Eltit emphasizes race as the
determining factor for acceptance into the sacred family of the nation, and thus
foregrounds the racial oppression that also structured the colonization of Latin
America. More than in any other of her novels, it is in this novel that Eltit
scrutinizes the link between the discourses of race and nation.

The Paternal Bond of Love

Coya resides within a web of Oedipal family relations that are predicated on
her desire for and love of her father. Hers is an affection that continually borders
on the violation of the incest taboo, the principal taboo that underpins the
Symbolic order and prohibits sexual exchange among family relations. Although
Coya's desire for her father is represented in incestuous terms, the question of
whether the father–daughter relationship is ever consummated is one that is
never explicitly answered.

It is in the first section of the novel, after the fatal wounding of Coya's father
by the military, that the relationship between father and daughter is most fully
depicted. Coya had previously been in her father's bar, performing an erotic
dance with her mother, which is suddenly ended as the moan of a disembodied
male voice calls out for her: 'Coa, Coya [...] Sí, alguno del reservado yacía
clamándome en su final' (p. 26). The act of naming of this unidentified male

---

[36] Tierney-Tello, p. 102.
[37] Piña, p. 240.

body, whose final climax foreshadows the finality of the death of Coya's father, echoes her father's subsequent instruction that she return home, 'el clamado de mi padre' (p. 27). This male act of naming pushes Coya, whose name represents a line of female, indigenous nobility, to accept her descent into the increasing social and linguistic degradation represented by the name Coa. Her previous, singular identity is now replaced by a subjectivity that is twofold and defined in linguistic terms: 'Esa noche de la tragedia, alguien acabó en mi nombre y desde entonces respondo dual y bilingüe si me nombran Coa y Coya también' (p. 27). As she subsequently confronts the slow death of her father, the fragmentation of her identity results in the unsettling of linguistic and syntactical norms, and the blurring of the boundary between high/low culture.

What I wish to highlight here is the disruption of kin and gender positions that occurs as Coya tends to her father. Coya indicates that her father has suffered a wound that she was powerless to prevent, even had she wanted to: 'Aindiado como era no pude ni quise prevenirle el corte, el terrible tajo que le hicieron, no el boquete de la bala, los golpes' (p. 35). Although no direct reference is made here to castration, the implication is that the wound inflicted on Coya's father results in his emasculation. As noted previously, Richard argues that state violence resulted in a 'feminization' or symbolic castration of its male victims. By foregrounding the father's indigenous features, Eltit adds a racial dimension to Richard's argument, highlighting race as a fundamental category of military oppression.

In Freudian terms, castration would signify the foreclosure of the father's position as a masculine subject and his expulsion from the social and cultural domain. The final hours of Coya and her father are therefore characterized by the inversion of the founding principle of family relations, the division between the sexes, as Coya's feminized father recoils to the Kristevan realm of the semiotic *chora*, searching for the pre-Oedipal mother through the body of his daughter. The dying wish of this father-child is that Coya attend to him as if she were his mother: 'Háblame como si fueras mi mamá, tú sabes' (p. 42). The father can thus be seen to seek comfort and oneness with the mother through his daughter, returning to his first love: the love for the mother. The symbolic place of the mother is here portrayed as fluid and not confined to an individual as Coya assumes the role of her father's mother, that is, her grandmother, which suggests an undifferentiated female or nurturing presence and a maternal genealogy, or matriarchy.

At a linguistic level, alliteration serves to illustrate the performance of the maternal function by Coya as she tends to her father: 'Lo paré, levanté su cabeza y le di un agua caliente [...] Lo parí. Estuvo atascado todo un día sin querer salir' (p. 42). On a physical level, the intertwining of the bodies of father and daughter is mingled with a childlike suckling that endows Coya's body with the maternal role of nurturing, where the mother's milk is replaced by the father's blood: 'Besados, yo nada palabra supe qué decir, más que niñita al hombre mío, al padre mío que se bajó hasta mi pecho languándome la sangre suya misma' (p. 35). It is, however, only their torsos that are joined together;

their genitalia remain apart: 'Parada ante la mesa, sin la prenda de arriba, me traspasaba en rojo […] pero abajo no pude' (p. 36). Her father reprimands Coya for exposing herself in this way, thus taking up once again the paternal function through the regulation of her desire. Coya is aware that her desire has the potential of violating the sanctity of family relations and describes such actions as a sacrilege, yet she pleads with her father to reciprocate her physical affection: 'un poquito la mano en mi pecho, por una vez y sin pecado, un tantito no más la boca en el pecho, una fugaz como si no fuera cierto, como si nunca papá mío fuera' (p. 38).

The shadow of incest thus haunts the physical proximity between daughter and father, in their assumed roles of mother and female infant respectively. The father's desire to be nurtured by the maternal body is foreclosed and Coya's wish to be close to her father as he dies is impeded. The incest taboo is exposed as a sinister law that forbids closeness and comfort between family members even in the most desperate of circumstances. Although the mother–child relationship is mapped onto the relationship between Coya and her father, the father, in his role of feminized child, does not wholly relinquish the authority of the paternal function that mediates the relationship between mother and child. The paternal function thus remains intact, which illustrates the difficulty in separating the paternal body from paternal law.

Also problematic here is Coya's conscious decision to omit her mother from her performance of the maternal role. She informs her father: 'pero nada más que usted en la pieza mía, no la madremía en la pieza, no sus partes. Nada de ella ahora. Nunca' (p. 38). While the fluctuation of kin and gender positions grants representation to the mother–daughter relationship, Coya pushes aside her own mother to usurp the maternal role. Her actions thus reflect what Irigaray has termed the symbolic 'murder' of the mother.[38] Father and daughter may stage the absence of the mother, but their performance is ultimately founded on the mother's erasure from representation.

Coya's ululation celebrates the unconditional love that she holds for her father-lover-child: 'es el amor mío que crece, se agranda sublevado, acosado, si en esta tierra hasta el don lo niegan' (p. 34). The term 'don' refers to a gift, which is symbolized later in the novel by the ruby red ring that Coya had earlier bestowed on her father, the colour of which foregrounds their blood ties. The term also refers to a natural gift or ability, a point to which I will return. Significantly, the term 'don' is a prefix given by Coya to her father's name to bind their relationship; a prefix that implies honour and prestige, which have been brutally wrested from him by the military. Although Coya employs this term as a means to endow her father's death with dignity, her use of it ultimately upholds the paternal law that is founded on the Oedipal pattern of desire and the division between the sexes, in the sense that it foregrounds her father's sexed body as the object of her desire: 'Don, que nada ni la herida de los malos pasos se lo quiten' (p. 36).

---

[38] *The Irigaray Reader*, p. 36.

In Freudian terms, Coya's desire for her father signifies penis envy. Freud argues that the little girl hopes (in vain) to be endowed with the male organ and so she deflects her desire away from the mother and towards the father, with the aim of obtaining from him what she lacks.[39] Freud states that only after repeated opposition from the father does the daughter's desire to have a child replace the desire to obtain the penis from the father, and she then directs her desire towards another man, who will act as a paternal substitute.

Coya, however, is unable to reproduce. As she states: 'soy completamente huera y me pongan al interior lo que me pongan, no hay ninguna posibilidad' (p. 161). It is, we learn, her mother who is responsible for her sterility: 'si ella misma me hizo este trabajito' (p. 161). By imposing a non-reproductive sexuality on her daughter, the aim of Coya's mother can be read as a drastic means of wresting motherhood away from the masculinist political discourse that venerated the mother as the reproducer of sanctioned concepts of gender and nationhood. She thus flouts the socially sanctioned representations of the maternal figure as the reproducer of authorized social roles by imposing Coya's sterility; an act which is celebrated by the corvine army of mothers who hound Coya throughout the novel, and who have been compared by Eltit to the Harpies or the Furies of Greek mythology.[40] Irigaray has described the Furies as women who cry out for vengeance, 'in revolt, rising up like revolutionary hysterics against the patriarchal power in the process of being established'.[41] In Eltit's novel, the army of phallic, shaven-headed mothers are angry to the point of madness, furiously denouncing the appropriation of their male children by the state, as well as their sons' treacherous collusion with the military.

In Freudian terms, Coya's sterility results in her inability to deflect her desire away from her father. Notably, Coya refers to her sterility as a natural gift through the use of the term 'don': 'Bueno, mujeres, no es culpa mía, es un don que tengo y un honor para ustedes, alguien debe portar algún beneficio' (p. 161). Describing her sterility in this way echoes the manner in which Coya would address her father, 'don que tanto el pecho me penetraste' (p. 34), which binds her sterility with her love for her father in an unending circle of misplaced desire.

As noted earlier, it is Juan, the representative of the state who has been continually unmanned by Coya, who seeks to recover his virility by facilitating the military raid. His aim is to rupture the web of Oedipal desire that binds Coya to her father and so usurp the position of the authoritative father figure. As such, Juan would also hope to be addressed by Coya in the manner in which she addresses her father; that is, as don Juan. The implicit reference to the infamous philanderer of Spanish Golden Age literature mockingly contrasts in

---

[39] Sigmund Freud, 'Femininity', in *The Standard Edition of the Complete Psychological Works of Sigmund Freud*, ed. by James Strachey, vol. 22 (London: Hogarth Press, 1964), pp. 112–35 (p. 128).

[40] Morales, *Conversaciones*, p. 39.

[41] *The Irigaray Reader*, p. 37.

the novel to his contemporary Chilean namesake, for whom an erection is no longer possible.

The male rivalry and aggression that underpin Oedipal structures are thus pushed to the extreme by Coya's inability to deflect her desire away from her father, which spurs Juan's betrayal of his community. Juan's treachery ultimately stems from the actions of Coya's mother, in the sense that it is she who is responsible for Coya's non-reproductive sexuality. The aim of her mother has been read above as a drastic means of transgressing paternal law. Indeed, by forcibly jamming the flow of her daughter's Oedipal desire towards the paternal body, her aim can once again be seen as the prevention of her daughter's submission to paternal law. As Jane Gallop explains in relation to Freudian psychoanalysis: 'The seduction which the daughter desires would give her contact with the father as masculine sexed body. The seduction which the father of psychoanalysis exercises refuses her his body, his penis, and asks her to embrace his law, his indifference, his phallic uprightness.'[42] However, in a context in which the paternal body and paternal law are inseparable, the potentially transgressive actions of Coya's mother founder. They result only in tragedy, since they push Juan to abet the violence of a male-centred political order as a desperate means of imposing the narrative of heterosexual romance.

Coya flatly and tersely relates the death of her father: 'En ese tiempo forzaron la puerta a culatazos y sin que mediera vacilación alguna le dieron el golpe de gracia a papá' (p. 47).[43] Like Antigone, Coya is haunted by the unburied corpse of her male relative, her father. It is the fate of his corpse that intensifies her lack of allegiance to her homeland, and she becomes a 'hero', like Antigone, by defying the patriarchal state that prohibits her from burying her father.[44] Problematically, however, Coya is able to come to terms with her father's death only by glorifying his memory, a point that is referred to again below.

The Mother Tongue and Mother–Daughter Separation

Unlike the Oedipal story, which erases the maternal figure, the mother is the starting point of Eltit's novel. Both by her presence and her absence the mother is included in a position of centrality. The novel opens with a childlike repetition of the first syllable of the maternal address 'mamá', which links from the very start the acquisition of language to the maternal body and firmly grounds the novel's linguistic prowess on the metaphor of the mother tongue:

[42] Jane Gallop, *Feminism and Psychoanalysis: The Daughter's Seduction* (London: Macmillan, 1982), p. 75.

[43] Coya later portrays her father as a petty criminal who used his bar as a front to run his shady operations, rather than as a political activist, highlighting the earlier point made by Eltit regarding the collapse of the boundary between politics and criminality.

[44] For an analysis of how the historical figure of Antigone can be seen to influence the position from which Eltit writes, see Cróquer Pedrón, pp. 23–30.

ma ma ma ma ma ma ma ma ma ma ma ma ma ma ma
ma ma ma ma ma ma ma ma ma ma ma ma ma ma ma
am am am am am am am ame ame ame ame dame dame
dame dame dame dame dame madame madame madame
dona madona mama mama mama mama mama mamá
mamá mamá mamacho el pater y en el bar se la toman y
arman trifulca. (p. 1)

These opening lines signify the maternal body as one of origins, and throughout the novel Coya's mother comes to embody origins, not only in terms of kinship and language, but also in terms of race. The lines perform a series of disrupting aural and visual effects that serve to emphasize the ideological transformation of the term 'mother' over time. The maternal bedrock that underlies language, the mother tongue, is here penetrated and obfuscated by the father, thus foreclosing what Irigaray terms 'this first body, this first home, this first love'.[45] Superimposed onto the maternal body are paternal language and law, which results in debauchery and violence centered on the mother.

Throughout the novel, Eltit unearths depraved and monstrous facets of maternal subjectivity as a means to highlight the complexity and ambiguity of the maternal role and the mother–daughter relationship, reflected in Coya's uncertainty in narrating the shifting connection with her mother. Their relationship is fractured by three instances of separation in the novel, all of which result from paternal mediation, and which are examined here. The first instance of separation occurs during childbirth. In a seemingly impossible account, Coya narrates the scene of her own birth from within her mother's womb.[46] Even prior to her birth, Coya presents the mother–daughter relationship as ambivalent. Residing within a maternal body sodden with alcohol, Coya's pre-natal act of suckling aims to extract alcohol, not milk, as a source of nourishment as she struggles against her mother's violent rejection of her primary needs: 'mamo y la boca se me abre en balde. No hay trago y la matona me pega, me empuja el vientre que se le hincha' (p. 16). Coya attempts to extend the excruciating birthing process for as long as possible, and she describes her enclosure within her mother's body in terms of a maternal homage: 'Yo estoy en cruz en el revés de mi mami. Yo honro su cuerpo, la expando con creces, la hambreo con ganas' (p. 16).

The voracious hunger incited in Coya can be read, as throughout Eltit's *oeuvre*, in terms of sexual desire. The maternal body is thus located as the object of Coya's desire and her position within her mother's womb is described in terms that are reminiscent of the timeless image of Christ on the cross.[47] In Christian terms, it is the death of Christ that leads to eternal life, but here the

---

[45] *The Irigaray Reader*, p. 39.

[46] The seemingly inconceivable position of a foetal narrator is explored further by Eltit in her following novel, *El cuarto mundo* (see Chapter 3).

[47] The gender transformation of the Christ figure is an image reworked by Eltit in her sixth novel, *Los trabajadores de la muerte* (see Chapter 6).

sacrificial image of the suffering Christ is embodied by a female foetus and the scene of crucifixion is inserted into the womb, which inscribes the maternal body as the site of new life through birth, not death. Coya here acknowledges the debt owed, not to the paternal body as in Christianity, but to the maternal body as the giver of life, and each of her following separations from her mother is marked by a maternal homage ('un homenaje materno').

Under the ironic title of 'EL EXTASIS DEL AMOR MATERNO' (p. 192), Coya makes evident the murderous maternal hostility unleashed towards her immediately after her birth, which confounds cultural expectations of natural maternal love. Indirectly citing her mother, Coya underscores her mother's frustrated hopes for the birth of a male child: 'Quiere un soldado que le dé arma, lo quiere armado, ceñido, señero quizás. Quiere, quiere al bastardo: la bastarda sale cabeza afuera' (p. 192). The little soldier boy, who in Freudian terms would give the mother the penis that she desires, depicted here in terms of the phallic arm, turns out to be a little girl. Coya thus unveils maternal complicity in the propagation of patriarchy and military bloodshed through reproduction. However, the use of the terms 'bastardo/bastarda' simultaneously confounds paternal law. By highlighting her daughter's illegitimacy, the mother disinherits the father from the process of reproduction, while also throwing into question the issue of an official paternal line and subverting the continuation of the patronymic name.[48]

The mother's fury at the birth of her female child is compounded by her daughter's dark skin, a racial trait that she immediately attempts to erase:

> Hierve su pecho y moja de leche la testa, lava a su niña de leche para limpiar morenita:
> – Leche blanquea, dice la madre de la madre. (p. 193)

Incited by her own mother, Coya's mother uses her breast milk not to nurture her daughter, but to wash away her indigenous traits and so transform her into a socially acceptable embodiment of femininity. Coya's mother, described on the first page of the novel as an 'india putita teñida' (p. 13), similarly attempts to hide her own indigenous roots by bleaching her dark hair: 'Caderas amplias de buena madre y mancha ese centímetro de raíz negra de mamá mala, su pelo grueso y tosco, no como arriba que es rubiecito: ondas y crespos de su infinita bondad' (p. 13). The novel thus opens by immediately confronting the myths of 'good' and 'bad' motherhood that lie at the heart of militaristic discourse and which are shown to be determined by racial origins, and not in terms of nurture and love. While the mother's dyed blonde hair and child-bearing hips epitomize those attributes deemed to denote a 'good' mother, the indigenous features which underlie her 'imported' appearance, notably her dark pubic hair, vilify her maternal nature. Unable, then, to fully disguise her identity as a

---

[48] Sonia Montecino argues that the origins of Chilean culture are founded on the bastard offspring ('huacho') of an indigenous mother and absent Spanish father. See *Madres y huachos: alegorías del mestizaje chileno* (Santiago: Sudamericana, 1991), p. 49.

'machi', Coya's mother must endure the insults directed towards her, since her attempts to identify herself in Western terms are shown to have failed.[49]

The ambiguous nature of the mother–daughter relationship is again made visible as the impending military violence unfolds. Coya is shown to draw strength from her seemingly inconceivable memories of her mother's failed attempts to keep her inside her womb, which highlights the potential of the maternal body to act as a source of succour and courage: 'Tuve un segundo plano, la imagen de mi mam mamá tapándose la entrepierna con las dos manos para tenerme adentro: es mía, es sólo para mí la paria, decía, la parida no me gusta, no quiero partir sola de nuevo' (p. 32). In contrast to the repetition of the syllable 'ma' that opened the novel, the mother's paraphrased play on words (*paria/parida/partir*) all begin with the first syllable of the paternal address, 'pa'. Paternal law is thus shown to sever the intra-uterine relationship between mother and daughter, foreclosing any period of unmediated attachment between them, a point that will be discussed again.

The second instance of mother–daughter separation occurs just prior to the death of Coya's father, after their dance in the father's bar (referred to above), which reframes the mother–daughter relationship within an erotic context. This event is recounted twice by Coya, and the interchangeable use of past and present tenses in both accounts blurs the standpoint from which she narrates. There are slight differences between the two versions put forward, but in both Juan mediates the dialogue and physical intimacy between mother and daughter, acting as a mouthpiece for Coya's father by relaying his instruction that she return home.

In both instances the dance performed by Coya and her mother portrays the mother as a powerfully stifling entity who threatens her daughter's subjectivity. In Irigaray's terms, the confusion of the boundaries between self and other that occurs marks the mother–daughter relationship as unsymbolized.[50] Swallowed into the maternal embrace, Coya and her mother become physically intertwined, which leads to a vertiginous sense of suffocation on Coya's part.

As Coya leaves her mother to attend to her father's call, she marks her departure in terms of a maternal homage: 'Cortesanamente reverencié a mi mami antes de la salida y la dejé enclavada a Juan por el clamado de mi padre' (pp. 26–7). The ludic use of the adverb 'cortesanamente', which plays on the words 'cortés' and 'cortesán', brings to mind the historical figure of Hernán Cortés, the conqueror of Mexico, and his infamous courtesan and indigenous translator, la Malinche. Perceived by generations of Latin Americans in terms of betrayal, abandoning her racial origins to become Cortés's aide, la Malinche also bears the blame for founding the 'mestizo' race, initiating the fusion of indigenous and Spanish blood through the birth of the offspring fathered by Cortés. Arrate observes that it is ultimately Juan, not the mother, who is the figure of betrayal in this novel, but Juan nevertheless links the abandonment

---

[49] A 'machi' is an indigenous female healer or shaman.
[50] *The Irigaray Reader*, p. 35.

and treachery associated with la Malinche to Coya's mother, who briefly disappears after Coya leaves the bar.[51] Following her father's death and the subsequent military raid, Juan emerges to order the chaos that surrounds the absence of Coya's parents, insisting that she rewrite the events preceding her mother's disappearance in terms that reflect la Malinche's historical scene of betrayal, categorically declaring that 'Tú mamá se fue con un eslavo y tu papá partió detrás' (p. 49).[52] Although Coya contests Juan's words, she herself had previously mocked her mother's seductive approach towards the 'eslavos' and 'zarcos' who infiltrated her father's bar in the weeks prior to his death, which illustrates once again her inability to grant their relationship a meaningful narrative pattern. However, as Tierney-Tello points out, by locating the mother as the site of the interpretative struggle between Juan and Coya, Eltit foregrounds the mother's potential for social disarray.[53]

Coya's uncertainty regarding the maternal figure is compounded during the terrifying events that lead up to their third and final separation. Reunited in the father's bar during the military raid, it is here that the mother–daughter relationship is most fully depicted. The re-emergence of Coya's mother precedes a narrative style and structure that are characterized by their excess and chaos. As the external violence intensifies, mother and daughter's grip on language increasingly falters and the first of several linguistic slippages occurs as Coya questions her mother about her recent absence: 'Explícame, háblame de qué manera pariste [...] No, me erré, quiero decir partiste' (p. 83). Coya inadvertently links the events which surround her mother's absence to the scene of her birth. Not only was this the first instance of the separation of mother and daughter, but the first syllable of the paternal address, 'pa', is again shown to mediate their relationship here.

As the military encroaches, the physical proximity between Coya and her mother intensifies into an abject need that collapses the corporeal boundaries between them. Coya huddles close to her mother, her eyes squeezed shut in fear. Subsequently, she opens them to six hallucinatory visions. These are described by Coya through a rich and highly ambiguous language that can be read in terms of the Kristevan semiotic, in the sense that it attempts to accommodate the unspeakable, repressed desire between mother and child, but Eltit's aim here is to articulate the desire specifically between mother and daughter. The fragmented and elliptical visions offer an important insight into this relationship, and their hallucinatory nature reflects the relationship between madness and desire that Irigaray has identified in the child's relation to the mother.[54]

The second of Coya's visions is entitled 'Por la patria', a titular dedication writ large in the novel's title, and the ironic nature of which is intensified

---

[51] Arrate, p. 43.

[52] The terms 'eslavo' and 'zarco' are used throughout the novel to refer to the Caucasian features of male military commanders.

[53] Tierney-Tello, p. 118.

[54] *The Irigaray Reader*, p. 35.

through the hallucinatory and erotic desire between mother and daughter that is played out here. The vision is framed by two sober addresses that are ultimately eclipsed by Coya's six dedications to her mother, which are increasingly fragmented in syntactical, linguistic and typographical terms. The maternal figure is prominently and repeatedly lauded as loved, worshipped and self-sacrificing, these praises appearing on the page in bold capitals. As Tierney-Tello notes, the military's glorification of motherhood collapses into a parody, in which 'the maternal ideal is here mocked and regarded as a lie, a discursive invention'.[55] In the novel, the linguistic juxtaposition of the terms 'madre' and 'patria' breaches the gap between the disembodied notion of woman as mother invoked in militaristic discourse and the corporeal pulsations and desire of the maternal body configured in a situation of bleak terror.

The text that follows each maternal dedication subverts any attempt to romanticize the mother or nation, as Coya intermingles her obscenely intimate depictions of her bodily fusion with her mother with her descriptions of treacherous nation. Her maternal dedications contain furious and sardonic plays on the theme of honour. Traditionally the core value instilled in any soldier, the soldiers that intrude into Coya's bodily relationship with her mother are shown not to fight with honour, or for the honour of the nation, but to fulfil the bloodthirsty commands of the 'eslavos' and bankers who seek to protect the 'honour' of thugs and traitors.

The metaphor of the mother tongue as the language first learned by a child, and which framed the opening of the novel, is rendered liberally in this vision with sexual attributes. It is the mother's tongue, delving deep inside Coya's body, which allows for the enactment of their repressed mutual desire, articulating the lingual and linguistic intimacy of mother and daughter through an erotic language that is inseparable from the body. Coya again unsettles kin relations by taking on the maternal role in relation to her own mother, offering her nipple to her mother as she did to her father prior to his death, and the physical intimacy previously denied to Coya by her father is now lavished on her by her mother. Coya is sent into a spiral of sexual arousal as her mother thrusts her tongue into her daughter's genitalia, and even the imminent arrival of the military does not prevent her from attaining *jouissance*, collapsing onto the floor in ecstasy:

en fin mamita tu

lengua

me lleva

al suelo. (p. 97)

---

[55] Tierney-Tello, p. 117. One of the ironic maternal dedications, 'BUSQUEMOS A LA MAMA MEJOR DEL MUNDO QUE ESTA EN ESTE PAIS' (p. 101), brings to mind the award presented by the Nazi government to the best Aryan mother. The Nazi government offers another example of a regime that appropriated motherhood as a political tool in nation-building, similarly equating 'good' motherhood with the reproduction of racially pure Aryan traits.

It is from within her sexual being that Coya enacts her revolt, declaring a call to arms that consists of splitting the very adjective that affirms her nationality:

> En el pubis mío la comezón del acero y en el centro pubial y nupcial el odio contra la patria:
>   CHILE-NO, grité el levantamiento.
> Y le largué una última mirada de deseo a mi madre la vasta bastarda.
> (p. 115)

Coya's rebellion against the 'patria' thus explodes by making manifest her forbidden desire for her mother, whose description as a 'bastarda' also locates the mother as the offspring of an illegitimate union with no official paternal line, thus emphasizing a matrilineal order.

It is at the end of Coya's hallucinations that the novel most prominently equates the symbolic paternal repression of the desire for the mother and the mother's own desire with external state repression. In the absence of a father figure, the state intervenes as the paternal authority to carry out the normative function of prohibiting the child's access to the mother as a sexual object. Boundaries between family and nation founder as Coya's bodily encounter with the mother is violently mediated by the entrance of the military into the father's bar. The 'bad' mother, who embodies social, sexual and linguistic disorder, and thus transgresses the female ideal championed by the military, is cast into oblivion, and the mother–daughter bond is ruptured and subordinated to an oppressive, male-centred political order. The 'matricide' that Irigaray has equated to the establishment of social order is framed in terms of the mother's disappearance, a fate that was dealt to thousands of victims by the dictatorships of the Southern Cone.

Representing the Mother–Daughter Relationship

The insuperable loss involved in Oedipal structures of identification, which require separation from the mother, and the intense grief inflicted by authoritarian violence are conflated in the second section of the novel, which opens with Coya's reiterated lamentation: 'No veo a mi mamá' (p. 164). Both Irigaray and Kristeva draw on the distinction made by Freud between mourning and melancholia to insist that female sexuality is melancholic because the little girl can never mourn the loss of the mother, a point that here thrusts Coya into a state of melancholia.[56] This section of the novel is divided into three chapters. The title of the first, 'Ella siempre tiró pa reina', not only alludes to the past, noble, indigenous heritage of Coya, the Inca queen, but also transposes the title of Mistral's well-known poem, 'Todas íbamos a ser reinas', into third-person

---

[56] Irigaray, *Speculum*, p. 68; and Kristeva, *Black Sun*, trans. by Leon Roudiez (New York: Columbia University Press, 1989), p. 29.

singular, contemporary Chilean slang ('coa'). Mistral's poem, the first verse of which is included as an epigraph to this chapter, portrays the nostalgia and disillusionment of four young women whose childhood aspirations remain unfulfilled. Their dream of growing up to become queens is given a shocking twist in Eltit's novel, since the fate that awaits Coya and her three close friends, Flora, Berta and Rucia, is a horrific assault upon the childhood innocence depicted by Mistral.

The frenzied narrative pace and style of the previous section of the novel is in contrast to the painful and truncated first-person narrative that portrays Coya's bodily collapse, illustrated through her repetition of the phrase 'Yo nada.' Her increasing disassociation from her own body means that survival becomes less a matter of conscious will and more to do with the stubborn beating of her heart, which persists in pumping blood in its autonomous state. This vital organ, usually considered the seat of life and emotions, is reduced to a process of survival in an environment in which love is impossible.[57]

The initial pages of this section make no direct reference to Coya's abrupt and violent separation from her mother, but maternal imagery abounds, as the description given by Coya of her entry into the concentration camp illustrates: 'Salgo expulsada en el pujo' (p. 169). Her entry is described in terms that suggest an expulsion from the maternal body; her 'rebirth' signifies the ultimate separation from her mother and her arrival in a hellish environment of physical and psychological violation. Coya's separation from her mother is inscribed directly onto her body as she regresses to a pre-Oedipal stage as an initial process of survival, curling up in the foetal position and drooling from her gaping mouth.

It is shortly after enduring appalling torture and gang rape that Coya begins her writing. Unlike the first instance of writing in the novel, which was instigated by Juan as a means to rewrite the tragic events that had befallen her, it is now Coya who initiates and takes control. Her aim is to give voice and agency to her female inmates. The title given to her writing, 'Parlamentos, documentos, manifiestos' (p. 212), reflects the title of the fifth and final chapter of the first section of the novel, 'TESTIMONIOS, PARLAMENTOS, DOCUMENTOS, MANIFIESTOS'. The latter is composed of a series of mother–daughter dialogues between Coya's three friends, Berta, Flora and Rucia, and their respective mothers, and also between Coya and her own mother. Their dialogues are interspersed with phrases that cruelly remind the reader of the ongoing military raid, bringing to the fore the paternal mediation of the mother–daughter relationship. I read the mother–daughter dialogues in the fifth chapter as forming part of the subsequent corpus of writing initiated by Coya in the prison camp. By inserting these dialogues into the past and into a previous section of the novel, which had as its backdrop the military raid of

---

[57] The description given by Coya of her relationship with her heart, 'latimos juntos en la noche como gemelos en el pariente' (p. 173), offers a preview of a uterine relationship between twins, one male and one female, which is developed by Eltit in *El cuarto mundo* (see Chapter 3).

Coya's neighbourhood, Eltit, like Irigaray, can also be seen to perceive the potential for transforming political and symbolic structures by granting representation to the mother–daughter relationship, as we shall see.

The mother–daughter dialogues included in Coya's writing are by no means idealized. The dialogues of Berta, Flora and Rucia are structured around their childhood memories, all of which occur in a domestic environment in which the father is absent, and from which all three women are banished by their mothers at an early age because of their sexual transgressions. Coya's own dialogue with her mother is framed by the bellicose discourse of maternity propagated by her grandmothers, who instruct Coya to rebuff her own mother's pleas for affection, as the following dialogue between them illustrates:

> – Quiéreme, me suplicaba.
>   Estamos en guerra, le contestaba. (p. 156)

Coya's subsequent process of writing thus uncovers the repression of the maternal bond of love that is deemed necessary by mothers to survive in their savage environment. In Coya's marginalized community it is mothers who expose the sham of political discourses that venerate maternity as an ideal of femininity, refuting this myth with one sharp phrase: 'No hay marido legal, animal estado las espera la panza' (p. 158).

Coya's representation of the mother–daughter relationship makes evident the impossibility of a nostalgic return to the maternal body. Indeed, she later describes her pitiful attempts to return to her mother's womb as a young child. Butting her head against her mother's vagina, with her mother desperately clawing at her vaginal walls to open a passage for her daughter, Coya would attempt to crawl back into the dank warmth of her mother's body in a reversal of the scene of birth. However, they weep at the realization of the impossibility of their joint endeavour, which reflects the point made by Irigaray: 'If you are born a girl, the question is quite other. No return to, toward, inside the place of origin is possible unless you have a penis.'[58] Both Coya and her mother find that the maternal body is now accessible only through male penetration: 'Se había recompuesto férrea los canales y sólo hombre, apenas mano podía tragar' (p. 194).

Central to Coya's writing is the ordering of the collective memories of the women and the imposition of a hierarchy of maternal relations among them. The power granted to Coya by her writing allows her to place herself at the head of the other women. She assumes the position of 'madre de madres' and defines herself as the self-appointed Madre General who commands the mother tongue that guides the strict, hierarchical structure of her maternal troops. Coya invalidates the very etymology of the maternal function since she is sterile, but she redefines the maternal role so that it is based on the ability to speak. It is only Coya, as Mother General, and a select few of her maternal comrades

[58] *Speculum*, p. 41.

who are granted speech; those further down the hierarchy emit only guttural sounds.

Coya's writing is problematic for two reasons. Firstly, the vertical relation between the women is identical to a male, military hierarchy, which has been shown to rupture family relationships and mediate the mother–daughter bond. The structure of Coya's maternal troops also replicates the hierarchy of the corvine army of mothers who ferociously pursue Coya, referred to above, who in turn are also structured akin to a military hierarchy.

Secondly, although this section of the novel opens with Coya's desperate search for her disappeared mother, she becomes progressively hostile towards the ambivalent memory of her mother, which once again foregrounds her inability to meaningfully represent her mother and so mourn her loss. The stability of Coya's maternal position is attained only by casting out the maternal figure who threatens boundaries and blurs distinctions, as Coya once again usurps the place of the mother while leaving unresolved the relation to her.

Coya turns instead towards the glorified memory of her dead father, who appears not as the dependent, needy father of their final encounter, but as the armed, dapper dandy of an earlier time. It is this earlier phallic paternal figure to whom Coya remains bound, as she declares her love for her father's 'herramienta' or 'arma' (p. 197). The symbolic phallus that upholds paternal order is thus exposed as the underlying structure of Coya's writing. Her attempts to rewrite the maternal function and grant representation to the mother–daughter relationship are thus undermined, since her writing leaves intact a patriarchal and militaristic order that is founded on the mother's absence and negativity. It is only at the end of the novel, after the dramatization of the moment of Coya's conception by her friend Rucia, that Coya is able to rearticulate the Freudian telos that emphasizes separation from the mother as the essential rupture which allows the formation of a mature subject position.

Through her astonishing enactment of the primal scene, Rucia performs the primal trauma of infantile fantasy, an act that has haunted Coya since the beginning of the novel and which Coya has tried, but failed, to reconstruct. It is her reconstruction of the primal scene, Rucia hints, which will disarticulate Coya's triangular, Oedipal relationship with her parents: 'Ya lo vas a ver, ya vas a ver la escena completa. Estás en la pira, en la pirámide destruida' (p. 269). Rucia gives prominence in her performance to Coya's mother, which reverses the description given of her on the first page of the novel and outlined previously: 'Mujer tramposa de arriba, ser verídico de abajo' (p. 271). Rucia thus emphasizes the authenticity of the dark hair that belies the mother's indigenous blood and which she herself had attempted to disguise. She also foregrounds the mother–daughter relationship by reclaiming the pleasure of the bodily contact between mother and daughter, which had been erased from Coya's memory. The first syllable of the maternal address, 'ma', is reinvested by Rucia with its primal significance, which is that of the maternal body and the mother tongue, as Coya's stuttering paraphrasing of Rucia's speech indicates: 'Habla de ella y yo, de nosotras. De la lengua confinada sobre mi carne y refinada encima mío, mi ma ma madre' (p. 271).

Kristeva posits the fantasy of a father–mother conglomerate united in complete satisfaction as a means to reconceptualize the primal scene and redress the absence of the mother in current symbolic structures.[59] However, in contrast to Kristeva, Eltit does not portray the primal scene in terms of a union of complete satisfaction. Rucia depicts Coya's mother as sexually insatiable, and the inability of Coya's father to satisfy the mother's sexual demands leads to the collapse of their pleasure into recriminations. Coya's mother mocks the father for his 'lack', which foreshadows the dysfunctional gender relations that will later be played out by Juan and Coya:

> El encuentro de goce pasa a guerra:
> – No puedes, le dice.
> – Aguántate, le contesta.
> – No sirves. (p. 272)

In spite of their recriminations, Rucia makes visible the love expressed between Coya's parents during a time in which their relationship was not shaped by the triangular family structure that would later frame it. For the first time, Coya is forced to confront their expressions of mutual love:

> Y el amor que se tenían me remece otra vez [...] Por el amor que se tenían retumban las palabras de la Rucia y sus respuestas: el abandono a mí, que me empujaban atrás de todo procedimiento y decoro. (p. 273)

Until Rucia's dramatization, Coya had nurtured the fantasy of her participation as a foetus in her parents' sexual acts. She describes how, from the moment of her conception, she would open her legs to her father within her mother's womb, vying with her mother for her father's affection and usurping her mother's place. This startling image implies that even before her birth Coya had never experienced a sexually neutral, pre-Oedipal moment. Even as a foetus, Coya complies with Oedipal paradigms, a point that confounds established psychoanalytic frameworks and which is discussed again in Chapter 3. My point here is that paternal mediation forecloses any attachment between mother and daughter, which results in a mother–daughter relationship that is always and already fractured by rivalry. By locating this rivalry within the womb, Eltit dramatically emphasizes how Oedipal patterns of desire give rise to dysfunctional relations between mother and daughter, which forces readers to question the constructed nature of family relations. As Diana Fuss puts it: 'Why is the daughter's resentment and bitterness surmised to be directed toward the mother as competitor for the father's affections and not towards the father

---

[59] 'Interview with Julia Kristeva', in *Women Analyze Women*, ed. by Elaine Baruch and Lucienne Serrano (New York: Columbia University Press, 1987), pp. 241–50 (p. 249).

as interloper into the mother–daughter relation?'[60] By forcefully highlighting that there is no moment of mother–daughter symbiosis, Eltit unequivocally illustrates that the social and symbolic structures that uphold the nation, patriarchy and authoritarianism, are both founded on the violent repression of the mother–daughter relationship.

As noted above, Rucia's dramatization of the love that existed between Coya's parents induces in Coya a devastating feeling of abandonment, in a reflection of the point made by Kristeva that in relation to the fantasy of the primal scene, the child perceives itself as excluded. To counter its exclusion, she argues, the child turns to the loving imaginary father, a point that is challenged here by Eltit.[61] The collapse of the primal fantasy harboured by Coya thrusts her towards the maternal body, which, as Brito observes, also embodies the repressed racial history of Latin America: 'Victimada en el soplo: viuda de mi padre, viuda de mi madre, enlutada, me recojo hasta mi propia fundación, anterior al bar, ensañada en la selva oscura de mi madre' (p. 277).[62] Confounding kin relations once again in her role as widow to her parents, Coya moves beyond the paternal domain of the bar to conflate her moment of origin with the conquest of the Americas. She envisions an unbroken genealogy of indigenous mothers, exhausted by incessant childbirth and victims of male domination, both indigenous and colonial. Their precarious maternal existence is counterpoised by Coya to that of the women who will subsequently come to embody 'good' motherhood: 'han opuesto a ustedes extranjeras arrogantes, insinuantes y banales' (p. 276). Motherhood is shown to be appropriated as the exclusive prerogative of white male colonizers, while the indigenous mothers portrayed by Coya are relegated to the culturally abject in their role as founders of the 'mestizo' race. This pushes Coya to vent her fury at her mother for concealing her entanglement of dark pubic hair, and so occluding the representation of her indigenous, maternal heritage and making visible only her Spanish, paternal heritage.[63]

In Irigaray's terms, Rucia's rearticulation of Coya's primal scene allows Coya to perceive her mother as both mother and sexual being, and so symbolize her mother's identity in terms that are not reduced to the maternal function. This subsequently permits Coya to differentiate herself from her mother and initiate a search for an autonomous sense of self that is founded not on maternal repression, but on the reconstruction of an unbroken, symbolic umbilical cord that reunites her with the repressed maternal heritage of her continent. Eltit's stance here is close to that of Irigaray, who also asserts the existence of a genealogy of women as a means to rearticulate and symbolize the relation between mother and daughter.[64] Coya's representation of a maternal line that

[60] Diana Fuss, *Identification Papers* (New York and London: Routledge, 1995), p. 63.
[61] *Tales of Love*, pp. 34–5.
[62] *Campos minados*, p. 141.
[63] Montecino also foregrounds the repression of a maternal indigenous ancestry in Chilean society from an anthropological perspective. *Madres y huachos*, p. 189.
[64] *The Irigaray Reader*, p. 39.

structures the mother–daughter relationship, and which has hitherto been absent from the paternal Symbolic, results in the creation of a new psychic formation that allows her to flee the constricting definition of Oedipal structures in which she has been incarcerated, and which had denied her any access to the maternal body and to the repressed maternal origins of Latin America. As Berta declares: 'Te libraste, supiste hacerlo a tu medida, impresionaste hasta a la Rucia que es muy dura' (p. 279). Eltit thus portrays the return to the mother as positing a new feminine subjectivity.

Coya's psychic liberation also leads to her physical liberation. It is only now that she is able to negotiate an 'amnesty' with Juan, who returns in his role as prison guard to rekindle their relationship. This leads to Coya's release, along with her maternal troops. The etymology of the term 'amnesty', meaning a general pardon, is the Latin adjective 'amnēstia', which signifies oblivion or forgetting.[65] The use of the term in the novel is thus extremely ambivalent, since Juan has constantly aimed to usurp and obliterate Coya's memory. Their amnesty is founded upon Coya's acceptance of the validity of the following declaration made by Juan: 'que soy, que fui, que seré tu contramemoria y el viso de realidad que te afirma' (p. 290). Coya acknowledges that Juan must be taken into account in any attempt to rethink the feminine, since they are, as Tierney-Tello points out, 'a priori and almost tragically intertwined and inter-dependent'.[66] They are the other against which each is defined and only when there is mutual recognition, rather than the annihilation of whatever is consti-tuted as other, can there be any reconciliation of the binary logic that underpins patriarchy. Ultimately, then, the novel does not posit the notion of an unviolated female past, but reflects Richard's argument that the historical tensions and multiple discourses of oppression which exist in Latin America must be acknowledged in any attempt to open up a space to renegotiate the feminine.[67]

Sexual relations between Coya and Juan are now consummated, an act that is anticipated by Coya in terms of an epic. The epic thus emerges from a harrowing space of oppression and is founded on the reconceptualization of male–female relations in terms that suggest an archaic regression to the mother, corresponding to Kristeva's argument that the child is reconciled with its mother as an adult through sexual intercourse.[68] The codified order of desire structured through an identification with the father and separation from the mother is here transgressed by privileging a form of access to the maternal body. The incestuous and suppressed pre-Oedipal desire for the mother and the mother's own desire are inscribed directly into the corporeal union of Coya and Juan, as Coya searches through the body of Juan for a lost plenitude of

---

[65] Onions, p. 32. Specific to the Chilean context is the amnesty granted to the Chilean armed forces and enshrined in the 1980 Constitution. In addition, Amnesty International is a human rights organization.

[66] Tierney-Tello, p. 94.

[67] 'Feminismo, experiencia y representación', p. 741.

[68] *Tales of Love*, pp. 222–3.

maternal experience: 'Me tomó como mi madre, si lo fuera, cautamente y con liviandad' (p. 294). In turn, this allows for the renegotiation of Coya's relationship with Juan, which implies that only when the mother–daughter relationship is symbolized can the absolutely vital need to rearticulate dysfunctional gender relations occur.

Following this epic union, the women are subsequently released and return to their shattered community as an army of mothers with Coya at their head, pushing aside the corvine mothers that had previously intruded into the narrative. As Coya states: 'Me sentí rodeada de un ejército de madres caminando por calles extrañas [...] Somos madre general y madres 1,2,3,4,5,6, al destrone de las viejas y el nuevo símbolo de la parición invertida: la defensa' (p. 295). Their 'defence' is thus based on their refusal to service the process of male self-reproduction, emblematized by the maternal body of Coya which is stripped of the capacity for reproduction.

Coya and her friends emerge speaking the repressed, vernacular languages of Latin America and in so doing they extend the category of the feminine to include the marginalized sectors of Latin America. By granting orality an epistemic privilege they also foreclose any attempt to appropriate motherhood through their strategic use of a linguistic code that confounds dominant systems of representation. Limiting the reader's textual intimacy by privileging an argot that is unintelligible to many also serves to locate this novel as marginal, in the sense given by Sommer.

The closing lines of the novel portray the women as almost human, returning to administer the public space of the father's bar. As Coya proclaims:

– Se abre el bar, mujeres. Lo abrimos, lo administramos con jerarquía.
Y la sed se apoderó de ellas. (p. 297)

An acknowledgement of the significant challenge to authoritarianism posed by the political struggle of mothers' movements in Chile can be read throughout the second section of the novel, but I do not read such an acknowledgement as an uncritical celebration on Eltit's part. While the women in her novel assume authority in the paternal domain and renegotiate the maternal function so that it is based on a non-reproductive sexuality, they continue to be structured along hierarchical lines, their clearly differentiated categories of status a latent source of rivalry. However, their hierarchical structure can, perhaps, be viewed in strategic terms, since it grants individuation to the prototypical relationship between women, the mother–daughter relationship. This prevents the psychosis and fusionality that merges their identity and marks the mother–daughter relationship as unsymbolized.

The image of infinite thirst that closes the novel indicates the irruption of an oralized, primal desire associated with the mother, which rearticulates desire within a matrilineal order and posits these mothers as desiring subjects inside the symbolic paternal realm. Irigaray, however, equates oral avidity with the lack of representation of the child's separation from the mother.[69] So, while the transgressive potential inherent in rethinking mother–daughter relations may have been uncovered in the novel, further symbolization of the relationship to the mother is necessary to disrupt fully the underlying power structures of patriarchy and authoritarianism.

To conclude, the connection made in the novel between the nuclear family and authoritarian violence demands that the formation of family structures be reconfigured. Stable, middle-class family norms as established by Freud are shown to be inadequate and truly dangerous here, and the return to Oedipal family norms is impossible in a situation in which family members have been killed or disappeared. There is no family romance, only terror, chaos and a family nightmare. Rebellion against the fatherland and its heritage is thus located in the family and sexual realm, a point that is elaborated further in Eltit's following novel, *El cuarto mundo*. So, while the nuclear family is shown to be an artifice constructed on a foundation of repressed desire, most significantly that between mother and daughter, the most hopeful suggestion to emerge from this bleak underworld stems precisely from the collapse and rearticulation of patterns of desire within the family. By reimagining the premises of kinship and the maternal and paternal bonds of love, the notion of mother/fatherland may be refigured and the phrase 'por la patria' endowed with new meaning.

---

[69] *The Irigaray Reader*, p. 40.

3

Motherhood and Gender in *El cuarto mundo*

Body and Text in the Periphery

El cuarto mundo is, essentially, a fictional representation of the construction of gender.[1] The backdrop to the action of the novel is the increasingly enclosed space of, initially, the uterine chamber and then the family home, and the narrative is embedded in dysfunctional familial affiliations that become progressively intertwined with the public context. The narrative voices are those of fraternal twins, one male and one female, who narrate the first and second sections of the novel respectively, although there is a shift to an omniscient third-person narrator in the final two pages.[2] The narrative of the 'mellizo' consists mainly of his attempts to comprehend his relationship with his mother and twin sister. His ponderous and self-opinionated language, and his use of conventional syntax starkly contrast with the fractured and often obscure narrative style of the 'melliza'. While he aims to offer totalizing judgements and truths, the intention of his twin sister, she informs us, is to provoke and disturb. The novel ends with the birth of a baby girl produced by diamela eltit (the name given to the 'melliza' on the final page of the novel) and her twin brother: 'Lejos, en una casa abandonada a la fraternidad, entre un 7 y 8 de abril, diamela eltit, asistida por su hermano mellizo, da a luz una niña. La niña sudaca irá a la venta' (p. 159).

In contrast to *Por la patria*, which Eltit refers to as 'una obra más ... monumental', she describes *El cuarto mundo* as 'una obra menor pero bien hecha' and makes reference to the concision and craftsmanship of two novellas, by Carson McCullers and Yasunari Kawabata, as important models for her own work.[3] While drawing on themes previously explored in *Por la patria*, such as motherhood, the family, incest and sexual identity, Eltit has stated that her

[1] Throughout this chapter I refer to the second edition of *El cuarto mundo* (Santiago: Seix Barral, 1996). The novel was republished in 2003 by the Colombian publisher Norma in Buenos Aires and has also been published as a trilogy alongside *Los vigilantes* and *Mano de obra* as *Tres Novelas* (Mexico: FCE, 2004).

[2] Fraternal twins develop from two separate ova, each fertilized by a sperm, and may or may not be of the same sex.

[3] Morales, *Conversaciones*, pp. 40–1. Eltit refers to *The Ballad of the Sad Café* (1953) by McCullers and *House of the Sleeping Beauties* (1969) by Kawabata.

purpose in writing this novel was to create what she has called '"un doble relato". Uno que es bastante lineal [...] que es la historia de los mellizos; pero lo que más me importaba era hablar "materialmente" de cómo se escribía una novela.'[4] Eltit also explains that by using the metaphor of two foetuses of different sex, her aim was to explore 'la problemática de la pareja, que se considera como algo tan nuclear dentro de la sociedad [...] qué mejor metáfora [...] que estos fetos que se rozan, se molestan y se invaden mutuamente los espacios.'[5]

On one level, then, the novel consists of the story of the twins, which begins just prior to their conception and ends with the birth of their own child. In the previous chapter, I referred to the tradition of fraternal incest in indigenous culture, as well as Eltit's strategy of drawing on the metaphor of incest as a means to bring together two distinct discourses, two points which are also relevant here. In *El cuarto mundo*, the two differential categories that are brought together are those of sexual difference, and the central image of fraternal twins can thus be moved beyond its literal significance to address the status of male–female relations in Chilean society. On a second level, as stated above, Eltit's aim is to foreground the writing process (a common trait in her novels) and so uncover what she describes as 'las relaciones de fuerza que van entablando las voces femeninas, masculinas, voces incluso híbridas o andró-ginas'.[6] There is, however, yet another level to the novel, described by Eltit as follows: 'Pero hay otro nivel en que se representa la problemática de una novela que no se termina [...] Se trata en fin de una novela que va a la venta.'[7] Like *Lumpérica*, this novel is continually in process, as the end product – the baby girl – collapses into the novel itself, which enters as a commodity into market exchange.

El cuarto mundo is Eltit's third novel and it was selected to form part of the prestigious collection of the Biblioteca Ayacucho in Venezuela, which is made up of the seminal texts of Latin American culture. It has been translated into English and French, and is the first of Eltit's novels to be published by a major international publishing house (Seix Barral), opening up her writing to a wider readership beyond Chile, but also prompting a reflective tone in the novel regarding the commercial circulation of her work. The novel was published in Chile in 1988, the year of the plebiscite that heralded the end of the Pinochet dictatorship and a period in which Chile was traversed by the programme of mass privatization so central to the neo-liberal economic model imposed by the military. This social backdrop is reflected in the novel, since everything is shown to be up for sale. However, Jean Franco warns against reading the novel simply as an allegory of Pinochet's 'economic miracle', and

---

[4] Sandra Garabano and Guillermo García-Corales, 'Diamela Eltit', *Hispamérica*, 62 (1992), 65–75 (p. 69).

[5] Garabano and García Corales, p. 70.

[6] Garabano and García-Corales, p. 69.

[7] Garabano and García-Corales, p. 69.

focuses instead on the effects of discipline, repression, shame and marginalization on the bodies of a fragmented underclass with no stable identity.[8]

Eltit's writing of the novel coincided with a trip to France, where she first heard the term 'el cuarto mundo' applied to marginal swathes of industrialized countries. She describes the meaning of the phrase as follows: 'gente que se desocializa dentro de sus casas. Por ejemplo, pueden vivir con veinte gatos ..., treinta [...] Son formas de vida completamente desocializados.'[9] It was during this trip that, for the first time, Eltit realized she was viewed as coming from what the West terms the 'Third World'. For this reason, she states, she developed the term 'el cuarto mundo' to refer to a world that consists of 'las energías más oprimidas por la cultura'; a world made up of fragments and scraps ('escenas') rather than 'historias enteras o grandes relatos'.[10] Eltit also relates the term to what she describes as 'un mundo más oscuro que habita en cada uno de nosotros – dentro de lo cultural. Y a su vez, en ese mismo espectro, habría una referencia objetiva al Tercer Mundo que nosotros habitamos en Latinoamérica.'[11] She therefore aligns the term 'el cuarto mundo' not only with the less economically advanced area of Latin America, but also with all that is culturally repressed in society. Notably, the absolute poverty and marginalization associated with countries referred to as the 'Third World' often imply passive victimhood, but Eltit offers a disturbing portrayal of 'cuartomundistas' in her novel, binding them to the deliberate disruption of social/family order and self-marginalization.

Like Eltit, Richard applies an active and subversive quality to what she terms the periphery. As she states: 'The periphery has always made its own mark on the series of statements emitted by the dominant culture and has recycled them in different contexts in such a way that the original systemizations are subverted, and their claim to universality undermined.'[12] The following declaration by the 'melliza', 'Quiero hacer una obra sudaca terrible y molesta' (p. 114), illustrates her aim of using her narrative to challenge the often pejorative attitude of the West towards the so-called periphery, implied by the term 'sudaca', a term which Raquel Olea describes as emphasizing 'lo sudamericano como identidad margen, en desamparo, prostituible, minorizada'.[13] However, as Julio Ortega

---

[8] Franco, pp. 119–20. Franco's warning is reflected in Spivak's comments on the novel as foreclosing any referential connection in order to posit 'the infantile psyche that enters "social normality" precariously, in depression and mourning'. Gayatri Chakravorty Spivak, 'Three Women's Texts and Circumfession' in *Postcolonialism and Autobiography*, ed. by Alfred Hornung and Ernstpeter Ruhe (Amsterdam and Atlanta: Rodopi, 1998), pp. 7–22 (p. 22).

[9] Morales, *Conversaciones*, p. 69.

[10] Oquendo, pp. 114–15.

[11] Larraín, 'El trabajo es la vida y mi vida', p. 1.

[12] Nelly Richard, 'Postmodernism and Periphery', trans. by Nick Caistor, in *Postmodernism: A Reader*, ed. by Paul Docherty (New York: Harvester Wheatsheaf, 1991), pp. 463–70 (p. 470).

[13] Olea, *Lengua víbora*, p. 62. Ortega also stresses the derogatory significance of the term 'sudaca', which originates from Spain, in *Una poética de literatura menor* (see Lértora), p. 79.

perceptively notes, the novel also aims to foreground Latin American specificity through what he describes as 'la necesidad de gestar, de generar, una nueva respuesta desde la diferencia latinoamericana', but I would emphasize that the elaboration of such specificity is correlated in the novel to the narrative of the 'melliza', and thus to the category of the feminine.[14]

Eltit herself extends the term 'sudaca' to include what she refers to as its 'producciones sociales y culturales', and when used to describe the baby/novel, the term foregrounds the peripheral zone from which the writing process emerges.[15] There is, then, a fourth level to the novel, which concerns Eltit's position as a woman who writes from Latin America, and her comments on the inclusion of her name in lower case at the end of the novel (the name given to the 'melliza') foreground the cultural repression that she, as an author, faces: 'Utilicé mi propio nombre como hija para pasar a productora de textos, madre de textos, la novela sudaca [...] que desde el punto de vista narrativa elegido va a la venta teñida por su condición de desamparo y resistencia.'[16] Eltit here playfully throws the kin positions of mother and daughter into flux, firstly by conflating her authorial persona with the 'melliza' and then by locating herself as 'madre de textos'. Her comments clearly position the maternal body as the origin of the novel and occlude the father from the process of literary production/ procreation. She thus challenges the tradition of male authors who inscribe themselves in their novels as the product of their literary creation, perhaps the best example of which in Spanish literature is Miguel de Unamuno, whose ageneric literary text, *Cómo se hace una novela* (1927), collapses into the origin from which he emerges. The maternal body is overwritten in Unamuno's text, a point that is firmly contested in Eltit's novel, which foregrounds the maternal body as the underlying foundation of all representations, positioned as a creative source whose outlet is not only the production of a child but also a literary text. The maternal body is thus moved beyond the realm of biological procreation into the realm of culture.

The analogy here between motherhood and literary creation is one that Eltit has made explicit on several occasions.[17] Eltit frequently refers to her writing in terms of its 'artisanal' quality, a quality that she also describes as specific to both maternity and Latin American culture:

> Nuestro continente, aun en sus diferencias regionales, porta – a mi juicio – la marca de lo artesanal y en este hábito (lo digo en el sentido de la artesanía que comporta la escritura, por ejemplo), el pensamiento y el habitar concretos, nombran a una mujer que traslada en su cuerpo una particular manera de conectarse con la realidad. Una manera, por ejemplo, que se vuelve legible,

---

[14] Ortega, in *Una poética de literatura menor* (see Lértora), p. 79.
[15] Ortega, 'Resistencia y sujeto femenino', p. 236.
[16] Ortega, 'Resistencia y sujeto femenino', p. 238.
[17] See, for example, Eltit's comments in Larraín, 'El trabajo es la vida y mi vida', p. 5.

con la maternidad, artesanía privativa del cuerpo de las mujeres [...] Y en esa 'creación' define a la mujer latina por sus multiples gestaciones.[18]

Eltit thus brings together the spheres of female reproduction and Latin American literature and culture by stressing their local and homespun nature, which stands in contrast to the increasing global reliance on sophisticated technology. Eltit also stresses the importance of the relationship between Latin American women and the power of the female body to 'create' incessantly, but she stops short of idealizing this relationship. In *El cuarto mundo*, the highly positive – indeed, almost utopian – possibilities offered by the baby/novel may become perceptible to the reader at the very end, but the emphasis throughout is firmly placed on the physical and psychological suffering inherent in pregnancy and childbirth.

Eltit's alignment of the product of the relationship between the twins (the baby) and the novel that enters into market exchange positions the writer as analogous to a mother who carries her child in her body, gives birth to him/her and relinquishes the child to a society in which she is unable to determine the course of its development. Positing the female child as a commodity to be sold – given a price and put on the market – not only foregrounds the status of the female body as an object of exchange but also positions the baby/novel as a slave, which once again underlines Eltit's concerns regarding the commercial circulation of her work. However, by offering a grotesque and dystopian portrayal of a family unit, assailed by the pervasive market economy of Chilean society and flouting the social norms grounded in the Oedipus complex, Eltit's novel can be seen to counter what is probably the most commercially successful novel of Latin American literature: Gabriel García Márquez's *Cien años de soledad* (1969). While it is beyond the remit of this study to explore this point in further detail, it is worth pointing to Ana María Dopico's comments in her comparative analysis of García Márquez's novel and Donoso's *El obsceno pájaro de la noche*.[19] Dopico argues that Donoso's novel, in stark contrast to *Cien años de soledad*, annihilates 'the legend of the Latin American family as the vessel for a regional history', and reveals a world 'entombed from the export economy of magical realism, national allegory or historical novel' – two points that are extremely pertinent to any analysis of Eltit's reponse to García Márquez in *El cuarto mundo*.[20]

Eltit's novel can also be read as a response to the nation/family metaphor perpetuated by the Pinochet regime, which is the approach taken by both Lea Ramsdell and Anna Reid. Ramsdell argues that the fictional family/nation

---

[18] 'Acerca del hacer literario', in *Emergencias: escritos sobre literatura, arte y política*, ed. with prologue by Leonidas Morales T. (Santiago: Planeta/Ariel, 2000), pp. 177–85 (p. 183).

[19] Ana María Dopico, '*Imbunches* and Other Monsters: Enemy Legends and Underground Histories in José Donoso and Catalina Parra', *Journal of Latin American Cultural Studies*, 10 (2001), 325–51.

[20] Dopico, p. 326.

created by Eltit 'mirrors the violence and psychosis of power relations in the dictatorship', and Reid concludes that the nation/family formulations based on the family as the place of harmony and morals are subverted in the novel, since everything fragments at the end.[21] My reading also aims to focus on the representation of the family in the novel, but in terms of how this representation subverts what Richard refers to as the universal 'original systemizations' of dominant culture, specifically in relation to Western psychoanalysis. As Franco notes, the family members 'imperfectly live a version of the family romance that never conforms properly to the oedipal paradigm'.[22]

The third section of this chapter illustrates how Eltit radically uses her novel to disrupt and reverse Freudian etiology, since the twins fail to align themselves with paternal law and the family progressively disintegrates until it becomes unintelligible in Western terms. The maternal, and not the paternal, body is foregrounded as the central, informing presence in the family, and the maternal unconscious is prominently drawn into a narrative of subject-formation. This section of the chapter focuses on the distinct manner in which the twins relate to their mother, as well as the influence of the mother–child relationship on the formation of a gender identity. Perhaps the most patent example of the latter is the mother's conferral of the girl's name of María Chipia on the 'mellizo', an act that is central to his subsequent gender confusion.[23]

The following section of this chapter examines the representation of motherhood in the novel, which also forms the point of departure for the reading offered by Bernadita Llanos, who examines how the maternal subjectivity portrayed in the work resists traditional ideologies of motherhood.[24] The emphasis of my reading is on the representation of motherhood as depicted first by the 'mellizo' from within his mother's womb and throughout childhood, and then as represented by the 'melliza', who speaks as a mother and a daughter. The points of similarity and contrast between the two, often conflicting, representations are also highlighted here.

[21] Lea Ramsdell, 'Dysfunctional Family, Dysfunctional Nation: *El cuarto mundo* by Diamela Eltit', in *The Ties That Bind: Questioning Family Dynamics and Family Discourse in Hispanic Literature*, ed. with introduction and notes by Sara E. Cooper, pp. 103–25 (p. 103); and Anna Reid, 'Disintegration, Dismemberment and Discovery of Identities and Histories: Searching the "gaps" for depositories of alternative memory in the narratives of Diamela Eltit and Carmen Boullosa', *Bulletin of Latin American Research*, 17 (1998), 81–92 (p. 85).

[22] Franco, p. 119.

[23] Eltit explains that the names given to María Chipia and his younger sister María de Alava are 'borrowed' from a text by Julio Caro Baroja, and were the names of two women sentenced by the Inquisition for witchcraft. Morales, *Conversaciones*, p. 41, p. 66. Eltit does not give the title of the text to which she refers, but it is Caro Baroja's *Inquisición, brujería y criptojudaismo* (1970).

[24] Llanos, in *Letras y proclamas* (see Llanos), pp. 109–41.

The Representation of the Mother

As in the Freudian Oedipal story, the novel begins with the as yet nameless son who later becomes known as María Chipia. His account starts just prior to the moment of his conception, which results from a scene of domestic rape. It is thus the narrative voice of the 'mellizo' that gives birth to the novel, engendering the narrative without the help of his mother, within whose body he will shortly reside: 'Un 7 de abril mi madre amaneció afiebrada [...] Mi padre, de manera inexplicable y sin el menor escrúpulo, la tomó [...] Ese 7 de abril fui engendrado en medio de la fiebre de mi madre y debí compartir su sueño' (pp. 11–12).

The novel begins with a seemingly impossible account. In a parody of the biblical assertion that the Word was made flesh, here voice precedes body and person, and, once conceived, the omniscient embryonic narrator is endowed with a sex and a consciousness that a foetus does not have at this stage. As in *Por la patria*, by pushing back the point of sexual identity formation to within the womb, Eltit again challenges the existence of a moment prior to the construction of sexual difference, which dramatically emphasizes the extent to which the maternal body is territorialized by paternal law and patriarchal norms are inscribed in the psyche.

María Chipia's narrative aims to make visible that which Irigaray describes as 'The lapse in time between the moment of conception and consciousness', and which, she continues, 'can never be caught up with [...] The lapse is also expressed in the arrogance of a logos that remains unaware of the process of its gestation.'[25] María Chipia does, however, assume the authority to represent the 'lapse in time' referred to by Irigaray. His account of the origins of life and life inside the womb presents a narrative of the process of foetal and embryonic development that has so far eluded representation in multiple discourses. His categorical and pompous account of gestation and early childhood development draws on the classic, phallogocentric structure of the family romance, based on the nuclear configuration of the Freudian Oedipal triangle and the Lacanian Law of the Father, which is employed in the novel as a parody of the impersonal, universalizing master narrative of Western psychoanalysis. In Irigaray's terms, María Chipia's arrogant logos indicates that he remains ignorant of the process of his own gestation, a point that is continually ridiculed by the implied author, whose heavy tone of irony subverts his universal assumptions and questions his reliability as a narrator. Ultimately, the voice of the male narrator is employed strategically by Eltit to force the reader to question the constructed nature of discourse and social roles. Indeed, by deconstructing María Chipia's master narrative as the novel progresses, Eltit illustrates that what is accepted as the natural or logical order of things is not immutable and can be challenged.

María Chipia immediately aims to transform his mother's womb into the

---

[25] *Speculum*, p. 306.

locus of a monosubjective masculine culture, into which the subsequent arrival of his twin sister is clearly unwelcome. He acts as his mother's mouthpiece despite being in her womb, and seeks to control his mother's experience and representation through his male-centred logos and viewpoint as male child. His mother is portrayed solely as soma and as incapable of any independent identity or intellect, in contrast, of course, to the emphasis that María Chipia places on his own logic, rationality and intellectual superiority. In Kristeva's terms, his aim can be seen to discipline and repress the site of the maternal semiotic, and the mother remains an object of 'exploration' as described by Marianne Hirsch rather than a 'social, psychological and linguistic subject'.[26] Although, as Hirsch continues to argue, the mother produces and upholds the subject, 'she herself remains the matrix, the other, the origin'.[27] Indeed, while María Chipia describes his own conception using the passive tense ('fui engendrado' (p. 12)), his father is the active subject who brings about the conception of his twin sister after a similarly forceful sexual encounter the following day: 'ese 8 de abril mi padre había engendrado en ella a mi hermana melliza' (p. 13).[28] Conception thus takes place only when the mother, in her feverish and weakened state, is reduced to 'una masa cautiva y dócil' (p. 15), and her passive and fertile body is doubly and violently penetrated by the father.

According to María Chipia, rather than a symbiotic relationship developing between mother and foetuses, they are perceived by her in terms of aliens or parasites, and pregnancy is experienced in terms of suffering and infection. Not only is the mother's body shown to be under siege, but the twin foetuses eventually assume control even of her dreams. The mother meekly accepts their invasion of her unconscious, an apathetic stance that infuriates her son: 'Comprendí que mi madre era capaz de suspenderlo todo, incluso a sí misma, ante la más vaga amenaza' (p. 23). From his viewpoint, therefore, she fails in her primary role of protecting herself and her foetuses from any external (and internal) dangers, a point reinforced by María Chipia as the twins' birth draws nearer and their mother serenely resigns herself to the death that she views as the final destiny of her biological fate. María Chipia thus forges a connection between childbirth and women as agents of death: 'anuló nuestra existencia desde el instante en que nos incluyó en la ritualidad de su sacrificio' (p. 25). Childbirth as self-sacrifice, killing off the self for the other, the self without whom the other could not exist, illustrates the fusion of the identities of mother and foetuses, and foregrounds the psychic challenge that pregnancy poses to a woman's discrete subjectivity.[29]

---

[26] Marianne Hirsch, *The Mother/Daughter Plot: Narrative, Psychoanalysis, Feminism* (Bloomington and Indianapolis: Indiana University Press, 1989), p. 161.

[27] Hirsch, p. 168.

[28] It is possible for fraternal twins to be conceived during separate acts of intercourse. Indeed, there have been cases where fraternal twins have been conceived through their mother's acts of intercourse with two or more men, throwing the issue of paternity into crisis.

[29] The splitting of the subject during pregnancy has also been theorized by Kristeva in

It is only after their birth, states María Chipia, that his mother willingly embraces her maternal role, obsessively watching over her children and neglecting herself and her husband in the process. Her son approvingly acknowledges this belated and exaggerated surge of maternal love, declaring that 'Su experiencia con el amor materno fue la primera experiencia real que tuvo' (p. 29). He also proclaims that his mother's recognition of her social role has led to a state of internal purification: 'Su amor por nosotros la limpió como a una joven doncella' (p. 29). The word 'doncella', which denotes maidenhood or virginity, thus suggests that the mother's sexuality is inappropriate and superfluous to the maternal role that she now so enthusiastically assumes. She is repulsed by the shameful memory of her sexual intimacy with her husband; a viewpoint, of course, verbalized by María Chipia and which suits his perspective as male child. The maternal love that his mother now experiences, he unctuously explains, is the fulfilment of her feminine nature: 'Mi madre había encontrado, por fin, su razón sexuada' (p. 33). María Chipia thus presents motherhood as totalizing the woman in question, endorsing the Freudian idea that woman's emotional fulfilment comes not from her sexual relationship but from her maternal role, and specifically her attachment to her male child.[30]

The father, although cut out of the relationship between mother and twins, feels proud of his wife for so painstakingly assuming her maternal role. However, the discovery of a second pregnancy leads the mother to disrupt the harmonious climate that had encompassed the family home during the twins' early years. Having apathetically returned to her nuptial obligations, the mother is horrified to find herself once again pregnant, as María Chipia informs us: 'En vez de solidificar su impulso materno, se llenó de horror al darse cuenta de que estaba verdaderamente extenuada por entregarse a los caprichos de esas pequeñas vidas que ella misma había gestado' (p. 41). The mother actively participates in separating from her children by renouncing the maternal role that she had so recently embraced, since she is no longer willing to subordinate her desires to their demands. Hirsch argues that the mother's part in initiating the rupture from her children has been erased from theoretical and narrative representation, but by making visible the issue of maternal choice, Eltit reverses the Freudian image of an overly invested mother forced to separate from her child through the paternal realignment of the child's affections.[31]

According to María Chipia, it is after the birth of his younger sister, María de Alava, that his mother's acceptance of her maternal role irreversibly founders: 'El fervor maternal había cumplido un ciclo en ella' (p. 44). The obsessive love that she once lavished on the twins wavers, and María de Alava inspires in her mother only deep-seated feelings of hatred and repulsion. As María Chipia notes, the mother now begins to plot her escape from the house, spurred on by the frenzied sexual impulses that overcome her. From this point on, divisions

---

her essay 'Women's Time'. See *New Maladies of the Soul*, trans. by Ross Guberman (New York: Columbia University Press, 1995), pp. 201–24 (p. 214).

[30] Freud, 'Femininity', p. 134.

[31] Hirsch, p. 169.

and tensions increasingly cripple the family, and the breakdown of the parents'
relationship escalates with the realization that they are bound together in a web
of hostility because of their children. Patriarchal destiny is portrayed as flour-
ishing in inverse proportion to the creation of a victim of the mother since, as
María Chipia informs us, his father's sense of authority exists only in proximity
to the mother, and their hostile disputes are a necessary means of discharging
his aggression and shoring up his paternal authority.

The catastrophic climax of the first section of the novel is the discovery of
the mother's adultery, described by María Chipia in hyberbolic, biblical and
apocalyptic terms: 'Desplomó el universo, confundió el curso de las aguas,
desenterró ruinas milenarias y atrajo cantos de guerra y podredumbre. Mi madre
cometió adulterio' (p. 100). The profound waves of shock and shame that rever-
berate through the family members lead to their withdrawal into the home to
escape the whispers and mockery rippling through the city. It is the father who
discovers the mother with her lover, 'un conquistador de carne y hueso' (p. 101),
a flesh and blood lover who 'conquers' the mother's body. The reference to a
'conquistador' immediately brings to mind the Spanish conquest of the
Americas, and the mother's own reaction to the discovery of her adultery is
described by María Chipia in terms that link the enormity of her unfaithfulness
to the historical betrayal of la Malinche: 'Le parecía como si una nación entera
estuviese a punto de desaparecer' (p. 102).

Importantly, it is precisely through the cataclysm unleashed by the discovery
of her adultery that the mother now reaches an understanding of the nature of
her sexual desire. As the hurt and jealous father penetrates her in front of her
humiliated lover, it is through the fantasy of female masturbation that the
mother achieves orgasm, which indicates not only the singularity of *jouissance*,
but also the impossibility of its attainment within the circumscribed institutions
of motherhood and the family, founded on reproductive heterosexual relations.
The conflict between a maternal life and a female adult sexual life is thus
highlighted, and the impossibility for the mother of defining herself both as a
woman and a mother within the given social structures is foregrounded. Indeed,
María Chipia vocalizes his mother's awareness that a 'real' mother must
renounce her sexuality, since succumbing to sexual pleasure as a mother carries
with it the penalty of social exclusion: 'Entendió que el placer era una combi-
natoria de infinidad de desperdicios y excedentes evacuados por el desamparo
del mundo; entonces, pudo honrar a los desposeídos de la tierra, gestantes del
vicio, culpables del crimen, actuantes de la lujuria' (p. 104).

Maternal desire is thus associated with sin, criminality and vice, and so
linked to all that is socially disciplined. As noted earlier, Eltit aligns the term
'el cuarto mundo' with the most culturally repressed impulses of society, which
attain a subversive agency in the peripheral zone of the fourth world. In response
to Richard's assertion that the universality of dominant systemizations is undermined in the periphery, Eltit agrees that this is so, but she genders Richard's
argument by foregrounding the mother as the locus of that which is both
culturally repressed and dissident. In her novel, it is the eruption of the mother's

repressed desire which undermines her prescribed family role and subsequently instigates the dissolution of the family and paternal authority, and enables the advent of a female narrative voice.

The categorical and universal paradigms previously drawn upon by María Chipia can no longer address the dysfunctional and, in his terms, 'perverse' family members that he now perceives. It is at this point, when the 'shame' of the mother's adultery is such that it is visibly inscribed on her suppurating flesh and the disarticulation of the family reaches its culmination, that María Chipia cuts short his narrative in terms that concede a confession: 'Sintiéndome incrustado en un tiempo crítico, acepté depositar la confesión en mi hermana melliza' (p. 106). The 'melliza' is thus portrayed as the receptacle of his discourse, which is deposited in her body and fuses with her own narrative to produce the baby/novel itself. It is now, precisely at the moment of conception, that she gives voice to her story in the second section of the novel.

Like her brother, then, the 'melliza' begins with the description of a conception, but she speaks from the dual position of mother and daughter, and in relation to a conception that breaks the founding regulation of kinship: the incest taboo. The family is now pushed into further disarray by the unexpected outcome of the twins' union, which the 'melliza' describes in terms of a 'catastrophe' (p. 109). The etymological meaning of catastrophe is the denouement of a drama, or an event producing a subversion in the order of things, which reflects the aim of the 'melliza', outlined earlier, to produce a narrative that provokes and disturbs.[32]

Unlike María Chipia's narrative, this section of the novel includes the voices of different family members, particularly that of María de Alava, and there is a significant difference in the linguistic and typographical structure. The female narrative voice resists the linearity, rationality, logic and syntax heavily emphasized by María Chipia. While he had sought to repress the disruptive force of the maternal semiotic theorized by Kristeva, wrenching the story from his mother even though her body generated his narrative, maternity as represented by the 'melliza' acts as a counterpoint by privileging semiotic irruption, prominently drawing on the cultural unconscious as a creative source. What results is linguistic repetition and an excess of meaning that undercuts any textual unity. In her account, the maternal and all that it connotes – the feminine, desire, corporality and death – cut across the surface of her narrative, and the eruption of psychic pulsations, bodily drives and unsymbolized affects disrupt and confuse any attempts to signify. While the 'melliza' makes visible the enormous physical toll to which her progressively huge and distended body is subjected, a corporeal violence that she describes as 'el revés del placer' (p. 148), it is her sexual desire that dominates her disorderly narrative. Multiplicity and instability fragment her narrative voice, which attempts to 'speak' something outside the symbolic function of language – namely, maternal desire. Reference is thus made to the insufficiency of existing linguistic

---

[32] Onions, p. 152.

structures, a point made evident in the title of this section of the novel: 'Tengo la mano terriblemente agarrotada'.

María de Alava takes on a central role in this section. She acts as a 'confessor' for her older sister, who approaches her to assuage her continual feelings of guilt and shame for her promiscuous and telluric sexual desire. The confession, according to Foucault, acted as a precursor for psychoanalysis, a point that foregrounds maternal desire as the target of repression in both psychoanalytic and religious discourse.[33] Religious language and imagery pepper this section with the appearance of words relating to biblical sin and punishment recurring throughout, such as 'pecado capital' and 'la caída'. Notably, the description given by the 'melliza' of her confessions in terms of an 'inquisición', the admonitions and charges pronounced by María de Alava against her, and the images of burning stakes serve to conjure up images of the Spanish Inquisition. María de Alava is thus placed as the representative of religious and racial orthodoxy, as well as the embodiment of paternal law, and her initiation into patriarchal power structures illustrates that patriarchy does not refer necessarily to individual men, but is a system institutionalized in the family.

It is only now that we gain an insight into the mother–daughter relationship, which had been overwritten in María Chipia's narrative. In Irigaray's terms, the relationship between mother and daughter is enmeshed in fusion and thus unsymbolized, but their relationship also highlights what Irigaray describes as a lack of a model of love between women in religious culture and a lack of respect for feminine genealogy.[34] In a gendered inversion of the biblical stipulation that the sins of the father will be passed onto his sons, the mother's shame is passed onto her daughter, who is shown to confess on behalf of her mother as a means to alleviate the ignominy heaped upon her since her adultery.[35] As she declares: 'Pero aún debo disminuir la vergüenza de mi madre' (p. 120). The 'melliza' assumes the responsibility of shoring up the maternal body, literally carrying her mother as a mother would a child, and so inverting their kin positions. The father weeps for the mother's sins and blames her for the twins' acts of intercourse, since their bodies, observes the 'melliza', are imbued with her aberrant behaviour: 'nuestras figuras evacuadas por la pasión y traspasadas por el adulterio materno antiguo' (p. 111). The mother, now ancient and obscene, becomes the family scapegoat, and the constant references to her humiliation illustrate that she carries the burden of the biblical transgression of Eve and the historical betrayal of la Malinche. Mother and daughter are thus bound together in a web of guilt and shame, which forecloses any experience of love between them.

The lack of an emotional bond between mother and daughter also structures the relationship between the 'melliza' and her child *in utero*. The 'melliza',

[33] Michel Foucault, *The History of Sexuality: An Introduction* (Harmondsworth: Penguin, 1990), p. 67.

[34] Luce Irigaray, *Key Writings* (London and New York: Continuum, 2004), p. 35

[35] This biblical assertion is again picked up by Eltit with devastating consequences in her sixth novel, *Los trabajadores de la muerte* (see Chapter 6.)

speaking as a mother, describes her unborn daughter as an enemy within who is complicit with the belligerence of the other family members, which reflects María Chipia's representation of their own mother's hostile feelings towards her twin foetuses. Constant references are made to the horrendous physical wounds of the baby, reflecting the ruptures and gashes of the textual body, and offering a glimpse of a female 'sudaca' biological/cultural product that, as Ramsdell notes, 'will not be easily palatable to society'.[36] However, any references to the female progeny are always given briefly within parentheses and very little mention is made of the child other than as an increasing obstacle to the twins' attainment of sexual pleasure. Any maternal feelings of nurture or care on the part of the 'melliza' are subsumed by the endless and urgent demands of her genital drives. As she states: 'Aunque el niño estaba sufriendo, no pudimos ayudarlo [...] porque desde el día hasta la noche debí atender el pedido de mi sangre sudaca' (p. 152).

Maternal desire is here aligned with the racial lineage of the 'melliza', which is that of the peripheral 'sudaca' race, and both have previously been located as the site of cultural repression and dissidence. However, although this section of the novel once again foregrounds the transgressive agency of maternal desire, the self-representation of the 'melliza' portrays a disturbing inability to enter into human relations. Her unconscious pulsations take over her subjectivity and Eltit can be seen to illustrate the danger in isolating the maternal semiotic from symbolic processes. This, she suggests, results in the maternal body remaining outside of language and culture, trapped in the delirious chaos of the imaginary. Eltit can thus be seen to agree with Richard's assertion that the feminine emerges from a field of tension in which masculine and feminine are intertwined.[37] So, in order to represent motherhood and the mother–daughter relationship in meaningful and viable terms, the speaking female subject must emerge from the heterogeneous process of language, an important point to which I will return.

The (De)Construction of Masculinity

According to María Chipia, the twins' placental relationship is initially determined by their mother, who keeps them at a distance in her womb through the umbilical cords that secure them to the uterine walls, which illustrates the regulation and structure that exists within the maternal body. But as they grow bigger, the space between the foetuses narrows and their relationship, according to the male narrator, swiftly becomes one of antagonism. Although María Chipia aims to keep his distance, his twin sister tenaciously inches towards him, initiating a form of communication that he describes in terms of pre-linguistic 'pulsiones' (p. 15); in other words, a wave of corporeal drives that

---

[36] Ramsdell, in *The Ties That Bind* (see Cooper), p. 122.
[37] Richard, 'Feminismo, experiencia y representación', p.741.

corresponds to Kristeva's theory of the pre-Oedipal semiotic. It is through their bodily impulses that María Chipia becomes aware of the intimate relationship between his sister and their mother, and is furious to find himself excluded. Belying the authority of his master narrative, he admits ignorance of the nature of this feminine alliance, which has provided his sister with the key to unlocking the meaning of their mother's dreams: 'Por cierto, esas claves me eran insoportables y excluyentes. A partir de esa peligrosa exclusión empezó el acecho hacia mi madre (p. 17)'.[38] It is thus suggested that the uterine relationship between mother and child is determined by sex, and it is María Chipia's segregation which leads to the mother–son relationship collapsing into one of mutual suspicion and hostility, once again undermining his reliability as a narrator.[39]

María Chipia does, eventually, establish a tenuous form of communication with his mother, portrayed in terms of the first stirrings of his libido. His mother's dreams incite within him an unremitting hunger that symbolizes his incipient sexual desire: 'Mi ansiedad se traslucía en un hambre infernal que me obligaba a saciarla, abriendo compuertas somáticas que aún no estaban preparadas [...] En ese estado semiabúlico dejaba a mis sentidos fluir hacia el afuera' (p. 14). His libidinal impulses originate from and flow outside of the womb towards his mother, which places their relationship within the Kristevan semiotic and so presents the semiotic relationship between mother and child as an experience universal, but not identical, to infants, irrespective of sexual difference.

As the gestation period progresses, the restricted space of their mother's womb leads to the first physical contact between the foetuses. According to María Chipia, his twin sister shudders with envy when she rubs against him and perceives their biological difference. Describing the source of her rivalry in terms of 'mi incipiente pero ya establecido pudor' (p. 22), María Chipia implicitly refers to Freudian 'penis envy' to confirm the idea that the construction of gender is determined by anatomical distinction, whereby woman equates herself with lack. The male narrator asserts that it is the recognition of biological difference, represented by the male genital organ, that transforms the womb into the locus of a battle between the sexes, 'un explícito campo de batalla' (p. 22).

However, María Chipia's difference as a male is threatened by the constant rubbing together of the twins' bodies as they increase in size and by the dominant female forms that encompass him in the womb. He is spurred on by the need to define himself in opposition to his mother and sister, and attempts

---

[38] María Chipia's inability to interpret his mother's dreams is a challenge to the assumptions made by Freud in 'The Interpretation of Dreams', a challenge that is discussed again in relation to *Los trabajadores de la muerte* (see Chapter 6).

[39] Chodorow also argues that the mother–child relationship is determined by sex, but her study focuses on the post-natal, pre-Oedipal period. See *The Reproduction of Mothering*, pp. 92–110. Other points made by Chodorow are also reflected in the novel, such as the male child's cultivation of a contempt for the feminine as a means to separate from his mother and his own femininity, and the formation of a discrete identity as being harder for boys than for girls. However, Eltit explores these points through fiction as they occur within the womb.

to annihilate the circumjacent female forms through the emission of his 'marcas masculinas' (p. 24). The female forms that threaten María Chipia flow not only from his sister's body but also from the bloody fluids of the uterine chamber, and so, in his narrative, the female foetus is undifferentiated from the maternal body and the feminine is reduced to the (m)other against which the male foetus doggedly attempts to define his masculinity.

Trapped in a relationship described by María Chipia as 'un triángulo anómalo y desesperante' (p. 24), the Freudian post-natal Oedipal triad (father/mother/son) is here replaced by a placental triangular relationship between the mother and twin foetuses: two females and one male, as opposed to the two males and one female of Freudian paradigms. It is the male, in Eltit's novel, who has a harder time establishing his identity, since he can never completely isolate himself from the female-dominated influence of the family triangle. Indeed, María Chipia later links the failure of his attempts to construct a discrete identity to the nature of his mother's dreams during the gestation period. As noted previously, the foetuses eventually overpower their mother's unconscious, which grants María Chipia access to a previously inaccessible level of maternal experience and allows the twins to control the content of her dreams. María Chipia describes the dreams that they implant as 'híbridos y lúdicamente abstractos' (p. 21), but their hybrid and abstract nature ultimately reflects their mother's own dreams prior to the twins' usurpation of her unconscious: 'Sus sueños estaban formados por dos figuras simétricas que terminaban por fundirse como dos torres, dos panteras, dos ancianos, dos caminos' (p. 14).

Randolph Pope argues that the fusion of symmetrical figures in the mother's dreams dissolves the gender boundary between the twins, a point that is reflected in the novel through María Chipia's comments on his mother's dreams: 'Ella, que nos había domesticado a la dualidad, nunca abordó en sus sueños la diferencia genital, la ruptura desquiciadora oculta tras dos caminos, dos panteras, dos ancianos' (p. 31).[40] Although María Chipia later attempts to master language as a means to construct a coherent and transcendental sense of self, the 'flaw' contained in his mother's dreams results in his inability to separate from his twin sister: 'no había verdaderamente un lugar, que ni siquiera era uno, único, sólo la mitad de otra innaturalmente complementaria y que me empujaba a la hibridez' (p. 31). Eltit thus challenges the Freudian premise that the formation of subjectivity and sexual identity is ordained by the post-natal paternal function.[41] Their origin is located in the womb, and the

[40] Randolph D. Pope, 'La resistencia en *El cuarto mundo* de Diamela Eltit', in *Creación y resistencia* (see Lagos), pp. 35–52 (p. 43). Other critical readings, such as those of María Inés Lagos, Janet Lüttecke and Olga Uribe, also focus on how the novel aims to disarticulate the notion of 'difference', specifically sexual difference. See Lagos, 'Cuerpo y subjetividad en narraciones de Andrea Maturana, Ana María del Río y Diamela Eltit', *Revista chilena de literatura*, 50 (1997), 97–109 (p. 107); Janet A. Lüttecke, '*El Cuarto Mundo* de Diamela Eltit', *Revista Iberoamericana*, 60 (1994), 1081–8; and Uribe, p. 33.

[41] Sigmund Freud, 'The Ego and the Id', in *The Standard Edition of the Complete Psychological Works of Sigmund Freud*, ed. by James Strachey, vol. 19 (London: Hogarth Press, 1961), pp. 12–66 (pp. 31–2).

maternal unconscious is positioned as the foundation of the cultural and social construction of gender.

The hostility between mother and son reaches its climax at the twins' christening ceremony when the mother performs what María Chipia perceives as an act of revenge, presumably against his father, by slyly assuming the authority to rename her son and so usurp the father's name that had just been bestowed upon him: 'Su mano afilada recorrió mi cara y dijo: "Tú eres María Chipia"' (p. 29). The mother's act is witnessed only by his twin sister, and his father remains ignorant of it, continuing to call his son by the name given to him 'según la ley' (p. 29), but it is a name with which his son is unable to identify. It is thus the mother who prevents her son from assuming the father's name, which in Lacanian terms signifies his inability to acquire language and enter the paternal Symbolic.[42] Only when his mother suddenly embraces her maternal role is María Chipia able to respond to his father's name and assume command of language and the world around him. In so doing, and for the first time since his birth, he is able to make sense of his early childhood by drawing on Freudian paradigms. However, as their mother tirelessly conforms to her maternal duties, the emotional distance between the twins progressively increases, which suggests that the traditional, self-sacrificing maternal role not only upholds patriarchal structures, but also creates hostile relations between the sexes.

As stated earlier, the harmonious domestic atmosphere is shattered by the mother's discovery of her second pregnancy. It is the embryonic María de Alava, the twins' younger sister, who functions as the obstacle that forecloses the continued closeness of mother and twins, leading the mother to detach herself from the claustrophobic mother–child triad. In her embryonic form, María de Alava fulfils the paternal function of the Freudian family, which forces the twins to confront the need to surmount the Oedipus complex. However, whereas in Freudian terms the (male) child would reach maturity through an alignment with the father and a total separation from the mother, in Eltit's novel the twins compensate for the withdrawal of their mother's affection by reconstructing the physical and emotional dependency of their uterine relationship.[43] They thus substitute their original fraternal bond for the lack of maternal support, and from this point onwards, as the twins attempt to construct their identity through each other, the discourse of subject-formation seemingly goes beyond Oedipal patterns. Their relationship, states María Chipia, evolves as the enactment of a series of interchangeable male–female roles: 'esposo y esposa, amigo y amiga, padre e hija, madre e hijo, hermano y hermana [...] Jugábamos, también, al intercambio. Si yo era la esposa, mi hermana era el esposo' (p. 43). They are thus constituted as a play of mirror images, reflecting inventions of each other in a pantomime that not only illustrates the fluidity of familial roles, but also destabilizes any notion of an essentialist gender identity.

---

[42] Jacques Lacan, *Écrits. A Selection*, ed. by Alan Sheridan (London: Tavistock, 1977), pp. 1–7.

[43] Freud, 'The Ego and the Id', pp. 31–2.

With the withdrawal of maternal affection, at five years of age, it is thus to his twin sister that María Chipia turns to recover a sense of unity when faced with a situation of psychosis: 'Mi hermana melliza armó pieza por pieza mi identidad [...] Me obligó a separar el cuerpo de mi pensamiento y a distanciarme del orden de las cosas' (p. 48).[44] María Chipia's separation from what he has always accepted as the natural order of things intensifies his recognition of the instability of categories and relations, which results in the collapse of any unified sense of self. His mother, 'como fracaso de su propia institución' (p. 48), is blamed by her son for his crisis and it is only through the game invented by the 'melliza', '"¿Un padre no se rompe, ves?"' (p. 48), which they repeat over and over again, that he reconstructs a sense of self. Their game, which revolves around the notion of an indestructible father figure, can be contrasted with the 'fort-da' game described by Freud, which relates to the little boy's acquisition of language to compensate for the absence of the mother, and so allows the little boy to separate from his mother.[45] Eltit draws on the concept of repetition and game playing in Freud's account but associates it with the absence of the father, not the mother. The game played by María Chipia thus confounds Freudian norms by reinforcing his separation from his father and consolidating the fraternal relationship offered by his sister.

The twins' relationship continues as a series of games that they now play with each other's emotions, but it is during a confrontation later in the novel, just prior to their corporeal union, that the problematic nature of their fraternal relationship becomes most apparent. The 'melliza' here accuses her brother of conflating woman and mother. As María Chipia explains: 'Llegó a afirmar [...] que estaba cansada de nutrirme puesto que yo, consumido en un error sostenido durante demasiado tiempo, la confundía con mi madre, traspasando no sólo su parte láctea sino, además, su limitado e inestable ser' (p. 100). This implies that the subjectivity constructed by María Chipia continues to be founded on his reduction of woman to the (m)other, against whom he defines his masculinity. So, although the twins' reversion to the structure of their uterine relationship posits a discourse of identity that supposedly confounds Freudian etiology, it nevertheless reflects Irigaray's argument that within Oedipal structures the son seeks in other women a substitute for the mother, because the maternal body is eclipsed as the place of origin and the relation to the mother is left unresolved.[46] The twins' fraternal bond is thus structured along the lines of the mother–son relation and the subsequent consummation of their relationship thus collapses into maternal, and not fraternal, incest.

---

[44] The phrase 'el orden de las cosas' echoes the title of Foucault's study in which he aims to produce new interpretations and knowledge by illustrating the multiplicity and fragmented nature of names and categories that have been imposed by modernity. See *The Order of Things: An Archaeology of the Human Sciences* (London: Tavistock, 1970).

[45] Sigmund Freud, 'Beyond the Pleasure Principle', in *The Standard Edition of the Complete Psychological Works of Sigmund Freud*, ed. by James Strachey, vol. 18 (London: Hogarth Press, 1955), pp. 7–64 (p. 15).

[46] *Speculum*, pp. 31–2.

It is, however, through their corporeal union that the 'melliza' perceives a means to recover the memory of her origin. As María Chipia states: 'Pensó que consumarnos como uno podía traer a la memoria el impacto real del origin y el instante único e irrepetible en que el organismo decidió la gestación' (p. 99). Their physical union – the fusion that had structured their mother's dreams – thus again implies a return to origins, to the mother. However, the 'epic' that emerged in *Por la patria* from a return to the mother through adult sexual relations is destabilized in this novel. Problematically, the 'melliza' is clearly too dependent on her twin brother, as witness to the moment of her conception, to establish any relationship to her own mother, and thus to her own sex, which highlights the extent to which the access to origins is controlled by the phallus, a point to which I will return.

It is only in the opening of the second section of the novel, narrated by the 'melliza', that the outcome of the twins' nocturnal confrontation is disclosed: the conception of the female child, which, in turn, collapses into the novel itself. Boundaries between public and private also collapse in this section of the novel as the family home is besieged by the greed of 'la nación más poderosa del mundo', a term associated by Franco with transnational capital but one that is generally used in reference to the United States, so aligning transnational capital with US globalization.[47] While María Chipia had previously described the city in terms of an uncontrolled bacchanalia, pulsating with the libidinous traffic of the bodies of young 'sudacas', it is now depicted by the 'melliza' as a space of death and infection, littered with fires and reflecting the harsh urban landscapes of *Lumpérica* and *Los vigilantes*. The persistent ringing of horse hooves serves to conjure up images of military police on horseback or the arrival of the Spanish conquistadors, and the latter could also be associated with the threats of plague and pestilence that seep into the home. As in *Por la patria*, the conquest of the Americas is linked to authoritarianism, but in this novel it is specifically the analogy between the historical conquest and the intense programme of neo-liberalism washing over Latin America that is brought to the fore. Both result in the pillage and rape of the continent's vast resources, the imposition of another social and cultural model, and the poverty and exploitation of many of its citizens.

The threat to social values which is also prevalent in a context of globalization is reiterated by the 'melliza', who urgently makes reference to the political plot directed against the 'sudaca' family. It is María de Alava who declares that the threat from 'la nación más poderosa del mundo' can be countered only by a family homage, which the 'melliza' makes explicit as follows: 'Afirmó que sólo la fraternidad podía poner en crisis a esa nación' (p. 124). María de Alava's view is endorsed by the 'melliza', who expresses the supreme power of fraternity: 'Le hablo, otra vez, del poder de la fraternidad sudaca y de cómo nuestro poder podría destruir a esa nación de muerte' (p. 134). Fraternity, of course, is the foundation of the bond that exists between the

---

[47] Franco, p. 119.

twins. So, in the face of endemic globalization, Eltit focuses on the potential agency inherent in the rearticulation of gender relations in terms of a fraternal relationship and thus, in Irigaray's words, 'as horizontal and reciprocal relations between persons'.[48] It is, then, by shifting gender relations beyond hierarchical subject-object paradigms that Eltit perceives a means of resisting the devastation encroaching on the marginalized zone of the fourth world.

I have already referred to the problematic nature of the twins' fraternal relationship in terms of María Chipia's inability to perceive his female twin in her own terms, and not merely as the (m)other who defines his difference. Throughout the novel, the female name assumed by María Chipia and the interchangeable male–female roles that he performs with the 'melliza' suggests that his gender identity is mutable and shifting. However, in spite of his inability to align himself with paternal authority, the 'melliza' makes clear that María Chipia's virility remains intact: 'Vimos que la virilidad seguía aparentemente correcta e igualmente dañina' (p. 111). Although superficially María Chipia's masculinity is subsequently destabilized through his performance of gender, the primacy of the penis in the order of gender persists, and the descriptions given by the 'melliza' of their sexual relationship clearly indicate that it is structured by male possession and female submission. While María Chipia had previously perceived the 'flaw' in his mother's dreams as underlying his inability to construct an autonomous sense of self, in this instance the flaw can be seen to result in a corporeal fusion that leads to what Sylvia Tafra terms 'un proceso de indiferenciación violenta';[49] in other words, a loss of differentiation that annihilates feminine identity and thus positions the fraternal relationship along vertical, and not horizontal, lines.

It is only towards the end of the novel, when their parents and younger sister are forced by their consuming hunger and thirst to abandon the home, and recognizable social and familial systems disintegrate irreversibly, that we are offered a glimpse of the possibility of passing from a masculine culture into a culture in which an autonomous feminine subjectivity may emerge. All reference to sin and guilt now disappears, and compassion and love are shown to enter into relations between the twins for the first time. As the 'melliza' states: 'María Chipia mira compasivamente mis heroícos movimientos. Lo miro con el amor de la última pertenencia' (p. 155). The twins' subsequent dialogue, the longest in the novel, takes on a tone of reciprocity and respect that had not previously existed, and which foregrounds the possibility of a meeting between the sexes within a language that emerges from the fertile and dynamic intercourse of male and female voices.

Eltit thus points to the primacy of the phallus as the root cause of damaging gender relations, locating the perpetuation of phallic authority and power within the family sphere. Only now can social relations be transformed, since even

---

[48] *Key Writings*, p. 173. In her reading of the novel, Norat traces the significance of fraternity as a call for solidarity among writers in Latin America. Norat, pp. 121–49.
[49] Tafra, p. 80.

within a mother-centred nuclear family, in which the father is largely absent, the gender roles that perpetuate patriarchy continue to function. Eltit thus points to the potential inherent in the dissolution and transformation of existing social structures, even though, as Donetta Hines notes, the wave of economic devastation that globalization brings in its wake, also portrayed in the novel, offers 'a decidedly negative vision'.[50] In more positive terms, however, Eltit postulates that only outside of Oedipal family structures can the hierarchy of sexual difference be addressed and resolved, and dysfunctional gender relations be reconceptualized, an important point that was also central to *Por la patria* (see Chapter 2). In *El cuarto mundo*, it is from within an isolated and precarious house on the outskirts of the city, 'abandonada a la fraternidad' (p. 159), that the baby/novel emerges, the product of a relationship between the sexes that has as its basis respect, interdependence and creativity. The utopian possibilities of the twins' creation has thus been emphasized by Aurea María Sotomayor, who draws on Irigaray's concept of the divine to describe the baby/novel as 'una puesta en escena estética del engendro procreado por "la divina pareja"'.[51]

By shifting the focus from the gestation and birth of a child to the engendering of the text itself, Eltit uncovers the process of bringing a novel to fruition. The novel/baby incorporates the repressed pulsations and desires of the semiotic terrain of the maternal body within signifying practice and represents the place of origin as the mother's womb, thus positing a relation to maternal origins that is not mediated or occluded by Western phallocentric discourse. As such, the subversive nature of the 'sudaca' novel can be seen to lie in its unveiling of the relation to the mother. This, in turn, is capable of producing new psychic and social structures, and a model of gender relations that moves beyond base genital drives to be founded on mutual love, acceptance and support. Disturbingly, however, Eltit's following novel, *Vaca sagrada*, makes evident that the possibility of shifting gender relations beyond the level of genital drives is only a transient possibility, as we shall see.

To conclude, I do not suggest that Eltit unproblematically links writing to the sex of the author. The baby/novel emerges from the interplay of two sexed bodies, and from the interplay of the categories of masculine and feminine, challenging the idea of binary oppositions and gendered writing. The date of the baby's birth is also relevant here, since it highlights, in temporal terms, the gap or the schism that separates the sexes. As a means to breach this gap, and as in *Lumpérica*, Eltit again points to the threshold of the symbolic and semiotic functions of language as the site from which the speaking subject emerges.

---

[50] Hines, p. 68.
[51] Aurea María Sotomayor, 'Tres caricias: una lectura de Luce Irigaray en la narrativa de Diamela Eltit', *MLN: Modern Language Notes*, 115 (2000), 299–322 (p. 312).

4

Vaca sagrada: Violence, Abjection and the Maternal

Woman's Abject Body

Vaca Sagrada (1991) was the first novel published by Eltit during the Transition and it occupies an anomalous position within the trajectory of her narrative.[1] It was the first of her novels to be published outside Chile (in Buenos Aires) and was widely marketed by the publishing house Planeta as part of the boom of the *nueva narrativa*, a term generally used to describe the literary work of young Chilean authors who emerged at the beginning of the 1990s. The prove-nance and composition of the *nueva narrativa* have been widely debated in recent years, and many writers and critics in Chile, including Eltit, agree that the disparate quality and diverse thematic and stylistic preoccupations of the novels included under the label throw into question the bracketing together of authors whose differences far outweigh their similarities.[2] As a result, the concept of the *nueva narrativa* has come to be seen as a marketing ploy on the part of the publishers Planeta and Alfaguara, who were successful, for a limited time, in achieving increased sales of contemporary Chilean novels to a notoriously small reading public in Chile.

Eltit has stated that her novel emerged at a time of great transition in her life. She has spoken of the personal, psychic and territorial changes that formed the backdrop to her writing, including her departure from Chile to take up the post of Chilean Cultural Attaché in Mexico City.[3] The novel's title, comments Eltit, alludes to the double-edged meaning of the phrase 'vaca sagrada' (sacred cow), which simultaneously implies reverence and degradation. While it is used figuratively to imply a powerful or revered person, custom or institution, Eltit notes that women are often insulted through the use of animal names: 'Siempre la mujer es definida, popular o cotidianamente, con el nombre de un animal: "es una mula, es una vaca, es una yegua, es una perra". Entonces, okey: la

---

[1] A second edition of *Vaca Sagrada* remains unpublished to date. The novel has been translated into English.

[2] For further details, see Eltit's essay 'La compra, la venta', in *Nueva narrativa chilena*, ed. by Carlos Oliváres (Santiago: LOM, 1997), pp. 57–60.

[3] Ana María Larraín, 'El cuerpo femenino es un territorio moral', *El Mercurio*, 5 January 1992, section Revista del Libro, pp. 3–5 (p. 4).

mujer es una vaca ... pero sagrada.'[4] In the case of 'vaca', women are associated with a female animal characterized by its udders and milk. So, while Chilean women may be revered as mothers in official discourse, the conflation of the reproductive attributes of cows and women in popular parlance belittles women by equating their reproductive functions with those of a beast.

Representing woman in terms of a cow also portrays the female body as signifying a collapse of the boundaries between the human and the non-human; that is, between human and animal. The location of the female body on the boundary of two categories and in an in-between place brands woman as abject, in Kristeva's terms: 'The abject confronts us, on the one hand, with those fragile states where man strays on the territories of *animal.*'[5] Kristeva's concept of abjection has as its basis the demarcation of the abject (non-human) element in society and the subsequent expulsion of that element, where the abject is defined as 'what disturbs identity, system, order. What does not respect borders, positions, rules. The in-between, the ambiguous, the composite.'[6]

The analogy drawn in Chilean popular discourse between woman and animal, which reinforces the phallocentric notion of female sexuality as abject, is central to Eltit's novel, which I read as enacting what Kristeva describes as a 'descent into the foundations of the symbolic construct'.[7] Eltit deliberately unearths culturally defined images of abjection, such as menstrual blood, putre-fying flesh and rotting food, to challenge and redraw the boundaries that underlie social structures. We are taken to the very limits of what is socially and aesthetically deemed as permissible in order to rethink the cultural taboos that currently debase woman and place the female body as the site of the struggle between the subject and the abject. Descending into the foundations of the symbolic construct may make the experience of reading the novel an uncomfortable one, but Eltit suggests that it is only by working though symbolic and imaginary processes that the abject may be confronted and woman's sexuality reconceptualized. In short, Eltit focuses on the hierarchy of sexual difference in her society to contest the manner in which woman's abjection serves to found the patriarchal Symbolic order.

The novel focuses on the relationships formed by the protagonist, Francisca, with her two male lovers, Sergio and Manuel, and her cousin, Ana. The narrative structure is scarred by the chaos and disintegration that engulf Francisca, and the plot is punctuated by analeptic prolepsis and anamnesis. Much of the novel is located within the public and liminal spaces of the bars and streets of an unnamed city, which perpetuates feelings of terror, death and vertigo. The city is traversed by a sense of decay, and poverty, alienation, alcoholism and violence are paramount. The hostile urban environment is exemplified by Francisca's sensation of being watched and followed through the streets, and the pervasive

---

[4] Larraín, 'El cuerpo femenino es un territorio moral', p. 4.

[5] Julia Kristeva, *Powers of Horror: An Essay on Abjection*, trans. by Leon S. Roudiez (New York: Columbia University Press, 1982), p. 12; emphasis hers.

[6] *Powers of Horror*, p. 4.

[7] *Powers of Horror*, p. 18.

sense of surveillance is anticipated on the first page by reference to a terrifying, disembodied eye, 'un ojo escalofriante' (p. 11).[8] Emphasis is placed throughout on the act of survival, an act usually associated with the animal world, which is made even more precarious in the tense city.

Critical readings to date include that of Sandra Garabano, who argues that the novel accentuates the emptiness and impossibility of utopias and history, a reading that complements Claudine Potvin's examination of how the dislocated concept of utopia destabilizes space and body in the novel.[9] Luz Ángela Martínez traces the representation of the city as the site of a political conflict that permeates the most intimate level of subjectivity, but it is specifically female experience that forms the focus of my reading. Other critics have also approached the novel in this way, such as Fernando Moreno, who examines the pleasure and transgression associated with the female body.[10] My reading, however, emphasizes the representation of woman as abject in the novel, which I argue is always founded on her mothering and reproductive functions. Kristeva's work on maternity and abjection, which aims to challenge the oppression that results from woman's association with reproduction as a means to reconceptualize motherhood, is drawn on throughout this chapter, but before outlining my argument further it is useful to summarize Jo Labanyi's reading of the novel, since she also draws on Kristeva's theory of abjection, alongside Mary Douglas's *Purity and Danger*, which informs Kristeva's own work.[11]

Labanyi equates horror with the feminine in the novel by drawing a link between political terror and the female body. For Labanyi, the central image of menstruation is a means of exploring horror. As she explains:

> Eltit's novel suggests that woman's exploration of the abject is not an expression of a 'maternal' desire to shore up male authority [...] but that it is a way of dealing with her own precarious sense of self: a self constructed through a bodily relationship not only to men but also to the *polis*.[12]

Labanyi points out that, unlike Kristeva, who confines the source of horror to projected inner drives, Eltit also places horror within the material, political

---

[8] Surveillance is a theme that recurs in Eltit's novels and will be discussed in further detail in relation to *Los vigilantes* (see Chapter 5).

[9] Sandra Garabano, '*Vaca Sagrada* de Diamela Eltit: del cuerpo femenino al cuerpo de la historia', *Hispamérica*, 73 (1996), 121–7; and Claudine Potvin, 'Nomadismo y conjetura: utopias y mentira en *Vaca sagrada* de Diamela Eltit', in *Creación y resistencia* (see Lagos), pp. 55–66.

[10] Luz Ángela Martínez, 'La dimensión espacial en "*Vaca sagrada*" de Diamela Eltit: la urbe narrativa', *Revista chilena de literatura*, 49 (1996), 65–81; and Fernando Moreno T., '*Vaca sagrada*: goce y transgresión', in *Una poética de literatura menor* (see Lértora), pp. 167–83.

[11] Jo Labanyi, 'Topologies of Catastrophe: Horror and Abjection in Diamela Eltit's *Vaca Sagrada*', in *Latin American Women's Writing*, ed. by Anny Brooksbank Jones and Catherine Davies (Oxford: Clarendon Press, 1996), pp. 85–103.

[12] Labanyi, in *Latin American Women's Writing* (see Jones and Davies), p. 89; emphasis hers.

reality of the social. She concludes by arguing that the permeable boundaries of the female body force woman to self-identify with horror in order to complete the abjection process. In turn, the female body is portrayed as replicating the horror outside.

Labanyi's reading is insightful and I would agree with her on most of the conclusions she reaches. However, while Labanyi refers to the link between abjection and the maternal body in Kristeva's work, she does not examine the significance of this same link in Eltit's novel. I perceive the relationship between the female protagonist, Francisca, and the maternal body that underlies the novel as fundamental to any discussion of abjection here. Labanyi argues that woman is portrayed as constructing her precarious sense of self on 'a bodily relationship not only to men but also to the *polis*'.[13] In contrast, I read Francisca's precarious construction of identity as emerging from an abjection of self that is founded on what Kristeva describes as 'the immemorial violence with which a body becomes separated from another body in order to be'.[14]

Kristeva stresses that separation from the mother is a necessary precondition of the social. Abjection, for Kristeva, is central to the separation of mother and child, but she argues that only the male child can experience the mother as abject and so take up a subject position founded on normative, masculine sexuality. If the daughter attempts to abject the mother, argues Kristeva, she will also abject herself because of her bodily identification with the maternal body.[15] In Eltit's novel, the loss of the maternal body is shadowed by such an immense 'immemorial violence' that it prevents Francisca's abjection of the mother. This, in turn, forces her to self-identify with abjection and her abjection of self is shown to have profound and violent consequences for subsequent social relations. The primary mother–daughter relationship is thus paramount for understanding woman's cultural representation as abject and it is this relationship that forms the starting point of my reading.

Firstly, though, let me briefly outline the structure of the novel and its key imagery to situate my reading. The novel consists of eleven chapters of varying length, some carrying titles and others untitled, and the oscillation of the narrative voice between first- and third-person frequently confuses the reader as to the narrator's identity.[16] The notion of a single and univocal narrative perspective is thus thrown into question, a frequent trait of Eltit's writing. The first chapter, which is just one paragraph in length, opens with the following statement made by an anonymous female narrator: 'Duermo, sueño, miento mucho' (p. 11). The narrator's predilection for lying and inventing untruths is thus immediately highlighted, as it is when the narrator can be identified as Francisca. The assertion of the narrator's participation in the manipulation of fiction forces the reader once again to adopt a critical and reflective attitude

[13] Labanyi, in *Latin American Women's Writing* (see Jones and Davies), p. 89.

[14] *Powers of Horror*, p. 10.

[15] *Black Sun*, pp. 28–30.

[16] For Eltit's comments on the ambiguity of the narrative voice in this novel, see Morales, *Conversaciones*, p. 43.

towards Eltit's writerly narrative, and has led critics, such as Norat, to read the novel's textual artifice in terms of postmodern narrative strategies.[17] I would also point out that the questionable integrity of the narrator immediately locates her in the realm of abjection since, as Kristeva notes, abjection is that which 'does not respect borders, positions, rules [...] The traitor, the liar.'[18]

Eltit has stated that while the motif of menstrual blood is central to the novel, her aim was to move it beyond the biological. She has discussed the significance of the menstrual blood that flows from Francisca's body as follows:

> usé la sangre menstrual porque es una sangre poco escrita. [...] El rito femenino es sangriento y, en último término, es secreto y eludido por la cultura en algún punto. Pero además la sangre menstrual es la sangre del fracaso, porque la gente que sangra es gente que no engendra [...] Entonces, en ese sentido me pareció bien importante [...] descomprimir esa sangre, hacerla salir de su propia biología y desplazarla a todos los sitios posibles: a la erótica, a la violencia, a la memoria.[19]

Eltit thus makes direct reference to the cultural taboo surrounding menstrual blood. While menstrual blood flows from the fertile female body on a monthly basis, it is rarely spoken about in a social context and is disguised in the circulation of visual images that patently refer to menstruation. Eltit also points to the cultural norms that symbolize menstruation as a cyclical reminder of the female body's failure to reproduce. According to these norms, Francisca would be viewed as the embodiment of a non-reproductive sexuality and as 'non-mother' rather than woman. By introducing the motif of menstrual blood into spheres such as those of erotic pleasure and memory, Eltit's aim can be seen to endow female blood with a meaning that is not confined to reproduction. Her strategy, as Eltit states, corresponds to an attempt to move female specificity away from the biological, challenging the conflation of woman and mother without renouncing the procreative potential of woman. In this sense, Eltit and Kristeva correspond in their aim of reconceptualizing woman's relation to the maternal.

Eltit's focus on menstrual blood can also be read as an attempt to symbolize woman's sexuality in its own terms, thus moving beyond the phallic mode of discourse that reduces female sexuality to the lack that upholds masculinity, and challenging the widespread view of menstrual blood as what Kristeva terms a 'polluting object'.[20] As Olea observes, the representation of the female body in Eltit's novel subverts 'el carácter impuro de esa construcción cultural que esconde ese cuerpo que sangra'.[21] Eltit's aim of reversing cultural images of

---

[17] Norat, p. 152.
[18] *Powers of Horror*, p. 4.
[19] Lazzara, pp. 32–3.
[20] *Powers of Horror*, p. 71.
[21] Olea, in *Una poética de literatura menor* (see Lértora), p. 94.

menstrual blood as disgusting and contaminating can also be identified in her comments on the corporeal intimacy and pleasure that it incites: 'Yo pienso que eso era un poder de la sangre … que estaba escamoteado por la cultura, que le quitaba el goce secreto … de un roce muy genital, muy estratégico … una sangre que te roza lo genital […] Quise trabajar ese sentido y trabajarlo más como poder … dar un poder a esa sangre.'[22] Eltit's comments here reflect the terms used by Irigaray to discuss the image of the 'two lips', which also posits a model of female sexuality that is self-sufficient and defies binary categories, in the sense that the lips are neither clearly inside nor outside.[23]

Eltit thus locates the flow of menstrual blood as a potentially powerful marker of feminine subjectivity. It is juxtaposed in the novel to the male signifier *par excellence*, the phallus, which is relentlessly symbolized through the euphemisms 'el pájaro' or 'el pajarito', which are used in Chile to denote its biological attribute, the penis.[24] I have already argued that collapsing the boundaries between woman and animal not only degrades women, but also portrays them as abject. Eltit can be seen to use a similarly vulgar strategy here in an attempt to demystify the cultural authority wielded by the phallus/penis, reducing man to his genital function through animal imagery to contract the boundary that demarcates the human and the animal. However, the failure of this strategy becomes disturbingly apparent in the novel, and is a point to which I will return.

Francisca and Sergio: Abjection and Castration

As stated earlier, the starting point of my reading is the primary relationship between Francisca and the maternal body, represented in the novel by the suppurating and bleeding body of Francisca's ill and dying grandmother. There is, therefore, a jump in generation between the two women, as the mother–daughter relationship is portrayed in terms of the relation between grandmother and granddaughter.[25] In general terms, Eltit could be pointing to the mobility of the maternal role and highlighting the close bond that often exists between children and the grandparents who raise them. In relation to Chile, the absence of Francisca's mother (and father) could be read as a reference to the legacy of the Pinochet dictatorship. Although published in the early years of the Transition, the novel is permeated by the horror, loss and destruction caused by military violence.

---

[22] Author's interview with Eltit, 1 November 2000, Santiago.

[23] *This Sex Which is Not One*, p. 24.

[24] See Eltit's comments on the use of these colloquialisms in Piña, pp. 249–50.

[25] I deliberately avoid mention of Eltit's biography throughout my readings, but it is worth pointing here to her published comments on the relationship with her own maternal grandmother: 'Lo que yo tengo con mi abuela es una historia de amor de proporciones, una historia de amor intensísima. Es mi madre, es mi todo, es mi mundo. Yo fui hija única, mi madre era hija única. O sea, no hay tía, no hay primos, no hay … Lo único que había es un amor irrestricto que yo tengo con mi abuela.' Morales, *Conversaciones*, p. 221.

The relationship between Francisca and her grandmother is uncovered primarily in the fifth chapter of the novel, entitled 'Francisca', and is shown to underpin the subsequent relationship between Francisca and Sergio. The chapter is divided into four sections, which follow a tripartite structure. Each section begins by recounting the inception and development of the relationship between Sergio and Francisca, narrated in the third-person and forming the bulk of the four sections. Underlying the representation of their relationship is a short dialogue between Francisca and her dying grandmother. Each section then briefly concludes with Francisca's tortuous memories of her grandmother's suffering and imminent death, narrated in the first-person and included within parentheses in the text. The inclusion of her memories within parentheses may be read as the repression that Francisca seeks to enact on the ties that bind her to the abject but all-powerful matriarchal figure of her grandmother. I examine the tripartite structure of the fifth chapter in reverse order, to illustrate more clearly the manner in which the abject mother–daughter relationship shapes Francisca's subsequent relationship with Sergio. Since the structure of the ninth chapter is similar to that of the fifth chapter described here, I also refer briefly to the descriptions given by Francisca of her dying grandmother in the ninth chapter, to better illustrate my argument.[26]

Francisca's memories of her grandmother's moribund body are shot through with disgust and horror, and revolve around the nocturnal vigils that she kept at her bedside. She obsessively reiterates descriptions of her grandmother's wasting body, wracked by pain and disintegrating before her: 'Botaba sangre por todos los orificios del cuerpo, mientras yo, horrorizada, le estancaba la hemorragia con un paño' (pp. 161–2). Her memories always conclude with the image of a flock of birds wheeling overhead, awaiting the carrion that her grandmother will soon become: 'Una bandada, imaginé la bandada alejándose con la carroña atrapada entre sus picos' (p. 69). Flocks of scavenging birds are associated with death and destruction throughout the novel, and have been linked by Eltit to the formation of military aircraft in flight.[27] As stated earlier, 'el pájaro', a Chilean colloquialism used to refer to the penis, appears throughout the novel. The avian imagery in both instances thus serves to indicate that a militaristic and phallic violence forms the backdrop to the relationship between Francisca and her grandmother.

Preceding Francisca's memories of her bedridden grandmother are a series of brief verbal exchanges between them. Their dialogues revolve around the

---

[26] As in the fifth chapter, Francisca's memories of her dying grandmother are included within parentheses at the end of the first eight sections of the ninth chapter, which have as their focus male–female relations. What emerges is the reduction of gender relations to brute biological difference, and sexual relations as savage and debased.

[27] Author's interview with Eltit, 1 November 2000, Santiago. In this interview, Eltit commented that she was struck by the way in which the hierarchical structure of military aircraft in flight shadowed the formation of a flock of birds. She also discussed the linguistic proximity of 'la bandada' and 'la banda', the latter being associated in Chile with the military edicts ('bandas militares') enforced during the dictatorship.

grandmother's illness and the preparations that she wishes to make for her approaching death. For example, she instructs Francisca to help organize her papers and photographs so that they will be left in an orderly manner when she dies. Francisca's hesitant or negative responses can be read in terms of a delaying strategy and a refusal to countenance her grandmother's death, and she accuses her grandmother of deliberately willing her death in order to leave her utterly alone: 'Está llamando a la muerte, la llama desde hace años. Lo que quiere es dejarme sola, irse y dejarme sola, llevándose los papeles. Si usted pudiera se llevaría hasta mis recuerdos' (p. 64).

The maternal body is certainly represented as a figure of extreme abjection in the novel, but this is not enough to ensure Francisca's separation. While the grandmother attempts to relinquish her hold over her granddaughter, it is Francisca herself who obstructs their separation. Although overwhelmed with compassion at her suffering, she refuses to allow her grandmother to leave her: 'Habría hecho cualquier cosa para que ella no sufriera, pero nunca, a pesar de la atrocidad que la invadía, acepté que me dejara' (p. 158). Francisca's terror of separation can be seen to lie in the threat of psychic obliteration ('Si usted pudiera se llevaría hasta mis recuerdos'), which reflects Kristeva's argument that women are unable to complete the abjection process successfully because of the threat of loss of self.[28]

However, as in *Lumpérica* and *Por la patria*, Eltit brusquely discounts Kristeva's notion of a loving imaginary father who can facilitate the child's separation from the mother. The grandmother's body may be abject, but in a context marked by the absence of Francisca's biological mother and father it is all that she has to cling to. There is, simply, nobody else for her to turn to and nowhere else for her to go. What emerges in the novel is a damning critique of the paternal order, symbolized in official discourse by the military and represented here through the image of a voracious flock of vultures. The military's brutal disarticulation of family structures forecloses any loving support that could mediate the separation of mother and child. In addition, the horror and death that shapes the paternal order, which is supposedly responsible for the institution of civilization, alienates any sense of identification on Francisca's part. To construct an autonomous identity, in Kristeva's terms, Francisca must separate from her grandmother, but she is unable to work through 'the immemorial violence' that shadows this separation. As with Coya in *Por la patria*, her sexuality can thus be defined as melancholic, in the sense given to this term by both Irigaray and Kristeva.

Richard is one of several critics to discuss the melancholic dilemma of the post-dictatorship subject in Chile. Drawing on the work of Alberto Moreiras, Richard points to the tension between the 'assimilating' (remembering) and 'expulsing' (forgetting) inherent in melancholia.[29] However, Eltit can be seen to gender Richard's argument by suggesting that melancholia is primarily an

---

[28] *Black Sun*, p. 29.
[29] *Residuos y metáforas*, p. 37.

experience centered on the female body, a point discussed again in the third section of this chapter. Francisca's inability to mourn, and so abject, the mother is shown to have severe consequences for gender relations, as is seen here through an examination of the relationship between Francisca and Sergio.

Sergio develops a sinister obsession for Francisca when they first meet at school, and he immediately begins to watch her, stalk her and fantasize about her. The violent motives for his actions are foregrounded by the third-person narrative voice, which refers in militaristic terms to his 'persecución' and 'acecho' of Francisca, illustrating that Sergio conforms to the virile construction of masculinity propagated by the military, as described previously by Richard. Sergio, we learn, aims to capture, possess and attack Francisca, and although it is implied that she is complicit in, and even grateful for, his obsessive behaviour, she clearly demarcates a limit to her own involvement: 'aunque agradecía su obsesión, existía un límite y su pasividad era el único intercambio en el que aceptaba participar' (p. 59). It is, then, by strategically deploying the attribute traditionally associated with the feminine, passivity, that Francisca stakes a border between them which demarcates the male subject and female object. It is the existence of the border, Kristeva argues, that is the foundation of an organization that is 'clean and proper', and the subsequent breakdown of the border between Sergio and Francisca radically alters the structure of their relationship.[30]

Sergio's approach towards Francisca is described in animalistic terms, and for a whole year their relationship is founded on the absence of verbal communication and on the fantasies that Sergio elaborates at night, in which Francisca is included as the object of his sexual desire. The distance between them, upheld by Francisca's passivity, allows Sergio to perceive in her the specular relationship theorized by Irigaray: 'En la cara de Francisca estaba leyendo su propia historia, lo que iba a ser la deriva de su historia' (p. 62). However, when Sergio concludes that Francisca has bedded another man without his knowledge, the gulf between the 'imagined' woman and the 'real' woman that he encounters shatters the specular duplication that she had provided and collapses the boundary between them. They are thrust into the realm of abjection and the structure of the primary relationship, outlined earlier, is mapped onto their relationship.

Sergio now begins to view Francisca in uncertain and shifting terms. His former feelings of domination and control are replaced by fury, jealousy, hatred and humiliation. While Francisca is afraid of Sergio, she also laughs at him, taunts and ridicules him, and revels in her own effrontery.[31] The desperation that Sergio experiences at her hands is described in terms of a violent abandonment: 'Sergio experimentó la violencia que significaba ser abandonado' (p. 62). The

---

[30] *Powers of Horror*, p. 100.

[31] The overwhelmingly negative feelings that invade Sergio because of Francisca's behaviour towards him reflect the structure of the relationship between Juan and Coya in *Por la patria* (see Chapter 2). The relationship between Francisca and Sergio is later referred to as 'una poderosa batalla genital' (p. 67), and as in *Por la patria* and *El cuarto mundo*, relations between the sexes are portrayed in warring terms.

terrifying sense of abandonment suffered by Francisca as she watched her grandmother die is now experienced by Sergio, who is pushed into the position of a
child forced to countenance its separation from the abject mother. The abject,
according to Kristeva, 'simultaneously beseeches and pulverizes the subject',
and Sergio is certainly portrayed as a subject who is both fascinated and intimi-
dated by Francisca's abject body.[32] He is mesmerized by her propensity to
self-destruction, but is also horrified to note that she aims to use him to grant
representation to her unbounded self: 'Sabía que ella estaba tejiendo algo caótico
para otorgar sentido a los extremos marginales de su cuerpo y, después,
abandonarlo en esquinas siempre distintas' (p. 70). Sergio is drawn to Francisca
as the abject element necessary to define his identity, but he is also fearful of
her potential to trigger his own self-annihilation. Francisca, in turn, uses Sergio
as the abject mother uses her child, in Kristeva's terms 'as token of her own
authentication'.[33]

Sergio describes the link between them in terms of the primary link that unites
mother and child during gestation: the umbilical cord. However, rather than
transmitting oxygen and nourishment, the cord that unites them is deadly: 'había
contraído un vínculo prematuro y asfixiante' (p. 67). Sergio's fear of her is not,
as Freud would have it, based on her position as castrated other, but on her
embodiment of a maternal figure who represents castration, suffocation and
death. In Kristeva's terms, Sergio's fear stems from the threat of 'his very own
identity sinking irretrievably into the mother'.[34] I thus challenge Labanyi's
reading, in which she concludes that 'Eltit is not arguing that women's bodies
have been made into an image of horror by men afraid of being engulfed by the
maternal body, but that both men and women turn the female body, with its
bleeding wound, into an image of horror that helps stave off political terror.'[35]
The link between the female body and political terror is complex and is examined
in the following section of this chapter. My point here is that the female body
is branded by men as abject and as 'an image of horror' precisely because of
its association with the horror symbolized by the maternal in symbolic structures
and the threat of engulfment that the mother signifies for men.

Sergio's fear of Francisca is described in unlimited terms: 'El le decía que
sí por miedo. Su miedo ondulaba en esa zona oscura, sin bordes, que se desataba
en hoteles baratos, en calles oscuras, en camas prestadas' (p. 72). He is forced
into increasingly sordid spaces where he experiences an internal scission,
induced by Francisca's provocations and sexual humiliations. The extreme
confusion that he suffers during one of their sexual encounters leads him to
fall and break his arm. Encased in plaster, his broken arm subsequently hinders
the sexual movements that Francisca demands of him, serving as a metaphor
for his castration and firmly locating Francisca once again as castrating (m)other.
Sergio's need to avenge his abject humiliation pushes him to punch Francisca

[32] *Powers of Horror*, p. 5.
[33] *Powers of Horror*, p. 13.
[34] Freud, 'Femininity', p. 125; and Kristeva, *Powers of Horror*, p. 64.
[35] Labanyi, in *Latin American Women's Writing* (see Jones and Davies), p. 102.

in the eye, thus inflicting the visual mutilation that haunts Francisca throughout and which, in Oedipal terms, metaphorically symbolizes castration. Only now does Francisca allow their sexual relationship to be fully and perfectly consummated: 'y sólo entonces ella se aferró a él para lograr la unión más perfecta que tuvieron' (p. 73). While the castrating violence that underlies their union brings serenity to Francisca, it consolidates Sergio's determination to flee from her. Shattering his plaster cast against a tree, he finally breaks the stifling link between them, portrayed in terms of the act that signifies a child's primary separation from the maternal body: 'consiguió romper hasta la médula el cordón infectado que lo había unido a Francisca' (p. 73).

The superimposition of the mother–child connection onto the relation between the sexes thus shapes their relation in terms of castration. Francisca, grounded in abjection, seeks through Sergio the physical mutilation that would signify her symbolic castration, and thus her separation from the maternal body. The underlying foundation of female sexuality is now presented as a woman's need to seek through sexual relations a means of separating from the mother, rather than effecting a reunion with the mother, as previously put forward by Eltit in *Por la patria*. Although Francisca is initially complicit in conforming to traditional representations of passive femininity, Sergio's inability to relate to her as a woman in anything other than passive terms thrusts her into the only other feminine role available: the maternal. The fear and horror associated with the mother are unleashed as Sergio sees in Francisca the embodiment of the castrating mother, and Francisca is forced to self-identify with abjection by assuming a role defined by the abject body of her grandmother. Relations between them thus collapse into a re-enactment of Kristeva's 'immemorial violence with which a body becomes separated from another body in order to be'. The paternal violence that formed the backdrop to Francisca's relationship with her grandmother means that she is unable to conceive of her separation from the mother in anything other than violent terms, and she thus incites the physical mutilation that would symbolize her castration. Sergio shatters the plaster cast on his arm in order to mark his separation from Francisca and regain his autonomy, thus successfully completing the process of abjection. Francisca, however, is trapped in a role that compounds her failure to abject the mother, since she herself is reduced to the abject maternal body from which Sergio separates in order to be.

Francisca and Manuel: Abjection and Menstruation

For the first time in her novels, in *Vaca sagrada* Eltit offers an explicit portrayal of a feminist movement. However, while women may be portrayed as forming a labour union to demand improved employment and social rights, Eltit suggests that they have missed the point. Members of the female trade union brand tattoos onto their thighs as part of their protests, but their tattoos also cover over 'el centro mismo de la nalga' (p. 132). They thus obscure the natural scar of the umbilical cord that represents the child's primary separation from the maternal body, which forecloses any attempt to grant symbolic representation to the mother.

This section of the chapter examines how Eltit attempts to symbolize feminine subjectivity and woman's relation to the mother through the motif of menstrual blood, and draws on the representation of the relationship between Francisca and Manuel as a means to illustrate my argument. Their relationship is underpinned by a series of harrowing memories from Francisca's past, which emerge as a torrent from the unconscious when Francisca hears of Manuel's detention in the south of Chile in the fourth chapter of the novel. The memories are fused together in the text almost as a single experience and I read them as a representation of the imaginary that underpins the Symbolic order.

The first image to resurface is Francisca's recollection of cutting her leg on a pane of glass, causing a wound so deep that the flesh gaped open. From her bleeding leg she jumps to the memory of the heavily pregnant bitch that lived in her grandmother's house. The bitch is too old to bear pups and her bleeding body is equated by Francisca with a woman's sick and injured body.[36] Although about to give birth, the blood that trickles from the bitch's underbelly is associated by Francisca with death, and the bitch does indeed die after giving birth to five pups: two male and three female. As with the bitch's prior litters, Francisca's old and ailing grandmother decides which pups will live according to their sex. As she is now bedridden she instructs Francisca to drown the female pups, which Francisca does while sobbing uncontrollably.

The next recollection to surface is that of a filthy old man who pulls down his trousers in the street in front of Francisca; this act exposes her to the male genitals for the first time: 'El no esperaba nada más que yo certificara que era un hombre, no cualquier cosa, no un animal ni una basura, sino un hombre de verdad. Y así lo hice' (p. 46). Francisca's exposure to the male organ powerfully structures her relation to sexual difference. As she states: 'no recuerdo nada como no sea su parte indudablemente masculina [...] sabiendo que desde ese día en adelante nadie me podría engañar' (p. 46). His skin may have been putrid and punctured by oozing sores, his legs covered in pus and dried blood, but he was still the proud owner of a body part which, while referred to by Francisca as 'un pájaro en agonía' (p. 47), irrefutably upheld the boundary that separates the human and the non-human, so preventing his fall into abjection.

Four images now emerge that are not separated in terms of paragraph division, as occurred previously. Francisca's first recollection is of some sort of medical intervention, possibly an abortion, being carried out on her by a harsh and unsympathetic woman. Francisca is bleeding heavily between her open legs and the woman takes obvious pleasure in directing a surgical instrument between them, which Francisca describes in terms of the voracious pecking of birds: 'me asombraba ante la frialdad de la mujer y su inacabable

---

[36] Note the relevance of the term 'bitch' to the comments made by Eltit earlier in this chapter, in which she refers to the use of animal names to degrade women.

picoteo con los instrumentos' (p. 46). The association of the woman with a pecking bird, when read in terms of the Chilean colloquialisms used to denote the penis, thus defines her as a phallic woman.

Francisca's memory of her bleeding, prostrate body in a surgical environment is fused with the recollection of a blow to her head and the sensation that her eyeball has burst, which almost results in the loss of her vision. She attempts to reconstruct what she describes as 'el momento del golpe' (p. 47), which is not only another example of the images of visual mutilation that recur in the novel, but also brings to mind the military coup. A link is thus made between the coup, the blow to Francisca's head and the near loss of sight, which suggests that military violence is played out directly on the female body.

Another image now suddenly resurfaces which Francisca tries, but fails, to repress. A woman's body appears on a hospital stretcher and Francisca attempts to cover her: 'Busqué ocultar con mi cuerpo su figura, porque me pareció que estaba demasiado visible a lo largo de la sala de hospital, pero no alcancé a protegerla' (p. 47). She witnesses a needle puncturing the body's right arm, bringing forth a torrent of blood. The body becomes identifiable only later in the novel, during one of the brief dialogues between Francisca and her grand-mother in the fifth chapter. In this dialogue, her grandmother reluctantly allows Francisca to give her an injection to help her sleep: 'Bueno, pero que me las ponga en el otro brazo, en el derecho' (p. 60). The body on the hospital stretcher can thus be identified as that of Francisca's grandmother through the puncture marks and bruising on her right arm, which are the result of previous injections. Finally, Francisca is brought back to the present by the recollection of Manuel's detention in the South, and the stream of images come to an abrupt close with the following words: 'Pensé en la muerte' (p. 47).

Kristeva discusses the impurity that is associated with blood in Genesis because of its inherent animality, and she describes blood as a vital element that also refers to 'women, fertility, and the assurance of fecundation. It thus becomes a fascinating semantic crossroads, the propitious place for abjection where *death* and *femininity*, *murder* and *procreation*, *cessation of life* and *vitality* all come together.'[37] Throughout the imaginary process outlined above, female blood is conceptualized as signifying horror, humiliation and death, as well as procreation and femininity. Blood from Francisca's own wounds is shown to mingle with the blood of a pregnant animal and her dying grand-mother's own blood, and woman is shown to self-identify as an abject creature not far removed from animals because of her bodily reproductive attributes, symbolized by menstrual blood. Although the putrid male body referred to above is represented in terms of a collapse of corporeal boundaries, which is fundamental to Kristeva's notion of the abject, the cultural authority wielded by the phallus is shown to overcome abjection and grant symbolic representation. In the face of such authority, woman is reduced merely to the embodiment of a human/animal figure against which sexual difference can be defined.

---

[37] *Powers of Horror*, p. 96; emphasis hers.

The series of images that resurface in Francisca underscore the extent to which the imaginary is mediated by the phallus, which reflects Irigaray's argument that there is no place for woman in the (male) cultural imaginary, resulting in woman's suppressed sexuality being buried deep beneath patriarchal representations of the feminine.[38] However, what makes the imaginary process so disturbing here is the extent to which woman is shown to be complicit in the phallocentric construction of sexual difference. The grandmother firmly positions herself on the side of patriarchal law by valuing the male pups over the female pups, simply because of the difference that allows the latter to give birth. The phallic woman who 'pecks' at Francisca's body takes pleasure in the affliction caused by a bleeding wound that marks Francisca's body as abject. Francisca herself, although distraught at drowning the female pups, nevertheless carries out her grandmother's instructions. She is also complicit in guaranteeing the symbolic representation of the male body and in occluding the representation of the maternal body by shrouding it from visibility. Woman's socially inferior status is thus linked to her complicity in a patriarchal ideology that forces her to self-identify with abjection. In a context in which the paternal figure is absent, the patriarchal and phallocentric system nonetheless continues to function in and through woman.

As stated earlier, it is Manuel's detention in the South that sparks the emergence of these distant and disparate memories, and it is the motif of menstrual blood that structures his relation with Francisca. Prior to his detention, Francisca and Manuel had formed a friendship based on a mutual understanding of their shared flaw of inventing untruths. Their relationship is thus defined as abject from the start since, as Kristeva argues, abjection besets 'the shame of compromise, of being in the middle of treachery'.[39] Francisca uses Manuel to shore up her fantasies and lies, and he, in turn, uses Francisca to corroborate his projected fascination for the South, centered on the town of Pucatrihue, from whence he originates.[40] The nostalgic and utopian descriptions given by Manuel of his place of origin are belied by Francisca's private acknowledgment that he hates its consuming and hellish nature: 'Pucatrihue era el infierno. Su mar encabritado consumía los cuerpos y los árboles retorcidos emitían figuras espectrales' (p. 19). The bond between them rests on their complicity in burying each other's horror and self-deceptions. As Francisca states: 'Pero sumisamente decíamos que sí, decíamos que sí, transfigurando todo aquello que nos

---

[38] *This Sex Which is Not One*, p. 30.

[39] *Powers of Horror*, p. 2.

[40] Pucatrihue, states Eltit, is a coastal community in the south of Chile where the indigenous huilliche population carry out maritime rituals, which she witnessed. Manuel's place of origin thus takes on indigenous connotations. See Morales, *Conversaciones*, pp. 43–4. Labanyi points to the contradictory image of the South in Chilean culture, both as the place of 'idyllic, unspoilt nature', as propagated by Neruda, and as the base for several concentration camps set up by the military after the coup. Labanyi, in *Latin American Women's Writing* (see Jones and Davies), p. 51 (n. 5). Indeed, Eltit has commented that multiple images of the South exist, which go beyond the romantic vision of Neruda: 'Mi sur no es el de Neruda, es otro sur el que yo veo'. Pino-Ojeda, p. 147.

horrorizaba y, de esa manera, fuimos ordenando una alianza tramada en los compromisos que iban encubriendo el espesor de las mentiras' (p. 19). While Francisca's repressed horror can be associated with the 'immemorial violence' of the loss of her grandmother, I read Manuel's ambivalent relationship with the South in terms of his relation to the archaic mother, portrayed as the devouring and inhospitable place of origin, and the primordial abyss from which life originates and to which life returns.[41]

When the relationship between Francisca and Manuel moves into the sexual realm, the female body is once again located as the site of the struggle between the subject and the abject. Manuel's aggression may be superficially disguised, but his violence surfaces during intercourse when he debases Francisca with the following words: 'Perra malagradecida. Eres una perra malagradecida' (p. 23). His use of the term 'perra' brings to mind the pregnant and bleeding bitch, which locates Francisca on the boundaries of the animal world because of her reproductive functions. Francisca's negation of his utterances illustrates a dissolution of self, but also marks the attainment of their *jouissance*, described as an act of falling: 'No soy, no soy, no soy [...] Y en el éxtasis caímos juntos' (p. 23). It is, then, only when they are confronted with the abject – that is, when the female body is pushed towards 'those fragile states where man strays on the territories of *animal*' – that they fall together into *jouissance*.[42]

The sense of destabilization experienced by Francisca during their relationship, as she is increasingly forced to self-identify with abjection, results in her reduction to a body defined only by the sum of its sexual functions: 'En esos meses logré ser sólo un cuerpo que cumplía diversas obligaciones amplificado por el lenguaje arcaico que lo envilecía' (p. 24). The heat generated between the bodies of Manuel and Francisca – who are described as 'en celo' – denotes a sexual energy associated with animals during the rutting period. Like animals, their desire is intensified when Francisca is 'on heat': 'Era ahí, entre la sangre, cuando tocábamos el punto más preciso de la turbulencia genital' (p. 25).

Francisca stands over Manuel with her legs apart in order to cake him with her blood, which imbues their sexual union with an eroticism linked to contagion: 'Manuel pedía que le contagiara mi sangre. Se la entregaba cuando él la buscaba plenamente erecto para extraerla y gozar de su espesor líquido' (p. 25). She describes the sense of fusion and confusion incited in them by her blood, thus denoting the abject nature of their sexual relations through the collapse of gender boundaries, but she also emphasizes the power that it grants her, highlighting the potential to give life symbolized by menstruation. Although she appears to allow Manuel to share in this sense of privilege, she secretly resents the demands that he makes on her bodily fluid as the support for their sexual acts: 'Aunque fingía que era un privilegio de ambos, un espacio de mi mente se empezó a resentir por el esfuerzo de construir una a una la perfección de esas escenas' (p. 25).

---

[41] For further details of the 'archaic mother', see Kristeva, *Powers of Horror*, p. 91.
[42] Kristeva, *Powers of Horror*, p. 25; emphasis hers.

Kristeva argues that when the abjection of flows from inside the body 'suddenly become the sole "object" of sexual desire', man is able to withstand the horror of the maternal body and immerse himself in the mother without the risk of castration. As she states: 'that immersion gives him the full power of possessing, if not being, the bad object that inhabits the maternal body. Abjection then takes the place of the other, to the extent of affording him jouissance.'[43] In Kristeva's terms, the eroticization of Francisca's menstrual blood allows Manuel to plunge himself into the devouring mother and confront 'the desirable and terrifying, nourishing and murderous, fascinating and abject inside of the maternal body'.[44] It is, then, by 'extracting' Francisca's menstrual blood that Manuel attempts to confront the horror of the maternal body, represented earlier in terms of the South. His possession of her blood disturbingly illustrates the danger of a masculine appropriation and recodification of a potentially powerful marker of feminine subjectivity. Menstrual blood is reduced to a channel through which man is reconciled with the mother and attains *jouissance*. Wallowing in her own blood merely pushes Francisca towards animality and abjection.

Manuel's subsequent decision to return to the South is welcomed by Francisca, who anticipates the autonomy that she will now be able to regain over a part of herself that has been lost and which may be read in terms of her menstrual blood: 'Pensé que alejándome de Manuel iba a encontrar una parte perdida de mí misma' (p. 30). Manuel's decision to return, she states, is based on his need for reconciliation with his place of origin, and his appropriation of her blood can be seen as the trigger that sparks his decision. His detention upon his return turns his nostalgic reminiscences into a chilling reminder of the pervasive actions of the military, and confirms his repressed perceptions of the South as hellish and all-consuming. When read in terms of a return to the archaic mother, the maternal is emphasized as a destructive force linked to death, which reincorporates her offspring. When read in terms of a return to the mother/womb, Manuel's subsequent detention highlights the violence of the paternal authority that prohibits a reconciliation with the maternal body. Manuel is thus forced to pay a severe penalty for his eroticization of the abject, a penalty from which Francisca is not immune.

From this point on, the phrase 'Manuel había sido detenido en el Sur' is hauntingly repeated by Francisca, which constantly brings to the fore the political violence that surrounds Manuel's detention. Francisca is plagued by his detention, his spectral image looming before her at night, and she imagines him naked and moaning as he is chased by a flock of birds. She wills Manuel to stay alive through her nocturnal vigils and the flow of her blood: 'Manuel estaba detenido en el Sur y mi sangre conseguía suspender su muerte por una noche' (p. 51). Their relationship disintegrates into a re-enactment of the primary relationship, not only through the nocturnal images of vigils and death which are shadowed by flocks of birds, but also through the manner in which Francisca

---

[43] *Powers of Horror*, p. 54.
[44] *Powers of Horror*, p. 54.

had sought to eke out her grandmother's final nights: 'No me entiendes, es que ella se estaba muriendo y, si no inventaba, no iba a pasar la noche. Detuve su muerte por una noche, inventando' (p. 141). While Francisca had previously attempted to recuperate life through words, like Scheherazade in *The Arabian Nights*, she now consciously seizes control of her menstrual cycle as a means of ensuring the survival of another body. The affirmation of life over death is thus interwoven into the very texture of the narrative, since Francisca's journey through abjection subsequently collapses into the novel itself, a point discussed further below.

The flow of Francisca's blood is symbolized as an overwhelmingly powerful life force that opposes death and the phallic violence that is its precursor: 'la imagen de mi sangre reparaba a una multitud en vuelo' (p. 50). Just as she had previously incrusted Manuel's body with her menstrual blood, she now spreads her blood over her own body in order to stave off his death, placing herself within the realm of the abject through her immersion in bodily waste. Although bleeding, she is not dying, and the free flow of her blood signifies the revenge that Manuel calls out for her to enact on his behalf. Her blood is thus used to challenge and overcome male blood rites that endanger society. However, the power and privilege that Francisca had previously experienced soon disappear as her blood becomes infected by death: 'todos los meses llegaba la sangre y, en ese tiempo, la sangre había perdido en mí cualquier rango que no fuera su irreversible conexión con la muerte' (p. 51). Eltit's attempt to symbolize menstrual blood as a marker of feminine subjectivity thus increasingly founders, since it becomes imbued with horror and is appropriated for male purposes of resistance to the paternal order.

The 'immemorial violence' of the primary relationship continually emerges through the suffering and terror experienced by Francisca during Manuel's detention. Communicating through a form of telekinesis, she begs Manuel to breathe, since breath signifies life within the body. The devastating toll of Manuel's detention is played out directly on Francisca's body and she experiences abjection in terms of what Kristeva describes as 'an Other [that] has settled in place and stead of what will be "me"'.[45] Corporeal boundaries collapse as Manuel's disintegrating body fuses with her own, sucking out her vitality like a monstrous baby: 'Ya no era Manuel, era apenas un cuerpo que me provocaba para confundirse con el mío y succionar mi escasa vitalidad' (p. 77). Francisca is forced into the maternal role in order to keep alive the memory of a man exposed to paternal vengeance, and becomes the abject embodiment of the political violence that consumes the nation. Despite her attempts to secure Manuel's survival, he scornfully appears before her at night to insult her with the same words used to degrade her during sexual intercourse, 'perra malagradecida' (p. 77), trapping her in abjection.

The horror of Manuel's corporeal disintegration is increasingly internalized by Francisca and directed towards what she perceives as her deformed and

[45] *Powers of Horror*, p. 10.

imperfect body. She initiates a period of severe fasting, encouraged by Sergio, and the extremity of Francisca's fasting is such that she can clearly be identified as suffering from anorexia, even describing herself as an 'ayunante crónica' (p. 89). Her body becomes increasingly sapped of energy and her skin wracked by blemishes. Her aim, she states, is continually to heighten her alimentary privation in order to push her body beyond the brink of exhaustion. In this way, her waking hours will be diminished and the nocturnal demands made by Manuel will be silenced. Her extreme food loathing, which Kristeva categorizes as one of the most archaic forms of abjection, pushes her to consume putrefying meat that makes her retch, but she is desperate to find a means by which to separate from Manuel: 'Sin saber qué esperaba de mí, ensayaba distintas respuestas para que me abandonara' (p. 89).[46]

The shifting symbol of menstrual blood, depicted as active and dynamic at the start of the novel, loses its power as the novel progresses. Francisca states that menstruation no longer holds any pleasure for her: 'Sangraba sí, seguía sangrando, pero únicamente como el deber físico que me imponía una repetición biológica desprovista de toda utilidad' (p. 178). The cultural norms discussed at the beginning of this chapter, which associate menstruation with the female body's failure to reproduce, are here shown to overpower any attempt to move menstrual blood beyond the biological, reducing it to a stigma associated with repetition and waste. This biological reduction is linked to Francisca's inability to separate from the maternal body or to distance herself from the memory of the disappeared body of Manuel. As she states: 'Yo conocía bien el cuerpo en agonía, lo había visto descomponerse ante mis ojos. Esa agonía había quedado prendida de mis miembros y el precipitamiento de mi sangre había logrado distraerla' (p. 179). Menstruation, therefore, had previously alleviated the agony of 'the immemorial violence with which a body becomes separated from another body in order to be', and allowed a glimpse of how female sexuality may be moved beyond melancholia. However, the loss entailed for Francisca through menstruation is shown to be immense, since it involves shedding the disintegrating corporeal remnants of both her grandmother and Manuel. It is the inability to overcome this loss, and so symbolize menstrual blood as a marker of feminine subjectivity, that ultimately leads Francisca to question her position within the process of representation: 'Pero si ya no sangraba era necesario descubrir cuál era la realidad posible de una historia, cómo se llegaba a construir la farsa de una historia' (p. 179).

At the end of the novel, Francisca travels to the South to investigate Manuel's disappearance. She is disorientated by the unfamiliar landscape and overwhelmed by the flocks of screeching, migrating birds that overshadow her, characterized by their monstrous and indestructible nature and their ferocious survival instinct. Francisca comments on the self-serving nature of the birds' departure from a space of death and disintegration into warmer climes, and the scorn and disdain with which she watches their flight can be linked to the contempt induced in

---

[46] *Powers of Horror*, p. 2.

many sectors of Chilean society that were forced to witness the impunity with which the military retreated from government and into other institutions.[47]

Francisca's journey to the South is futile, as she states: 'Me recriminé [...] por la fantasía que me había llevado a pensar que yo poseía alguna garantía corporal. El Sur había destruido mi confianza al hacer evidente el placer inútil de mi hilo de sangre cuyo goce jamás podría compartir' (p. 183). The South, which I have previously read as representing the archaic mother, is here shown to be the locus of supreme phallic and militaristic power. Manuel's place of origin is thus portrayed as always and already appropriated for male purposes of violence. Against such an indestructible and pervasive phallic power, Francisca is forced to recognize her abject and fragmented corporeal structure, and the enormity of the task of granting symbolic representation to the female body.

Francisca now accepts the imperative of representing her own relation to origins: 'Sin ninguna claridad sobre cuál era mi lugar de origen emprendí una marcha agotadora hacia el anonimato del centro' (p. 184).[48] Writing becomes the means for her to seek her place of origin and she unearths the material proof that will form the basis of her text: 'Allí estaban las cintas, las cartas, las fotografías. Allí estábamos capturados en el cuadrante de la caja que empecé a catalogar con una obsesión que ya me conocía' (p. 188). This material proof can be read in terms of the papers and photographs that Francisca's grand-mother wished to organize before her death, suggesting that it is only after confronting abjection that Francisca can seek a reconciliation with the maternal body and so represent her relation to origins. Indeed, Kristeva argues that writing 'causes the subject who ventures in it to confront an archaic authority', an authority that she links to the maternal and which forces what she terms 'great' writers to come 'face to face with what we have called abjection'.[49] The end of the novel thus collapses into the origin of the journey through abjection that the reader has just completed, as the work folds back on itself in an endless cycle of confrontation with, and sublimation of, horror.

Writing is thus put forward as the means by which Francisca names and unveils horror. Although the possibility that writing offers of mapping out and breaking free from the abject images that confront her is a painful experience, it is essential if the abjection process is to be completed. Writing is portrayed as emerging from a space of liminality, and the risks and dangers that it entails

[47] As noted previously, the military put in place an amnesty law before handing over power to the Concertación in order to protect themselves from future prosecutions linked to abuses of human rights. Memory is an important topic in the novel, which attempts to work through the brutality of an era that is coming to a close, leaving uncertainty, distrust and sorrow deeply ingrained in the Chilean psyche.

[48] Note the shift towards the centre, and thus away from the margins, alluded to here. The question of positionality will be referred to again in relation to *Los vigilantes* (see Chapter 5).

[49] *Powers of Horror*, p. 75. Labanyi offers Eltit's novel 'as a case of the female abject writing missing from Kristeva's discussion'. Labanyi, in *Latin American Women's Writing* (see Jones and Davies), p. 89.

are not underestimated by Eltit, but she suggests that only from this liminal space can new forms and structures be identified that will allow woman to move beyond abjection. Fundamentally, writing will allow a reconciliation with the maternal body, which will enable woman to represent her relation to origins. First, however, it is necessary to endure an encounter with horror.

As throughout Eltit's narrative, in *Vaca sagrada* the domain of the female body points to the fragility of the Symbolic order. Eltit has commented on the centrality of the female body in this novel as follows: 'me sigue pareciendo que el cuerpo es un territorio moral donde ensayan su eficacia o su fracaso los sistemas de poder'.[50] Francisca's abject bleeding body is shown to defy the boundaries that delimit what Kristeva terms 'one's *own and clean self*', so subverting patriarchal and phallocentric systems of power.[51] However, I do not believe that Eltit offers abjection as a means of self-empowerment for women. Hovering on the boundary of animal and human merely reduces woman to man's abject sexual other, against which sexual difference can be defined. The abject female body constitutes a fearful and threatening form of sexuality for man, because of the conflation of female sexuality and woman's reproductive functions, and woman thus becomes the body through which masculine aggression is discharged. In a social context founded on the untouchable primacy of phallocentrism, Eltit illustrates the difficulty of representing feminine subjectivity in its own terms. In the novel, the potential marker of menstrual blood as a symbol of the feminine is contaminated and appropriated for male purposes of resistance to paternal law, a stance that is reworked and taken further by Eltit in her following novel, *Los vigilantes*.

Francisca's failure to abject the maternal body is shown to have serious repercussions for social relations. In turn, her inability to separate from the mother is compounded by the very structure of these relations, which force Francisca to replay the 'immemorial violence' of the primary relationship. Sexual relations are portrayed as grounded on horror, whereby each sex seeks to consume and possess the other, locating the very structure of gender relations as abject. Desire becomes subsumed in genital drives deprived of affect and respect, and the tragedy for humans is that they are unable to find the love they seek. Francisca, Manuel and Sergio may be bound in the novel by the phrase 'Caliéntame el corazón', but love is impossible in a climate in which the only heat generated is through the animalistic drives of their bodies.

The dictatorship may be coming to an end, but Eltit suggests that this will not automatically bring about the necessary redrawing of the boundaries that underlie social and symbolic structures. More than in any other of her novels, the need to challenge the hierarchy of sexual difference is portrayed as absolutely imperative in *Vaca sagrada*. Eltit's warning for Chilean women on the cusp of redemocratization is that sexual oppression continues to be the root of all other forms of oppression and cannot be ignored.

---

[50] Larraín, 'El cuerpo femenino es un territorio moral', p. 4.
[51] *Powers of Horror*, p. 65; emphasis hers.

5

Writing the Mother in *Los vigilantes*

Epistolary Writing and the Law

Los vigilantes, Eltit's fifth novel, was awarded the José Nuez Martín prize for the best novel published in Chile in 1994–95 and was written during Eltit's period of residence as the Chilean Cultural Attaché in Mexico City.[1] In her extensive interviews with Leonidas Morales, Eltit states that Samuel Beckett's *Molloy* and William Faulkner's *The Sound and the Fury* were two important references in her writing of the novel, as were certain elements of the work of Brecht and Kafka.[2] However, she also states that her main aim in writing this novel was to explore the idea of power, beginning from within the home and extending outwards into the social sphere, and she comments on the influence of the theoretical ideas of Foucault regarding power and surveillance.[3] The link between power and writing was another point that Eltit wished to interrogate. As she states: 'Estaba pensando en cierta escritura también: en la medida en que no pacta, sale.'[4]

Eltit has made reference to the huge effect that the change of political discourse in Chile had on her writing of the novel. It was written during the first government of the Concertación, and she describes her shock at the profound changes that intense neo-liberalism was effecting in Chile: 'estaban cambiando las relaciones sociales, la cuestión literaria. Se instalaba el mercado [...] en ese sentido me afectó, y lo vi más dramático, digamos, el retiro, la exclusión, la diferencia, la soledad.'[5] Eltit's perception of post-dictatorship Chilean society at this time as reified, acritical and depoliticized, and traversed by consumerism, competition and social inequality, is embedded within the novel. As she states: 'La sensación de desprotección urbana [...] fue recayendo en la novela [...] Fue recayendo incluso en la misma escritura como cerco, soledad y margen, como ajenidad en medio de sociedades que construyen su

---

[1] The José Nuez Martín prize is the first and only award to date that Eltit has received for her literary work in Chile and it was conferred by the Pontificia Universidad Católica in Santiago. *Los vigilantes* was first published in Chile by Sudamericana in 1994 and was republished by Norma in Buenos Aires in 2003. It has been translated into English.

[2] Morales, *Conversaciones*, p. 45, p. 50.

[3] Morales, *Conversaciones*, p. 47, p. 77.

[4] Morales, *Conversaciones*, p. 49.

[5] Morales, *Conversaciones*, p. 51.

orden a través del consumismo.'[6] The social effects of the market-orientated discourse of the Transition thus also came to constrain the writing process, and are directly reflected throughout the letters written by the mother in the novel (see pp. 118–26). However, Eltit's comments here can also be read as a reflection on the position of her own writing in a society where market forces determine which literary texts are published in terms of their potential to generate sales, regardless of their intrinsic quality.

Los vigilantes is divided into three parts. The main body is epistolary in content and consists of the letters written by a mother to the absent father of her son, which are clearly the mother's only means of communication with the man. Her name is given only in the final sentence of her last letter and the other members of the family remain nameless. There is, therefore, no named addressee or sender, and no dates to mark the passage of time. The father's replies are not included in the novel, but their content can be gleaned from the mother's letters, since his judgements, accusations and demands structure the content and tone of her own correspondence. As Guillermo García-Corales notes, the father's voice can be located in the novel as 'una voz silente'.[7] Although there is no traditional family structure in the novel, the paternal figure is shown to be simultaneously absent and yet still all-powerful, and nuclear configurations clearly continue to prevail as points of reference, even when they are distorted by the very discourses that aim to keep them in place.

The first and third chapters of the novel, which form a brief preface and postscript to the mother's letters, are narrated through the jerking body movements and babble of the mother's nameless son, who exists in the text as a polymorphous perverse bundle of drives. The son writhes along the floor, drooling and laughing unrestrainedly, and his extraordinary and chaotic discourse brings to mind the speech-inhibiting psychosis of autism, which starkly contrasts with the formal precision of his mother's writing. He empha-sizes at the very start that it is only his mother who writes: 'Mamá escribe. Mamá es la única que escribe' (p. 13). He also reiterates his inability to speak and his reliance on the kinetic discourse of the games he plays with his clay vessels as his only means of communication. However, the novel ends with a reversal of roles as the son assumes written control of the novel, and it is now his mother who drools and laughs uncontrollably, having lost the capacity to speak. As he informs us: 'Mi letra. Ahora yo escribo' (p. 126). The son's postscript portrays mother and son as physically collapsing into one another, a portrayal that not only suggests incest, but also a collapse into the Kristevan space of the semiotic.

Eltit has discussed the two meanings inherent in the title of the novel: 'Lo pensé en los dos sentidos, tanto en el sentido del que vigila y del que está en

[6] Eltit, 'Quisiera', in *Emergencias*, pp. 185–9 (p. 187).

[7] Guillermo García-Corales, 'Silencio y resistencia en *Los vigilantes* de Diamela Eltit', *Monographic Review*, 16 (2000), 368–81.

vigilia, el que no puede dormir.'[8] While external surveillance is paramount, the mother writes her letters from within the home that she shares with her son either as night falls, during the hours of darkness, or as the sun is rising, thus portraying a woman who maintains a nightly vigil.[9] The novel picks up once again on the themes of power relationships within the family and the fundamental importance of language in the constitution of power and subjectivity. Mother and son unite in their resistance to the father, and this mother–son dyad is replicated in the relationship between the father and his own mother, the mother-in-law, who helps to enforce the father's law.[10] Family hostilities are thus shown to fall along the lines of mother–son relations.

The law of the father is imposed directly on mother and son through the control that he assumes over their lives. The aim of his law is to discipline the mother and bring her into submission; breaking the law thus becomes an offence against a paternal figure. The absent father represents an impregnable system of control that relentlessly watches and polices the social body. His disciplinary power spreads from the mother's private domain into the city at large, but the target of his control never ceases to be the maternal body, which is always perceived by him in terms of disorder and disruption, and thus, in Irigaray's terms, as the excess that woman symbolizes in the Symbolic.[11] The father embodies an absolute power that allows for no compromise, and the mother's eventual refusal to accept paternal law and the norms of the city ultimately destroys her ability to act as a linguistic/speaking subject, a point that reflects Eltit's own comments on the position of the mother in the novel: 'Está en el "centro", entre comillas, pero sin embargo es desalojada por su diferencia. En la medida en que no hace pactos, que no obedece a pactos sociales, tiene que salir.'[12]

Nora Domínguez has placed the novel against the most emblematic example of a woman's epistolary writing in Latin America, that of Sor Juana Inés de la Cruz, to examine how Eltit reworks woman's historical link to the epistolary genre.[13] I digress slightly here to outline two other emblematic instances in which epistolary writing takes on a very specific meaning within Latin America,

---

[8] Morales, *Conversaciones*, p. 76. I would add that taking the law into one's own hands, denoted through the English phrase 'vigilante-style justice', is also of relevance to the actions of the neighbours who appear in the novel, as we shall see.

[9] The necessity of maintaining a nightly vigil was also emphasized in relation to L. Iluminada in *Lumpérica*.

[10] A euphemism for mother-in-law in Spanish is 'madre política', which conflates the realms of motherhood, law and politics, thus moving motherhood away from the realm of the biological.

[11] *This Sex Which is Not One*, p. 3.

[12] Morales, *Conversaciones*, p. 49. Eltit's use of the word 'pacto' here brings to the fore the pacts formed between democratic parties and the military prior to redemocratization, which were fundamental to the subsequent consensual style of politics of the Concertación.

[13] Nora Domínguez, 'Extraños consorcios: cartas, mujeres y silencios', in *Fábulas del género. Sexo y escrituras en América Latina*, ed. by Nora Domínguez and Carmen Perilli (Rosario: Beatriz Viterbo, 1998), pp. 35–58.

specifically in terms of its relation to the law. My aim is to foreground the politicized nature of writing in post-dictatorship Chilean society.

In *Myth and Archive*, Roberto González Echevarría traces the influence of legal discourse in the first narratives of Latin America, the 'cartas de relación'.[14] These were addressed to a source of Spanish authority and, as González Echevarría notes, they constitute a document that granted the writer a sense of emancipation. He includes a chapter on the *Comentarios reales de los Incas* (1609), an appeal to the Council of the Indies written by Garcilaso de la Vega, el Inca, to clear his father's name. In relation to this epistolary text, González Echevarría stresses that 'To write was a form of enfranchisement, of legitimation. The *pícaro*, the chronicler, and in a sense the whole New World, seek enfranchisement and a validation of their existence through the writing of their stories.'[15] The sense of legitimation that the writer attained through the power of the letter as a document, as emphasized by González Echevarría, can also be found in Eltit's novel. Only by maintaining epistolary contact with the father is the mother's existence validated, since she exists in the social realm only in so far as she responds to his questions or accusations.

Leonidas Morales links the colonial epistolary tradition in Latin America to the letters that he selected for inclusion in *Cartas de petición*, which includes a foreword by Eltit.[16] The letters included are addressed to various (absent) sources of military authority in Chile, and were mostly written by the relatives of those arrested between 1973 and 1983. The majority of the correspondence, which Morales found in the archives of the Vicaría de la Solidaridad in Santiago, seeks to petition the military as to the whereabouts of family members.[17] The letters are poignant and dignified; the rhetoric and syntax are impeccable; and they include a meticulous level of detail. Any replies received, which are few in number, are also included.

As Eltit points out in the foreword, the writers of these letters sought to open up a channel of communication with the perpetrators of abuses that extended violently and directly into the sanctity of their own homes, a situation that she describes as 'un diálogo humano en medio de una situación radical-mente inhumana'.[18] In a society where administrative and legal channels have been silenced, the writers are thrust into a desperate written relationship in which they hold no power, and Morales thus describes their position as analogous to that of the indigenous 'letrados' who sent 'cartas de petición' to the Spanish monarchy to petition such causes as the restoration of rights. The

[14] Roberto González Echevarría, *Myth and Archive: A Theory of Latin American Narrative* (Cambridge: Cambridge University Press, 1990), p. 10.

[15] González Echevarría, pp. 45–6; italics in the original.

[16] *Cartas de petición: Chile 1973–1989*, ed. by Leonidas Morales T. (Santiago: Planeta/Ariel, 2000). The writers of these letters were both men and women, and their names and addresses are included in their letters.

[17] The Vicaría de la Solidaridad was established in Chile by the Catholic Church during the dictatorship with the aim of defending human rights. Legal assistance in writing these letters was provided by the Vicaría.

[18] *Cartas de petición*, p. 10.

addressees in both instances were absent representatives of the state, and the sender a private subject whose only option was the deployment of discursive strategies that aimed to persuade the authorities to look benevolently upon their petitions. I perceive this one-sided correspondence to be reflected in the structure of Eltit's novel. It is woman, in her maternal role, who is forced to exculpate herself and seek reunification with paternal law by proving her worthiness as a mother through her written pleas and confrontations with the father of her child, whom we can now consider an absent representative of an absolute public power.

Several of the critical readings of the novel to date have focused on the representation of power within it, which is also an important aspect of my own reading. Alvaro Kaempfer examines the relation between the confined domestic space and the city through an analysis of the power relations between its inhabitants, while María Inés Lagos looks at the mother's resistance to paternal power through writing.[19] The first section of my reading also charts the process of the mother's resistance to the authoritative power of the absent father, following Foucault's well-known argument that 'Where there is power, there is resistance, and yet, or rather consequently, this resistance is never in a position of exteriority in relation to power.'[20] However, in contrast to Lagos, my focus on the mother's corpus of letters also examines the myriad power relations that they make evident, through which motherhood is shown to be constituted. The power relations portrayed reflect Foucault's concept of power as spreading from the micro-level into society at large. In Eltit's novel, it is the patriarchal structure of power within the family – in which woman, in her maternal role, is positioned either as the target of, or vehicle for, male domination – that enables the operation of wider networks of power in the social body. The novel thus offers a gendered critique of a supposedly democratic system of power, both in terms of its effect on social relations and its appropriation of marginal spaces and discourses.

As indicated above, the theoretical ideas of Foucault regarding power are pertinent to my reading here. Although the poststructuralist work of Foucault diverges from the approach taken thus far, it allows for an exploration of the specific and local mode of power relations and of the manner in which disciplinary power invests the body. However, as a number of feminist critics have pointed out, the immediate difficulty in Foucault's concept of power is that it fails to address power as gendered and rests on the notion of the body as sexually undifferentiated. As Rosi Braidotti notes: 'Foucault never locates woman's body as the site of one of the most operational internal divisions in

---

[19] Alvaro Kaempfer, 'Las cartas marcadas: política urbana y convivencia textual en *Los vigilantes* de Diamela Eltit', *Confluencia*, 16:2 (2001), 32–45; and María Inés Lagos, 'Lenguaje, género y poder en *Los vigilantes* de Diamela Eltit', in *Creación y resistencia* (see Lagos), pp. 127–45. For an exploration of the broader representation of power structures in the novel, see Norat, pp. 176–206.

[20] Foucault, *The History of Sexuality*, p. 95.

our society, and consequently also of the most persistent forms of exclusion.'[21] It is specifically the maternal body which is identified by Eltit as the locus of internal social division and exclusion in her novel, and the emphasis placed by Eltit on the gendered structure of power within the family highlights Foucault's silence on the subject of sexual differentiation.

The third section of this chapter focuses on the first and third chapters of the novel and explores the relationships within the family triangle from the son's viewpoint. My reading is framed by Kristeva's psychoanalytic work relating to the semiotic *chora* and centres on the representation of the mother–son relationship within the maternal realm. First, though, let me begin by offering a précis of Foucault's ideas regarding disciplinary power, which form the theoretical basis of the following section.

Power, Knowledge and Surveillance

Foucault stresses the importance of one instance in the history of repression: the transition from inflicting an exemplary penalty to placing people under surveillance. He states that surveillance emerged because it was 'more efficient and profitable in terms of the economy of power', and its efficiency and profitability would certainly complement the hegemonic economic ethos of neo-liberalism in Chile during the Transition.[22] Foucault continues by arguing that surveillance is made possible by the mechanism of panopticism, which automatizes and disindividualizes power, in the sense that power becomes disassociated from a centralized institution or apparatus, and functions as a set of constraints and regulations that govern the most intimate level of individual lives.[23]

Surveillance is essential to the exercise of discipline, which Foucault describes as 'a type of power, a modality for its exercise'.[24] As Jana Sawicki notes in her commentary on Foucault, disciplinary power functions through the establishment of norms 'against which individuals and their behaviors and bodies are judged and against which they police themselves'.[25] Disciplinary practice is thus a means of normalization and social control, dividing society

[21] Rosi Braidotti, *Patterns of Dissonance* (Cambridge: Polity Press, 1991), p. 87.

[22] Michel Foucault, *Power/Knowledge: Selected Interviews and Other Writings*, ed. by Colin Gordon (Brighton: Harvester, 1980), p. 38. Robert Neustadt also draws a link between social relations in post-dictatorship Chilean society and the mechanism of panopticism. Neustadt, *(Con)Fusing Signs and Postmodern Positions*, p. 63.

[23] Michel Foucault, *Discipline and Punish: The Birth of the Prison* (London: Penguin, 1991), p. 214. The Panopticon was designed in the eighteenth century as an all-seeing institutional building of surveillance that aimed to induce in inmates an awareness of their constant visibility, thus permitting power to function automatically.

[24] *Discipline and Punish*, p. 215.

[25] Jana Sawicki, *Disciplining Foucault: Feminism, Power and the Body* (London: Routledge, 1991), p. 68.

in terms of what is acceptable; that which is considered abnormal or different is disqualified and cast out.

Foucault also stresses the link between discipline and knowledge, arguing that disciplinary power is reinforced through the circulation of certain forms of knowledge. Ways of knowing are thus linked to ways of exercising power over individuals, and the effects of power and knowledge are relayed through discourse. As defined by Foucault, discourse is 'a space of positions and of differentiated functions for subjects', but his aim is to question its 'archaeology' – that is, the set of rules that at a given period and for a specific society define what it is possible to speak of, and thus what is constituted as the domain of discourse.[26]

In contrast to *Lumpérica* and *Por la patria*, in which military power and surveillance are visibly located in a technological apparatus or a centralized institution, *Los vigilantes* portrays the change of political discourse as initiating a change in the mechanism of power. The regime of power is now 'synaptic'; in other words, as Kaempfer also notes, power is no longer exercised from above through violence and repression but operates throughout the social body, functioning through what Foucault terms 'its capillary form of existence, the point where power reaches into the very grain of individuals', a point to which I will return.[27]

The epistolary body of *Los vigilantes* opens at daybreak. Thirty letters are written by the mother to the father of her son and, apart from the final letter, they are all similar in length. Interwoven into her text are carefully nuanced descriptions of the hostile and extreme climate. Until her penultimate letter, the mother refers to their son as 'tu hijo', a term which highlights the patrilineal bond of kinship and emphasizes the paternal duty that she feels she has a right to expect from the father of her child. Although she confides in the father the feelings of irritation and desperation provoked in her by their son, she also questions his right to usurp control of her progressively peripheral and enclosed home while failing to provide materially for his son. Her letters thus oscillate between a need to involve the father in her predicaments and a wariness of his role in overseeing what she describes in her first letter as 'nuestro hostil derrotero' (p. 25). So, from the very beginning, the mother foresees her eventual defeat at the father's hands and senses that a punishment inevitably awaits her. The novel can thus be read in terms of a tragedy, in the sense that the catastrophe that unfolds is inevitable.

The distance and distrust between the parents is made apparent in the mother's opening letter. She immediately refers to previous communication between them, berating the father for failing to prevent his son's expulsion from school, in spite of her warnings. Each parent blames the other for their son's expulsion, and although we never find out exactly why the son was

---

[26] Michel Foucault, 'Politics and the Study of Discourse', *Ideology and Consciousness*, 3 (1978), 7–26 (p. 13).

[27] Kaempfer, p. 32; and Foucault, *Power/Knowledge*, p. 39.

expelled, the mother makes no excuses for his actions: 'Lo que hizo sobrepasó todos los límites y yo me vi enfrentada a un conocimiento que me ha dejado demasiado avergonzada' (p. 27).

Their son's expulsion provokes a series of differing viewpoints between his parents and what emerges is a conflict over two different forms of knowledge. The father appears to accuse the mother of instilling in his son a system of knowledge that opposes his own. As the mother states: 'Si bien entendí tu reciente carta, te altera el que yo quiera promover en tu hijo un pensamiento que te parece opuesto a tus creencias' (p. 33). The son's system of knowledge is centered on the home and on his ability to refine his bodily senses, and the father clearly rebuffs the highly unusual manner in which his son's knowledge is evolving, as the mother makes evident: 'No se trata de una pérdida de todos los principios, como afirmas, el que adivine por el olor lo que nos alimenta' (p. 71). The son's acutely developed animalistic instincts all comprise a valid system of knowledge for his mother, and she questions the father's inability to comprehend this: 'Sabrás que también existen otros conocimientos además de los que imparte la escuela. Tu hijo aprende, por ejemplo, el impresionante dilema que contienen las habitaciones [...] el pasado que ofrecen los rincones' (p. 40).

The father thus endorses his son's development of an empirical knowledge that reflects his own, and which would be instilled in him in an educational institution through training, surveillance, punishment and control.[28] Paternal knowledge, which corresponds to the socially approved discourse and practice of a disciplinary regime, thus aims to normalize and homogenize the son. The mother, on the other hand, nurtures in her son an extremely anomalous sensory and intuitive knowledge, which in Foucault's terms can be described as subjugated, in the sense that it is part of 'a whole set of knowledges that have been disqualified as inadequate [...]: naive knowledges, located low down on the hierarchy, beneath the required level of cognition or scientificity'.[29] The son's subjugated knowledge thus stands in opposition to the father's normalized knowledge, and it is by disqualifying his son's knowledge, and thus the mother's practice of mothering, that the father aims to subject his son to paternal discipline.

Foucault also refers to subjugated knowledge as preserving 'the memory of hostile encounters which even up to this day have been confined to the margins of knowledge'.[30] In other words, the subjugated knowledge instilled by the mother in her son perpetuates the memory of conflicts and struggles that have been suppressed in normalized discourse and practice, a point that corresponds to Richard's assertion that memory has been sidelined during the Transition as a means to ensure social order and cohesion.[31] However, Eltit once again adds

[28] See Foucault's examination of disciplinary institutions in *Discipline and Punish*, pp. 170–94.
[29] *Power/Knowledge*, p. 82.
[30] *Power/Knowledge*, p. 83.
[31] *Residuos y metáforas*, pp. 27–73. The important theme of memory forms the focus

a gendered dimension to Richard's argument. While her novel highlights the repression of a form of knowledge that has the potential to polarize society, it prominently makes evident that this repression is based on disciplining the maternal body.

In her letters, the mother reiterates the difficulty that writing poses for her, and it is precisely by forcing her to communicate through writing that the father attempts to control the mother, since he monopolizes her time and labour. Writing can thus be viewed as a disciplinary mechanism to render her more docile. The mother's writing also uncovers the corporeal effects of the exercise of power, since it places an immense toll on her body, denoted through her numerous references to her increasingly stooped back and cramped hand. However, in spite of her physical deterioration and progressive emotional and psychological turmoil, the linearity and coherence of the mother's letters remain unaffected. She never ceases to comply with rhetorical, syntactical and lexical norms, and her letters maintain a formal register throughout, which reflect her submission to paternal power. Although the content and tone of her letters may frequently express her resistance to the father's orders, her correspondence nevertheless serves to augment the father's disciplinary power. The descriptions that the mother provides of her emotions, movements and material conditions allow the father to build up a knowledge of her body and modes of behaviour, and her letters are thus an effective instrument for the formation and accumulation of knowledge to be used by the father against her.

The mother is constantly frustrated by the father's disregard for her concerns, most notably in relation to their son's solitary games and unnerving laughter. She warns the father that their son's laughter is a potential affront to the laws being passed by her neighbours: 'Debo cuidar de que tu hijo no estropee con sus carcajadas las leyes que penosamente nos amparan' (p. 37). In a manner similar to his reaction to their son's expulsion from school, the father appears to ignore the mother's insistent warnings, even though she seeks his support in disciplining a body whose uncontrollable laughter, founded on vocal and corporeal spasms and pulsations, is an example of a semiotic operation that has the potential to disrupt social norms, thus placing the son in danger of social exclusion. However, the mother persists in confiding to the father the discomfort she experiences as she observes their son's lurching games, which revolve around the clay vessels that he furiously and obsessively orders and re-orders throughout the home. Her inability to understand his system of ordering the vessels serves only to provoke his shrill laughter. In contrast, she can clearly comprehend the rules laid down by the father in the games that he plays with her: 'entiendo la clave de tus juegos con mayor precisión que las adivinanzas que me plantea tu hijo' (p. 93).

We know from the opening chapter of the novel that the son cannot speak

of the reading by Idelber Avelar, who traces mourning and allegory in the novel to argue that there is simply no possibility of affirmation in post-dictatorial Chilean society. Avelar, pp. 178–85.

or write, and therefore has not acquired language. The ritual games that he enacts with his vessels may exist outside language, but they can be seen as the performance of a kinetic discourse, which is itself an instance of another semiotics, with its own logic, rules and grammar. The son's discourse is unintelligible to his mother and clearly flouts paternal knowledge and power, which are grounded in logical and rational language. In turn, the discipline that the father attempts to impose on the maternal space through the mother's writing is likewise shown to be alien to his son, as the mother indicates: '[tu hijo] parece ser contrario a entrar en un tiempo cuyas reglas desconoce' (p. 72). Once again, the discourses of father and son are shown to be mutually incomprehensible and exist in opposition. As I shall later argue, the mother is trapped between two opposing masculine discourses, and it is her body and corpus of writing that form the site of the struggle between father and son.

Although the father continues to question the interruption of their son's education, the mother appeals to him to protect them from her neighbour's persistent spying: 'Mi vecina me vigila y vigila a tu hijo. Ha dejado de lado a su propia familia y ahora se dedica únicamente a espiar todos mis movimientos' (p. 29).[32] The father seemingly justifies the neighbour's surveillance, stating that its purpose is to protect the mother from her inclination towards rituals that everyone now wants to forget. The mother makes clear that her neighbour is only one component in a network of surveillance that spreads throughout the city, in which families, friends and even strangers turn against each other and keep watch over each other's movements. It is the act of surveillance, the mother claims, that gives meaning to her neighbours' lives: 'Viven para vigilar y vigilarse' (p. 73). Indeed, she states that the neighbours' monotony, fear and greed lead them to circulate rumours that incite fear and panic throughout the city, the most persistent of which is the threat of plague and infection.[33] In Foucault's terms, their rumours can be read as a mechanism to attain further social control, since they intensify the execution of surveillance.[34] While the mother is able to perceive the constraining character of surveillance, the neighbours act as its very tools, which allows disciplinary power to function like a mechanical apparatus. The aim of the neighbours' surveillance is to guard against disorder and crime, but they are also their own overseers, in the sense that they police themselves and thus interiorize power. Power is revealed as circulating through a dispersed network of micro-powers, creating a homogeneous society that complies with social norms through the mistrust and estrangement induced by surveillance.

The neighbours' surveillance, states the mother, is linked to the imposition of law and order: 'Esta vigilancia que auspician los vecinos para implantar las

---

[32] The term 'neighbour' has biblical connotations that denote love and respect. The meaning inherent in the use of this term in the novel, however, is closer to the sense of neighbourhood propagated by the system of 'neighbourhood watch'.

[33] The threat of plague and infection is also shown to penetrate the family home in *El cuarto mundo* (see Chapter 3).

[34] *Discipline and Punish*, p. 198.

leyes, que aseguran, pondrán freno a la decadencia que se advierte' (p. 32). The mother soon suspects that the father's insistence on keeping her under his control is linked to the neighbours' imposition of social norms, collapsing the boundaries between private and public spheres: 'Es quizás arriesgado de mi parte aventurar un juicio sobre tu comportamiento, pero en ocasiones pienso que estás confabulado con las peligrosas normas que intentan imponernos' (p. 42). The purpose of their dangerous norms, she comments, is to construct an orderly social body, which will allow the neighbours to increase their material wealth and guard 'el destino de Occidente' (p. 65). So, the propagation of consumer culture is shown to be ensured through the establishment of a cohesive social body, which, in turn, is founded on the disciplinary apparatus of panopticism. The latter originates as a strategy of domination within the patriarchal family, in which the mother is positioned as the target of domination. Ultimately, then, it is the disciplining of the maternal body which is portrayed as underlying the social order that makes possible the global discourse of neo-liberalism in Chilean society.

The mother makes clear that the neighbours' laws make no sense to her and she refuses to participate in their social pact, describing their laws in terms that suggest authoritarianism and tyranny: 'lo que pretenden los vecinos es gobernar sin trabas, oprimir sin límites, dictaminar sin cautela, castigar sin tregua' (p. 41). Words and images are peppered throughout her letters which refer to the social pact in terms of interrogation, torture, fear and confession – terms that could equally be applied to the military's regime of repression – and the trite slogans that she encounters ('el orden contra la indisciplina'; 'la lealtad frente a la traición'; 'Occidente puede estar al alcance de tu mano') bring to mind the banality of the phrases endorsed by the military in public speeches, on posters and in texts. The boundary between democracy and authoritarianism is thus blurred, illustrating what Ana Forcinito describes as 'los residuos de la violencia dictatorial en las tecnologías del neoliberalismo'.[35] However, in democratic society hegemony is shown to be achieved through the complicity of the masses in their own oppression.

Excluded from the neighbours' social pact are the 'desamparados', the destitute and wretched beings who roam the city in search of food and shelter, haunting the success of the neighbours' social pact and feared by the latter as contagious insurrectionists.[36] Richard has referred in more general terms to such disinherited and voiceless sectors of post-dictatorship society as those who embody the past, making visible positions and memories that remain unrecon-ciled and in conflict, and who are simply inconvenient for a society of consensus.[37] The treatment of the 'desamparados' in Eltit's novel reflects

[35] Ana Forcinito, 'Cuerpos, memorias e identidades nómadas: Diamela Eltit y la ciudadanía cyborg sudaca', *Revista de estudios hispánicos*, 37:2 (2003), 271–92 (p. 272).
[36] Similarities can be drawn between the 'desamparados' and the 'pálidos' that appear in *Lumpérica*. Both terms refer to a group of homeless, voiceless, ghostly beings who congregate around a female body at night-time.
[37] *Residuos y metáforas*, p. 29.

Richard's critique of the Transition. With public refuges closed to the 'desamparados' during the harsh winter months, the neighbours pass a motion to deny them shelter within their homes. Aghast at the lack of social compassion, the mother declares that whole families of 'desamparados' are rumoured to have frozen to death in the streets, their bodies stealthily removed from public view during the night.[38]

Rumours circulated by the neighbours that the mother offered night-time shelter to the 'desamparados', in spite of their accord, soon reach the father, and he makes clear that the gravity of her transgression is such that she will be prosecuted through civil law. The mother, clearly terrified, beseeches the father to drop the charge against her. She justifies her 'crime' of solidarity through reference to the desperate physical state of the 'desamparados', but although she increasingly questions the validity of her prosecution, she is forced to confront the fury of a mob of neighbours. As she reports: 'Llegaron hasta mi casa dispuestos a convertirme en la primera víctima, a probar desde mi cuerpo la certidumbre de sus planes' (p. 77). If penal power during the dictatorship rested on physical torture, terror and collective horror, the aim in the 'punitive city' is to hold up the mother as a disrupting, disturbing and unassimilable element, whose punishment will serve as an example to all those marginal beings who refuse to heed the neighbours' laws.[39]

The mother now accuses the father not only of prompting the neighbours' actions, but of instigating a system of power that is illegitimate. She makes clear that paternal law exists outside of any recognizable legal code, and although in return for a pardon she eventually agrees to provide a written report detailing the entry of the 'desamparados' into her home, she states that, rather than serving to clear her name, her report will be used as proof against her. The content of her letters now collapses into the substance of her report, which leads the mother to describe her writing as 'redactando mi sentencia' (p. 99). In her final letters, the mother is no longer able to identify her accusers or even the father of her son, since he loses any human attributes and becomes dispersed throughout the myriad systems of power that he has established, corresponding to Foucault's description of the nature of power as diffused throughout society: 'No sé quién eres pues estás en todas partes, multiplicado en mandatos, en castigos, en amenazas que rinden honores a un mundo inhabitable' (p. 112). Punitive power is thus shown to originate from the patriarchal system of power instilled at the level of the family, from which it spreads throughout a society that penalizes any deviation from the norm. There is no judicial apparatus of objective arbitration; paternal penal power is functional and despotic, disturbingly reflecting the nature of military repression.

Intertwined in the mother's final letters are her reflections on the significance of her writing. Written language, she states, disqualifies her own experience as

---

[38] The removal of the bodies of the 'desamparados' not only brings to mind the disappearance of bodies during the dictatorship, but also contrasts to the visibility granted to the 'pálidos' at night-time in *Lumpérica*.

[39] I borrow the term 'punitive city' from Foucault. See *Discipline and Punish*, p. 130.

a mother, and she describes the space of writing in the following terms: 'un espacio oscuro e infértil, un terreno erial en donde dejan abandonada a la mujer sangrante' (p. 103). This image reflects the pollution rites carried out by certain communities to isolate women during their menses, and, as in *Vaca sagrada*, the abject female body is again shown to underpin hegemonic discourse. It is useful here to draw on Kristeva's theory of the heterogeneous nature of language to illustrate how the mother unveils the repression of the semiotic function in the economy of language. The maternal terrain has now become untenable in the nominal language and law that upholds social norms, that is, in the paternal, symbolic function.[40] As Kristeva argues: 'All networks of possible meaning must be exhausted beneath common sense, banal, vulgar, obvious meaning' – an argument that is echoed by Richard in her critique of cultural discourse during the Transition: 'Lenguajes estandarizados por el patrón comunicativo de vocabularios técnico-instrumentales y subjetividades normalizadas por el operador del consenso que disciplina lo heterogéneo.'[41] Both Eltit and Richard thus highlight the linguistic process as a means to uncover the disciplinary power of the politics of consensus of the Transition, which functions on the repression of a previous discourse of resistance: the semiotic.

Ultimately, the mother's downfall rests on her rejection of the language that upholds social norms. Aware that her writing will be labelled as anarchic, unintelligible and insolent, she stresses that the written word is imbued with a power and longevity that will stand as a testament to her impending fall from language: 'Te escribo ahora nada más que para anticiparme a la vergüenza que algún día podría llegar a provocarme el escudarme en silencio' (p. 111). As Domínguez observes, writing provides the means for the mother to break through the silence that will eventually be imposed on her, but it is here that I also note an element of self-reflection on Eltit's part regarding the marginal position that has characterized her writing in Chile.[42] In the novel, the reception of the mother's writing makes evident the power relations that govern the production of discourses, which, as Foucault argues, must be identified with social norms in order to circulate; those discourses that transgress disciplinary power are suppressed.

Strikingly, in her final letters, and in the face of certain censure, the mother adopts a swift change of discursive strategy by incorporating her son into her defiance of paternal power. She increasingly uses the first-person plural pronoun 'nosotros' to describe their actions, in contrast to her previous use of the singular subject pronoun 'yo', and no longer refers to her son as 'tu hijo' but as 'la criatura', cutting patrilineal family ties and depicting the son in terms of a newborn child. As such, he would be expected to exist in an anaclitic relationship with his mother, but it is she who grows increasingly dependent on her infant son. She lauds his skills and conspicuous masculinity, describing

---

[40] *Desire in Language*, p. 7, p. 138.
[41] Kristeva, *Desire in Language*, p. 181; and Richard, *Residuos y metáforas*, p. 243.
[42] Domínguez, in *Fábulas del género*, p. 45.

him as 'una criatura increíble y masculina' (p. 113), and together they give order to his vessels, which becomes their means of resisting paternal power. The mother, clearly, has learned to decipher the numerical rules of her son's previously alien discourse: 'He resuelto, al fin, la encrucijada aritmética de la ley que todo el tiempo me planteaba el juego de la criatura' (p. 116). So, in order to exist beyond paternal power and the norms of the city, the mother must submit to her son's law. She is thus forced to comply either with the discourse of the father or with that of his son; there is shown to be no space for her own discourse or subjectivity.

The mother writes her final letter leaning against a wall, illuminated by the rising sun of dawn.[43] Mother and son are now homeless and wander the streets like the 'desamparados', driven by no other purpose than their hunger. For the first and last time the mother depicts herself as a speaking subject by concluding her letter with her verbal response to a neighbour's questioning, reported in direct speech: 'Sí, esta criatura me pertenece. Sí, sí, mi nombre es Margarita, no sé ni cuántos años tengo' (p. 117). In order to name herself, then, the mother must leave the home, and bypass writing and the paternal power and discipline that this entails. She may attempt to use writing as a means of communication and enfranchisement, but ultimately she disappears from language and the social domain, and her writing remains solely as permanent testimony to her downfall.

The Maternal *Chora*

Kristeva argues that the semiotic function of language is located within the maternal space of the *chora*, a term that derives from Plato's *Timaeus* and which she describes as 'receptacle [...] unnameable, improbable, hybrid, anterior to naming, to the One, to the father, and consequently, maternally connoted'.[44] In other words, it is a term that denominates a maternal receptacle. For Kristeva, it is through the maternal prohibitions laid down in the *chora*, which regulate the semiotic activity of the child, that the infant is prepared for entry into symbolic language and law, a stance that is thwarted by the mother in Eltit's novel, as we shall see.[45]

In his study of the novel, Avelar reads the postscript, narrated by the son, as depicting the son's entry into writing and his acceptance of its law. As Avelar states: 'The only desire left is the mother's written desire, while the boy has submitted to the oedipal order, closing what had been the only space untouched by the grid of language, which is always, as psychoanalysis has taught us, the grid of Law.'[46] Avelar also points to the change in the son's language, 'which

---

[43] *Lumpérica* also closes with the image of the female protagonist, L.Iluminada, sitting in a public space and illuminated by the light of dawn.

[44] *Desire in Language*, p. 133.

[45] Kristeva, *Revolution in Poetic Language*, p. 27.

[46] Avelar, p. 185.

syntactically and lexically becomes indistinguishable from his mother's'.[47] However, I disagree with Avelar's reading here. The son may assume written control in the final pages, but I read his narrative as forming a direct challenge to paternal law. His writing in the final chapter remains syntactically and lexically identical to his chaotic corporeal expression in the opening chapter, and in no way corresponds to the precision and formality of his mother's written language.

In this section of the chapter, I argue that the novel ultimately portrays the mother's subordination to her son's semiotic discourse, rather than her son's submission to the Oedipal order, as put forward by Avelar. It is thus the mother's regression into the semiotic realm that marks her language as indistinguishable from her son's, a reading which is similar to that of Bernadita Llanos.[48] My reading also closely reflects the observation of Domínguez, who describes the space inhabited by mother and son at the end of the novel as 'un espacio irrepresentable pero exento de la metáfora del padre'.[49] However, while Llanos and Raquel Olea highlight the powerful potential inherent in the fusion of the discourses and bodies of mother and son at the end of the novel, I read the final pages as constituting not only a disturbing representation of the mother's disappearance from language and the Symbolic order, but also her submission to another system of power.[50] Although it is a system of power that is based on an opposing logic, order and knowledge to the father's, it is, nonetheless, a masculine and triumphant discourse that equally violently buries the mother.

As already stated, the novel opens with the non-verbalized, corporeal discourse of the nameless son, who repeatedly depicts his communication as based on muscular contractions and libidinal impulses: 'Mi cuerpo laxo habla, mi lengua no tiene musculatura' (p. 13). As he tumbles among his vessels, it is his mother's pimpled calf ('su pantorilla engranujada') that most frequently comes into view, and as he describes his romps it becomes clear that his vessels and his mother's truncated limb are indistinguishable to him: 'Mi lengua es tan difícil que no impide que se me caiga la baba y mancho de baba la vasija que ahora se ha convertido en una pantorilla y quizás así se me pegue un poquito de musculatura' (p. 13). The very artisanal quality of his clay vessels locate them as local artefacts crafted by potters, in constrast to the technological advances brought by globalization, but they are also a form of receptacle and, as such, can be read as a metaphor for the maternal receptacle that Kristeva,

---

[47] Avelar, p. 185.

[48] Llanos, in *Letras y proclamas* (see Llanos), p. 137.

[49] Domínguez, in *Fábulas del género*, p. 48. Lagos also argues that the father fails to submit the infant son to his law, but she perceives the son as acting to preserve and transmit, rather than appropriate, maternal discourse. Lagos, in *Creación y resistencia* (see Lagos), p. 136, p. 142. For her part, Forcinito concludes that the son resists 'capture' by dematerializing into the howl with which the novel ends. Forcinito, p. 277.

[50] Llanos, 'Emociones, hablas y fronteras en *Los vigilantes*', *Revista Casa de las Américas*, 230 (2003), 126–9 (p. 129); and Olea, *Lengua víbora*, pp. 78–9.

following Plato, has designated as the *chora*.[51] The substratum of the son's kinetic discourse, his clay vessels, is thus aligned with the maternal body and the games that he plays with his vessels highlight the control that he exercises over the maternal space of the *chora*.

It is by drooling onto his mother's leg that the son aims to extract from her body, in a parasitic fashion, a muscular system that will give strength to his tongue and so allow him to speak. He is clearly aware of the importance of language in the construction of identity and is so frustrated by his inability to speak that he is prepared to separate from his mother in order to enter into the symbolic function of language: 'En algún hoyito dejaré la pierna de mamá cuando consiga la palabra que aún no logro decir' (p. 16). The son thus desires to become a speaking subject, but he points to the existence of a violent maternal prohibition that prevents him from learning to speak: 'Si mamá me ve con la boca abierta intenta tirarme la lengua para afuera. Quiere arrancarme la lengua para que no hable. Hable' (p. 19). His mother is therefore intent on preventing him from acquiring language, and thus a form of knowledge that would submit him to paternal law and social norms. In Freudian terms, the mother prevents her son from surmounting the Oedipus complex and becoming an authoritative subject in his father's image. Instead, she traps him in a semiotic discourse that positions him as the other of the linguistic and social contract. By binding him to the primordial forces that hold him close to her body, the mother symbolically castrates her son and thus contravenes the maternal authority that Kristeva has located in the *chora*, since she refuses to prepare her son for entrance into the Symbolic.

The son's representation of his mother is predominately of a cruel and angry figure, who denies him the warmth of her breast so that he turns blue with cold. He indicates that he has to remind his mother of his hunger so that she will leave the home to search for food, depicting a maternal figure who fails to provide the most basic nurture and care. The son knows that his mother still retains a trickle of warm milk in her breast, and while she occasionally allows him to suckle, it is never enough to satisfy him. His fusion with the maternal breast does, however, grant him access to an intimate knowledge of his mother's thoughts and feelings: 'La leche de mamá tiene un secreto que yo debo vigilar. Ese secreto le provoca a mamá un estado malo. Malo. Mamá queda con el estado malo cuando ve cómo el hambre inunda las calles' (p. 21).[52] The son thus makes visible his mother's shame when she witnesses the hunger in the

---

[51] Erich Neumann illustrates how the female body has historically been perceived in terms of an elementary containing chamber or vessel. See *The Great Mother: An Analysis of the Archetype*, trans. by Ralph Manheim (London: Routledge & Kegan Paul, 1955), pp. 39–48. Interestingly, as noted in Chapter 3, Eltit consistently refers to her own writing in terms of its 'artisanal' quality. See also Eltit's comments on her perception of clay as emblematic of the cultural foundation of Latin America, and thus as one of the key motifs of her novel, in Morales, *Conversaciones*, p. 52.

[52] Note here the use of the verb 'vigilar' and the disturbing connotations of power that it subsequently takes on in comparison to its previous use when applied to the mother.

city, which leads her to hide any trace of the milk that signifies nurture and warm nourishment for her son. Notably, the knowledge that the son attains of the most instinctual level of his mother's body is transmitted through the semiotic pulses of her breast milk, which are unrepresentable in the symbolic realm of language and so inaccessible to his father. However, even the intimacy of the mother–son relationship is embedded in a system of power, since the son makes clear that his knowledge will be used for disciplinary purposes when he learns to speak: 'Cuando yo hable mamá temblará porque yo le adivino los pensamientos' (pp. 19–20).[53] The mother's prevention of her son's acquisition of language can therefore be read in terms of her fear that he will use his knowledge against her, and so expose the unconscious realm of the maternal terrain to disciplinary power.

As the mother writes her letters, she is perceived by her son as the embodiment of disorder, which infuriates him and confounds his capacity to express himself: 'Los dedos que tengo están enojados con su desorden. Cuando me enojo mi corazón TUM TUM TUM TUM y no lo puedo contener porque parece decir TON TON TON To' (p. 13). The son indicates that he uses his games and shrill laughter as ploys to distract his mother from her writing, actively competing with his father for her attention by biting her, and he emphasizes the resentment that his mother's written communication induces in him: 'Yo quiero ser la única letra de mamá. Estar siempre en el corazón de mamá TUM TUM TUM TUM y conseguir sus mismos latidos' (p. 17). Writing thus forecloses the son's desire for a profound corporeal proximity with his mother, which would reflect their symbiosis during gestation, since a child's first awareness of an other is through the rhythmic beating of its mother's heart. In order to regain a sense of oneness with his mother, then, the son must make her forget 'las páginas que nos separan y nos inventan' (p. 18). So, although mother and son are given symbolic validation through their submission to the paternal function of language, the son knows that his mother's writing forms a barrier that separates her from him, subordinating him to an inaccessible linguistic discourse which prohibits his pre-Oedipal desire.

Eltit here foregrounds the maternal body as the locus through which social and family structures extend their power into the semiotic *chora*. The mother's letters submit her to paternal law, while also introducing this law into the home, so mediating the son's desire. Two discourses of motherhood are thus shown to clash here. To conform to the social expectations of motherhood, the mother must respond through writing to the father's demands and neglect the nurture, care and attention expected by her son. To comply with her son's wishes, the mother must disobey the father's commands and renounce writing. Both father and son thus seek to project their desires onto a maternal body which, in both instances, represents excess and disorder, in order to control and ultimately

---

[53] The son's control over the unconscious impulses of the maternal body reflects the control usurped by the twin foetuses over their mother's dreams in *El cuarto mundo* (see Chapter 3).

obliterate the mother. So, while the mother is of central importance to father and son in the consolidation of their identities, she is ultimately reduced to the channel through which they play out their power struggle.

In the final chapter of the novel, the son continues to emphasize his inability to speak, while also making clear that his mother has lost the capacity to speak and write. The son is now clearly unable to distinguish his mother from the dark backdrop of their nocturnal existence: 'Pero mamá ahora no escribe porque busca confundirse con la noche. La noche' (p. 121). In Kristeva's terms, they are no longer 'illuminated by a subject master of language', but reside in the penumbra of the repressed semiotic, which stands in contrast to the transparency of a society that is 'all-seeing'.[54] Within this murky realm, it becomes impossible to demarcate two discrete subject positions for mother and son, since even their thought processes are shown to merge, as the son indicates: 'Mamá todavía conserva algunos de sus pensamientos. Los pensamientos que conserva son míos. Son míos. Yo soy idéntico a la uña, el dedo, la mano avasallada de mamá' (p. 121).

While the son portrays his mother's previous writing as arid and useless, he nevertheless attempts to grasp control of her disjointed hand, employing it as the instrument through which he might attain self-representation through written language: 'Debo tomar la letra de mamá y ponerla en el centro de mi pensamiento. Porque soy yo el que tengo que dirigir la mano de mamá' (p. 124). So, although he usurps narrative control, his written discourse is inseparable from the body of his pre-Oedipal mother: 'Escribo con mamá agarrada de mi costado que babea sin tregua y BAAAM, BAAAM, se ríe [...] Ahora yo domino esta historia. Llevo a mamá por mi propio camino' (p. 126). The maternal body, rather than the phallus, thus underlies the son's discourse, and his attempts to become a subject of writing are founded on his fusion with, rather than separation from, the mother. It is here that I challenge Avelar's argument that the son submits to the Oedipal order, since he clearly defies the paternal law that requires him to abandon the mother in order to enter into symbolic meaning and signification. The son's narrative authority is founded on his manipulation of an opaque semiotic discourse that eludes the paternal symbolic function. Rather than producing signifying knowledge, the son indicates that his aim is to enter a narrative void where meaning and communication are wiped out, so putting an end to the story and unequivocally removing his mother and himself from the reaches of paternal discipline: 'Quiero perderme con mamá en los instantes más extraordinarios de la noche. De la noche' (p. 122).

By the end of the novel, mother and son are engulfed in darkness and their bodily symbiosis appears to confound any possible separation: 'Su pierna y la mía se enredan, BRRRR, tiritamos juntos de hambre y de frío. TUM TUM TUM TUM, mi corazón, su corazón' (p. 128). The son thus attains his desired corporeal proximity with the mother: their hearts beat to the same rhythm, and they laugh and drool as one. Together they crawl towards the brilliant

---

[54] *Desire in Language*, p. 106.

constellation formed by the fires that are lit on the margins of the city, where they will finally be free of the paternal shadow: 'AAAAY, nos acercamos al fulgor constelado para quedarnos en este último, último, último refugio. Las miradas que nos vigilaban apabullantes y sarcásticas no pueden ya alcanzarnos. Alcanzarnos' (p. 129). The novel ends with the immolated and petrified faces of mother and son raised towards the most distant of the fiery heavens, howling like mad animals: 'como perros AAUUUU AAUUUU AAUUUU aullando hacia la luna' (p. 130).[55] Confounding all psychoanalytic interpretations, it is only now, from within a semiotic void that forecloses any symbolic legality, that the son's desire for oneness with his mother is overcome: 'Mamá y yo nos acercamos extasiados mientras yo olvido mi hambre por su cuerpo, mi deseo de fundir mi carne con la suya' (pp. 129–30). It is, then, through madness and psychosis, rather than through his submission to paternal law, that the son separates from his mother, but this separation nevertheless continues to be founded on the repression and annihilation of the mother.

Although there were loopholes in the previous regime of power that, paradoxically, allowed for a discourse of resistance to emerge, as made evident in *Lumpérica*, *Por la patria* and *El cuarto mundo*, there is simply no space in this novel for any expression of contestation. Difference is no longer a source of resistance, and Eltit's previous strategy of incorporating the semiotic into signifying practice as a means to enact symbolic change now founders. The novel suggests that the marginal realm of the semiotic has been politically co-opted, since the infant son precociously grasps control of the semiotic realm solely for male purposes of resistance to the paternal order. However, in Eltit's following novel, *Los trabajadores de la muerte*, roles are reversed as it is now the mother who employs the semiotic terrain of her body as a means to control her son's thoughts and actions for her own purposes, as we shall see.

---

[55] In Kristeva's terms, the blurring of boundaries between human and animal here positions mother and son in the realm of the abject (see Chapter 4).

6

The Myth of Motherhood in *Los trabajadores de la muerte*

Reappropriating Myth

Eltit's sixth novel, *Los trabajadores de la muerte* (1998), exposes the furious and vengeful facet of maternity that emerges from a narrative embedded in familial abandonment and betrayal.[1] Eltit has stated that she drew on a murder that occurred in Chile in the 1980s and was reported in the gossipy 'crónica roja' (tabloid press) to structure the plot of the novel.[2] The newspaper reports that generated Eltit's interest detailed the murder of a woman by her half-brother in the southern city of Concepción, after her attempts to bring their sexual relationship to an end.[3] The main body of the novel, framed by an epilogue and a prologue, is dominated by the ruminations of a nameless and abandoned mother in Santiago, deserted by the father of her two sons for a bride in Concepción. From the moment of his birth, the mother grooms her eldest son as the unknowing agent of retribution against the father for reneging on his paternal duties, later inciting her son to follow her urgently whispered instructions to travel to Concepción. There, he unknowingly has sexual intercourse with his half-sister, the offspring of his father's second marriage, and only later, during a feverish conversation with his lover/half-sister, does the son realize that his father did not die during his childhood, as his mother had told him, but moved to Concepción and started another family. His father, he now learns, died many years later.

The powerful sexual attraction between the son and his half-sister, whose names we learn only at the end of the main narrative, overpowers the taboo against incest, and their relationship intensifies for over a year. Only then does the half-sister attempt to end it. Pleading for one last meeting, the son sets the scene for his half-sister's ritual murder, stabbing her to death in a seedy room

---

[1] The novel was first published in Chile by Seix Barral in 1998. A second edition was published in 2001 by Norma in Buenos Aires.

[2] Morales, *Conversaciones*, p. 233; Lazzara, p. 70.

[3] Concepción is Chile's second largest city and is located approximately 300 miles south of Santiago. From 1565 to 1573 it was the political and military capital of Chile. 'Concepción' means 'conception', and the name thus fuses primal connotations of the maternal and the political, in contrast to the subsequent establishment of Santiago as the capital of Chile with its overtly masculine-paternal denomination.

in Concepción and thus enacting the revenge desired by his mother: the annihilation of his father's honour and the lineage ensuing from his second marriage.

Eltit connects the recent family tragedy in Chile with the myth of Medea in Greek tragedy: 'La madre vengativa, resentida y abandonada hizo que ese hijo emprendiera su viaje, que era la toca envenenada de Medea.'[4] In the novel, the mother's retribution against the father reflects the actions of Medea, who used her two sons as unwitting agents to bring about the murder of Jason's new bride, subsequently killing her sons to eradicate Jason's lineage.[5] The most notable divergence between the vengeful actions of these two mothers is that the mother portrayed in Eltit's novel sends her son to kill his father's daughter, not his second bride, after his father's death.

It is in relation to this novel that Eltit most explicitly comments on her aim to explore the violence inflicted on women, as mothers, through cultural narratives and social rituals:

> Quise trabajar cómo la cultura inocula la maternidad en el sujeto femenino, que es una forma también de violencia. Me interesaba cómo los hijos están ahí dando vueltas para siempre en el imaginario materno, sin crecer nunca – esas guaguas que las mujeres arrastramos, pero que es una violencia cultural en el sentido de que te dan toda tu biología (su vida, su salud, su muerte, su riesgo) [...] Entonces, más que la violencia inter-género, me interesaba especialmente la violencia que hay en la maternidad en nuestras sociedades.'[6]

However, in spite of the cultural violence that, Eltit argues, is inherent in the 'imaginario materno', the mother portrayed in her novel is unequivocally shown to be both victim and perpetrator of violence. While the lack of care and affection from the paternal figure may be largely to blame for the absence of filial respect and remorse, the mother's vengeance leads to an abuse of maternal authority, most prominently through the lethal secret that she withholds from her eldest son regarding his father's abandonment. As the title of the novel indicates, the maternal labours of reproduction and nurture can also be linked to death and destruction, underscoring the potential for chaos and violent agency inherent in the maternal role. By once again exposing the complexity of maternal emotions, Eltit illustrates that conventional expectations of motherhood are inadequate and even dangerous. Motherhood in Eltit's novel is portrayed as harsh, furious and self-absorbed.

Greek tragedy is also prevalent in the novel through the transposition of

---

[4] Lazzara, p. 70.

[5] While the myth of Medea has been rewritten throughout the ages, most translations and adaptations stem from the tragedy by Euripides (480–406 BC), in which Medea is forsaken by her husband, Jason, for the daughter of Creon, the King of Corinth.

[6] Lazzara, p. 66. 'La guagua' is the colloquial term used in Chile to refer to a baby. It is a feminine noun and, as Eltit notes, it is only through the appendage of the terms 'hombre' or 'mujer' that the sexual identity of the infant is defined. See Lazzara, p. 68.

the myth of Oedipus to a contemporary Chilean context. By drawing on Greek mythology to offer a mutant modern version of the Freudian patriarchal tragedy, Eltit proposes that the immense shaping power of myth, specifically in relation to male and female socialization, underlies a contemporary, globalized Chilean context. She can thus be seen to agree with Irigaray's assertion that the mythology underlying patriarchy has not changed.[7] In her novel, it is the son's ignorance of his origins that leads to his transgression of the incest taboo, which reflects the misfortune of Oedipus, who marries Jocasta unaware that she is his mother. As with *Los vigilantes*, the novel can be described as a tragedy, since it replicates the structure and key components of Greek tragedy, most significantly the inevitability of fate, as the mother's words make evident: 'Sabía que lo que iba a ocurrir ya estaba escrito. Antes que yo. Antes de mí' (p. 40).[8] The mother's eldest son is forced into the role of the tragic hero and his lover/half-sister is subsequently positioned as the antagonist, but ultimately their roles are manipulated by the mother and father respectively, who use their children's bodies to play out their cruel intentions. Both parents therefore perpetuate abuses on their children, and the result is a tragedy of catastrophic proportions.

Also noteworthy are the many allusions in the novel to the Bible and Spanish Golden Age classics.[9] As Francine Masiello comments in relation to the novel's prologue: 'The novel thus opens with an episode that takes place in a tavern, a site of reunion for travelers that, although situated in modern Santiago, surely recalls the popular gathering spots described in *Don Quijote* or the inns of *Lazarillo de Tormes* or *El buscón*.'[10] I read Eltit's appropriation of classical narrative structures and myths as a means to inscribe her novel within a longstanding literary tradition. In this way, her novel is distanced from the commercial literature so prevalent in market-driven Chile, where books that can be easily sold, consumed and discarded are the order of the day. In the novel, emphasis is placed on intertextuality, and ancient times, places and beliefs are projected into a contemporary context, challenging dominant literary trends by engaging with a literary history and cultural knowledge that the immediacy of the market seeks to erase. I would also add that the complex and fragmented narrative structure forecloses any rapid consumption of the novel, and thus defines it as a writerly text.

Few critical readings have been published to date, but both Juan Carlos Lértora and Leonidas Morales offer a good overview of the novel. Lértora points to the representation of the mother as both self-sacrificing and vengeful,

---

[7] 'The Necessity for Sexuate Rights', in *The Irigaray Reader*, pp. 198–203 (p. 199).

[8] The intervention of the gods and the oracle are other elements of Greek tragedy that appear in the novel.

[9] The novel also includes clear references to Lorca, especially *Bodas de sangre* and *Yerma*. The chiming of wedding bells that recurs in the mother's dreams is perhaps the most salient example.

[10] Francine Masiello, *The Art of Transition: Latin American Culture and Neoliberal Crisis* (Durham and London: Duke University Press, 2001), p. 211.

and also notes the novel's underlining pessimism towards the human condition, while Morales foregrounds violence and betrayal as key to the narrative continuum.[11] In turn, Masiello focuses on the challenge posed by the novel to 'the domain of the "market"'.[12] By returning to legends of classical antiquity, she argues, Eltit inserts popular subjects within enduring myths and destabilizes archaic narratives by illustrating the conflicts between storytellers. Masiello links narrative destabilization to the potential of the popular voice 'to undo the banality of the ready-made, to challenge the flatness of a neoliberal economy that [...] would make a pretense to a totalized social whole'.[13]

The reading offered here examines not the role of the market, but the challenge that the novel poses to archaic myths of origin.[14] In *Totem and Taboo*, Freud argues that the origins of social organization, moral restrictions and religion are founded on the murder of the primal father by his sons.[15] He points to the ambivalence of the sons' feelings after their act; while they had satisfied their hatred and fed their desire to usurp their father's power and sexual monopoly over the women in the primal horde, they were also overcome by remorse and guilt. According to Freud, their ambivalent emotions resulted in the creation of the two fundamental taboos of totemism and the Oedipus complex: the protection of the totem animal, equated by Freud with the primal father, and the prohibition against incest.

Eltit has referred to Medea as the most radical maternal figure, and by drawing on this most extreme of stories, in which woman unleashes a mighty and dreadful maternal power solely for her own purposes of revenge, she selects a myth of motherhood which explicitly subverts traditional representations of maternal feelings.[16] In the following section of this chapter, I argue that the myth of Medea functions in the novel as a counter-myth to Oedipus, in this way stripping the Oedipal narrative of its primary prestige and allowing Eltit to write the mother into the Oedipal story – a notable omission on the part of Freud for which he has been taken to task in the work of Irigaray and Kristeva, among others. Ana Forcinito perceives the use of the myth of Medea in the

[11] Lértora, 'Apuntes sobre un manuscrito: *Los trabajadores de la muerte* de Diamela Eltit', in *Creación y resistencia* (see Lagos), pp. 149–62; and Morales, *Novela chilena contemporánea*, pp. 99–111.

[12] Masiello, p. 207.

[13] Masiello, p. 208.

[14] Myth signifies a fictitious story that is always concerned with how something comes into being. See J. A. Cuddon, *The Penguin Dictionary of Literary Terms and Literary Theory*, 3rd edn (Harmondsworth: Penguin, 1991), pp. 562–3.

[15] Sigmund Freud, *Totem and Taboo: Some Points of Agreement between the Mental Lives of Savages and Neurotics*, authorized trans. by James Strachey (London: Routledge, 2001), pp. 166–7.

[16] Lazzara, p. 68. The fury repressed behind the maternal role and unleashed in the novel is also to be found in the myth of Clytemnestra, who murders her husband Agamemnon for his infidelity and the sacrifice of their daughter Iphigenia. The Furies are also avengers of crimes, specifically crimes against the ties of kinship, as illustrated in their haunting of Orestes, who killed his mother Clytemnestra in retribution for his father's death. Unlike Medea, the mythical women referred to here enact their vengeance on behalf of others.

novel as a means to recover 'la genealogía materna a través de la memoria histórica', a point reflected in my own reading.[17] By drawing on the story of Medea, Eltit puts forward a powerful myth which challenges the patriarchal monopoly on the origins and transmission of culture. In opposition to Freud, Eltit shows that culture begins at the mother's breast and that it is this primary relationship which encodes the infant's subsequent thoughts and actions.

The third section of this chapter examines how the novel re-enacts and rewrites the killing of the primal father elaborated by Freud. Irigaray has consistently argued that Western culture and discourse are founded not on patricide, as Freud would have it, but on matricide. In her novel, Eltit implies that this may be so, but she also suggests that in her society the mother is complicit in the hideous crime from which the origins of culture are derived. Freud may argue that culture is founded on the ambivalence of the father–son relationship, but Eltit categorically illustrates that its foundation hinges on the ambiguous maternal figure. In the novel, the semiotic terrain of the maternal body is the indisputable source of the misery and hatred that motivate the eldest son to murder his half-sister. This, in turn, collapses into the symbolic murder of his father, as we shall see.[18] It is, then, the mother who incites the enmity between father and son that is so central to Freud's elaboration of the Oedipus complex and the killing of the primal father.

Before beginning my reading, it is necessary to point to the Sphinx-like figure of the nameless girl with a mutilated arm ('la niña del brazo mutilado') who dominates the prologue and epilogue of the novel. In the prologue, she is portrayed as a soothsayer and an interpreter of dreams. Her presence upstages the stories of a nameless chronicler of dreams, known only as 'el hombre que sueña', and provokes disquiet in the vagrants who congregate in the modern-day tavern. Essentially, the prologue is used by Eltit as a means of unveiling the underlying conditions of narrative production, a point that will be referred to again.

The epilogue is set in the bustling commercial centre of Santiago where the girl with the mutilated arm, accompanied by her two disabled companions, shrilly begs for money. The transposition to an era of contemporary globalization is immediately made evident through the portrayal of street vendors who hawk their imported wares in front of shop windows which offer the originals of the pirated merchandise that they sell, their torsos covered with the global slogans and brands inscribed on their T-shirts. Similarly to Euripides' tragedies, then, Eltit's novel includes an epilogue and a prologue that are distanced from the subsequent/preceding action.[19] The significance of both is developed below.

[17] Forcinito, p. 286. The recuperation of a maternal genealogy and historical memory was also prominent in *Por la patria* (see Chapter 2).

[18] A more literal reading of the novel in terms of fratricide would, of course, disturbingly contrast with the positive conception of fraternity that was offered at the end of *El cuarto mundo* (see Chapter 3).

[19] Euripides also gave prominence to socially marginal actors in his tragedies, such as

The Vengeance of Medea

In the prologue, the epic dreams of the nameless man, 'el hombre que sueña', deal with anarchism. Masiello describes their content in terms of 'a rebellion of soldiers against their commanding officer, surreal mutations of animals and phantoms that threaten the leader's power'.[20] The nameless man accuses the girl with the mutilated arm of inciting the disturbed dreams that afflict him and the other frequenters of the tavern, and of destabilizing the order that he attempts to instil in public spaces with his epic. The male chronicler of dreams recognizes that the girl's subversive power emanates from her very visible dismemberment, which allows her to facilitate clandestine disorder on the streets. Indeed, the girl later undermines his authority directly by proclaiming her triumph: 'le asegura al hombre que sueña que ella lo ha vencido, que seguirá bajo su mandato la hegemonía de las calles' (p. 31).

The girl also undermines the narrative authority of the nameless man during their vigil in a public shelter by subverting the challenge laid down by him: to interpret his recent, recurring dream.[21] She insists that she will accept his challenge only by referring to the repetitive dream that has plagued her recently, thus interpreting her subjugated rival's dream by merging his dream with her own. It is from the intertwining of their dreams that the main body of the novel emerges. So, as in *El cuarto mundo*, the underlying conditions of narrative production are exposed as the interplay of two disparate and competing discourses: one masculine and the other feminine.

A link can be drawn here between the girl's dismemberment and the lack of a phallus. Her narrative is founded on oral culture rather than writing, reflecting the oral tradition of mythic material, and its purpose is to disrupt the Law of the Father and the literary institution shaped by the dominant male understanding. Although the man recounts his dreams orally, his heroic war adventures allude to the epics and legends that are intertwined with militarism and nation-building.[22] The girl's oral narrative, founded on the convergence of their dreams, emphasizes the primary relationships within the family, and specifically the mother–son relationship. So, by overwriting the man's lofty epic with the family tragedy that dominates the main body of the novel, the girl presents an alternative story of the origins of culture and nationhood.

women and slaves. See *The Oxford Companion to Classical Literature*, ed. by M. C. Howatson, 2nd edn (Oxford and New York: Oxford University Press, 1992), p. 226.

[20] Masiello, p. 211.

[21] In *Los vigilantes*, it was because of the closure of the city's public shelters that the 'desamparados' were rumoured to have frozen to death in the streets during the perishing winter (see Chapter 5). In *Los trabajadores de la muerte*, the opening of the city's shelters suggests a less hostile social environment, but the vigil that takes place continues to emphasize the need to keep careful watch.

[22] As Cuddon notes, epics narrate the actions of warriors and heroes, and they attain their national significance through a grandiose embodiment of national history and aspirations. Cuddon, pp. 284–93. The subversion of epic narratives was also discussed in relation to *Por la patria* (see Chapter 2).

Eltit can also be seen to subvert the institution of Freudian psychoanalysis by portraying the girl's power over the man and her hegemony of the streets as emanating from her ability to interpret the man's dreams, thus positioning her in the role of psychoanalyst. Freud defines the object of his investigation into the interpretation of dreams as 'the thoughts which are shown by the work of interpretation to lie behind the dreams'.[23] These dream-thoughts, states Freud, can only be interpreted if the dreamer elucidates the unconscious thoughts that inform the dream's content. So, by allowing the girl access to the latent content of his dreams, the man enables her to penetrate his unconscious thoughts. She is thus able to turn Freudian methods of interpretation on their head by imposing a new order, connection and meaning onto the man's dream-thoughts, and so disturbing the established order of unconscious thoughts. Her rearrangement of psychical material results in the construction of a new structure of the unconscious, in a reflection of Irigaray's argument that current (male) imaginary structures must be dismantled and rethought to effect a change in symbolic representations.[24]

The family tragedy that emerges from the convergence of dreams is precisely structured in the main body of the novel as a triptych, consisting of three chapters referred to as 'acts' – a clear nod to Greek tragedy that again foregrounds the diversity of genres that shape Eltit's fiction. Each act is divided into three sections, the first of which is dominated by the abandoned mother's repetitive and bitter deliberations and memories. The first section of the first act opens with a polyphony of voices, which suggests a play in prose, but with no textual markers to differentiate one voice from another. The moans of the mother and her eldest son are followed by the voice of the nameless father. The voice of a second-person narrator interrupts to taunt the mother, and the jeering tone of the taunts soon indicates that the voice is that of the nameless girl with the mutilated arm, since the tone directly reflects that of the taunts directed by her towards the eldest son in the second section of each act. The mother's voice, however, rapidly silences any but her own. Her obsessive thoughts of revenge against the father emerge in a stream of consciousness, interlaced with memories of his base insults and sexual demands; memories of their two sons, always as babies; and self-pitying observations on the toll that motherhood has taken on her now decrepit and flaccid body.

The second section of each act consists of a second-person narrative, the narrator of which can be identified as the girl with the mutilated arm. She states in the prologue that her aim during her vigil is to interpret 'las voces que se incuban en el interior del alma del que va a ser el próximo asesino' (p. 31). To this extent, she details the thoughts and experiences of the eldest son during his circular journeys to and from Santiago to Concepción. The bloody outcome of his journeys between two cities that denote the paternal and the maternal,

[23] Sigmund Freud, 'The Interpretation of Dreams', in *The Standard Edition of the Complete Psychological Works of Sigmund Freud*, ed. by James Strachey, vol. 4 (London: Hogarth, 1956), p. 135.
[24] *This Sex Which is Not One*, p. 25.

respectively, is anticipated by her in the prologue: 'dice que ya se empieza a establecer un sangriento puente entre Santiago y Concepción' (p. 31).

The observations and actions of the eldest son, narrated in the first-person, constitute most of the third section of each act. The nameless girl again intervenes here to bridge the voices of mother and son, intertwining references to the distant mother into her commentary on the son's journeys. She constantly stresses the inevitability of the tragedy that awaits the son and highlights his ignorance of his mother's predetermined vengeance, thus assuming the role of the Greek chorus, whose purpose was to comment on the action in the tragedy and fill in unseen details.[25]

The first section of the opening act is entitled 'La cigüeña', but the innocent myth of the stork as the bringer of babies in a basket is overwritten by the misery of a woman who has resentfully sacrificed her selfhood in order to comply with the social expectations of motherhood; ultimately she veers wildly from these same social expectations. While the mother's self-representation is of an unjustly injured wife and mother, the nameless girl underscores the mother's furious thoughts, scoffs at her exhausted body, and gleefully mocks her inability to distinguish the actions and physical attributes of her sons as babies. The ability to recall these details accurately is clearly a source of maternal pride, and reflects the 'imaginario materno' referred to earlier by Eltit. The mother defensively refutes the girl's barbed interjections, which increase in frequency and pace to probe the mother's confused and contradictory memories in a parody of the cultural violence linked by Eltit to motherhood.

Throughout her lengthy and prosaic interior monologues, the mother constantly links her current physical incapacity to the past toll exacted by the father, her sons and the harrowing pain of childbirth.[26] The mother's complaints of ongoing ailments indicate that she is speaking in the inclement days of the present, but the obsessive pattern of her memories of her infant sons, their father's sexual proclivities and the suffering caused by his subsequent abandonment suggest that her present life far from the family home is frozen in a time and place rooted firmly in the past. As she later indicates, the enactment of her revenge by her eldest son will allow her to reclaim a life that has been put on hold for many years.

The mother portrays motherhood as a condition violently imposed on her by the father of her sons, whom she refers to only as 'el hombre'. The father clearly perceives himself as the sole agent of reproduction, forcing the mother

---

[25] In Greek tragedy the chorus-leader conversed briefly with the characters, a point that reflects the girl's brief dialogue with the mother in the first sub-section of the first act.

[26] The mother's memories of the anguish of childbirth and her resentment of the maternal duties imposed upon her clearly defy the words of the Gospel according to John 16.21: 'A woman in childbirth suffers because her time has come, But when she has given birth she forgets the suffering in her joy that a human being has been born into the world.' The mother's memories are more closely linked to the curse of Eve in the Book of Genesis, where she is condemned to give birth with pain for trespassing and inciting Adam to eat the apple.

onto her hands and knees and declaring that 'te voy a hacer una guagua, quédate tranquila, mierda, ¿acaso no veís que te estoy haciendo una guagüita?' (p. 89). As in *El cuarto mundo*, conception is shown to result from a scene of domestic rape; the mother is erased from the primal scene; and maternal vengeance is played out through the body of her son. In *Los trabajadores*, the mother resentfully recounts the father's humiliations, which included spraying her with his semen, measuring its quantity as a marker of his masculinity. She links the father's propensity for saturating her with his discharge to the frequent vomiting of her babies, describing herself as a mere depository for their bodily fluids, abjectly stripped of any sense of self: 'para que en ningún momento yo me librara de recibir sus líquidos y me olvidara para siempre de un olor propio que alguna vez me hubiera emanado' (p. 150).

The mother laments the waste of eight years of marriage, at the end of which she was left physically devastated by the father's abuse and impregnation; in exchange, she experienced not one moment of pleasure. She tirelessly revisits the father's abasement of her body to fan the flames of her revenge, linking her brooding retrospection to her maternal labours: 'Un pasado que tengo que mantener y frecuentar y cuidar con la pulcritud con la que se cuida una guagua' (p. 149). Any maternal feelings are subsumed by her unabated thoughts of vengeance, and as the nameless girl indicates, she lives only to feed off the hatred embedded in her memories. The mother justifies her revenge through an indirect allusion to the myth of Medea: 'la venganza es una condición propia de mujeres. Porque ya está escrito, ¿no? Sí, de mujeres' (p. 39).[27] Indeed, the mother's details of her retribution directly reflect the actions of Medea, who sent her sons to greet Jason's bride with a poisoned wedding robe and headdress: 'yo enviaba a la guagua primera con el presente que había preparado para contribuir con esa ceremonia, el vestido de gala y la toca dorada, lujosa' (p. 147).

The mother also calls forth the divine intervention on which Medea was so dependent, turning to the gods that she has honoured since childhood to exact her wrathful retribution.[28] Like Medea, the mother uses the auguries of her gods to begin her vengeful plotting, forewarned in her dreams seven years beforehand of the father's future departure through the chiming of wedding bells in a distant city. She thus assumes what Freud has termed a 'prehistoric' view of dreams, which he describes as reflecting the attitude towards dreams of people of classical antiquity, who believed that their purpose was to foretell the future.[29]

However, unlike Medea, whose vengeance emanates from the spurning of

---

[27] The mother's words could also allude to many other female figures in mythology, including the Furies and Clytemnestra (see n. 16).

[28] For Lértora, the mother's dependence on auguries and gods locate her as a 'machi' within the indigenous tradition. Lértora, in *Creación y resistencia* (see Lagos), p. 157, p. 161.

[29] 'The Interpretation of Dreams', p. 2. Dreams are prominent in the Bible, in which they are also portrayed as containing prophecies and divine revelations.

her passionate love for Jason, the mother's resentment surfaces within a loveless environment and stems from the father's callous disregard for her maternal self-sacrifice. Perhaps the most disturbing discrepancy between the myth of Medea and the portrayal of the mother in Eltit's novel is the latter's chilling emotional impunity. Prior to her act of infanticide, Medea oscillates between the grief of mortally wounding her own children and her hostility towards them because they issue from Jason's seed. The only regret expressed by the mother here is that the father is no longer alive to witness her vengeance. She declares that she has every right to use her sons for her own purposes, since they emerged from her body, which nourished and sheltered them: 'Y porque las guaguas eran mías, alimentadas por mi propio cuerpo, yo era dueña de hacer con ellas lo que quisiera' (p. 45). The mother ruptures the bond between the father and his sons at the moment of their birth, and she draws on the patriarchal legal system of primogeniture to justify her firstborn son's position as the rightful heir to her vengeance. From this moment onwards, the mother visits on her son the future sins of his father, while simultaneously turning him into a deformed manifestation of herself by inculcating in him the hostility that will later incite him to transgress the Christian commandment 'Thou shalt not kill'.

Even prior to the father's abandonment, the mother's feelings towards her sons clash with any cultural stereotypes of inherent maternal love, as she indignantly undertakes the maternal duties thrust upon her: 'Dos críos obligatoriamente míos que se me agarraron con una fuerza que me dejó indefensa [...] sin posibilidades de escapar a esa violencia infantil' (p. 42). The mother blames her sons' 'infantile violence' for irreversibly deforming her body, since their incessant crying forced her to attend to them night and day. She is horrified by their dependency on her, a horror that transmutes into guilt when she is forced to heed her own bodily needs. Her guilt, in turn, stems from the terror that some calamity would befall her sons if she turned away even momentarily, portraying their 'infantile violence' in terms that are emotional as well as physical.

The mother makes apparent the ever-present threat of infection during her sons' infancy, exemplified by her attempts to exterminate a rat, which she believed emerged from the sewers into the home. However, the most lethal source of contamination to which her sons were exposed originated in her own body: 'Mi memoria, resto de alcantarilla [...] No puedo olvidarme de la difamación, de la traición, de la herida' (p. 36). The detritus of the sewers in which she imagines the rat lurks is linked by the mother to the abject nature of her memories, and it is through the milk that spurts from her breasts that the hatred of her dangerously infectious memories is instilled in her eldest son. The son himself describes his mother's milk as 'una leche no exenta de veneno' (p. 67), and even the mother acknowledges its inhuman nature: 'una leche que a mí no me parece nada de humana' (p. 100). The milk that usually signifies maternal nourishment is here dehumanised and polluted, used by the mother to nurture in her son her own misery. It is, then, precisely through the semiotic impulses of her breast milk that the mother sows in her son the emotions that will later result in murder. In short, she does not aim to appropriate male attributes to enact her vengeance but employs her maternal body.[30]

Like their father, the sons also incur the mother's wrath for what she bitterly perceives as their ingratitude towards her. It is through her dreams, at the level of the unconscious, that she gratifies her repressed desire for revenge through acts of violent, maternal abandonment. In Freudian terms, her dreams can be read as 'fulfilments of wishes', since they allow her to express her desire to flee the suffocating bond that ties her to her sons, symbolized in her dreams as an infected umbilical cord.[31] The mother is able to sever the suppurating cord in her dreams only towards the end of the first section of the third act, which coincides with her eldest son's imminent enactment of her vengeance: 'el mismo aire del sueño cuya velocidad me permitía cortar el poderoso cordón que amenazaba con estrangularme y lo corté, sí, lo corté, con un afilado cuchillo que venía por el aire, una hoja elegante y antigua' (p. 159). The razor-sharp dagger employed to cut the primary link is the very same dagger that had been presented to the mother by her gods in fragments of her dreams, and which she, in turn, transmitted through her dreams to her eldest son to wield for her murderous purposes. It is also the same dagger that was used by the mother to ritually cut her eldest son during his infancy, branding him as the sharp, phallic weapon of her vengeance with the very weapon that he uses to execute her revenge.

While the mother's dreams allow her to fulfil her wish to separate from her sons at an unconscious level, her desire for vengeance against the father is enacted at a conscious level but hinges on the unconscious emotions that she has embedded in her son's psyche, which permit her to foster him as the instrument of tragic fate. The dagger, an archaic and classical weapon, thus symbolically represents the manner in which psychical processes are transmitted from one generation to the next through the unconscious realm of the maternal body. Significantly, the psychoanalytic phallus is often portrayed metaphorically as a knife, but in Eltit's novel the phallus is brandished by the mother, not the father.

Underlying the mother's desire to break free from her sons and her desire for revenge against the father is her wish to liberate her bodily desires. The mother's account of the father's departure from the home many years previously is encircled by a poetic expression of the deep-seated sensations that surface as she explores her body: 'mi botoncito de rosa desprovisto, desaprovechado, despreciado, demasiado caliente para conseguir impedir el oleaje [...] las acometidas furiosas y rebeldes de una naturaleza (la mía, la mía), que no cesaba, que no cesaba de imprecar' (p. 161). The waves of volup-

---

[30] An interesting contrast can be made with Lady Macbeth, who demands that she be unsexed and her breasts emptied of milk before inducing Macbeth to commit regicide.

[31] 'The Interpretation of Dreams', p. 122.

tuous pleasure that wash over the mother are described by her as 'criminal' and 'insurreccional', reflecting the terms used in *El cuarto mundo* to emphasize the cultural repression of maternal desire. In *Los trabajadores*, the powerful orgasm that results from these previously disparaged sensations explodes in the mother's narrative simultaneously with the father's departure, but it is only through the irreversible separation from her sons and the enactment of her vengeance that the mother finally anticipates a means of fully gratifying her desire, as her following words make clear: 'al final de unos años incontables por fin podré tenderme como corresponde y dejar que mi cuerpo dé curso a sus deseos' (p. 97).

Irigaray has emphasized the fundamental importance of the severance of the umbilical cord in the formation of subjectivity, a point that has been overlooked by Freud through the stress that he places on the Oedipus complex and castration.[32] In Eltit's novel, the emphasis is placed on the severance of the umbilical cord as a means to allow the mother to express her unfulfilled desire. The cultural violence that, Eltit argues, is inherent in motherhood can thus be seen to consist of circumscribing woman in a maternal role that strangles her existence as a woman. The catastrophic consequences of the actions of a woman who refuses to accept a role in which she is stripped of desire and selfhood are examined in the next section of this chapter.

The Killing of the Primal Father

The eldest son's first-person narrative emerges at night-time, when he withdraws into a hostile space where signs unravel in an endless signifying chain. This space, he states, is unintelligible to anybody but himself and he reiterates that he is 'un hijo de la noche', since the dark, nocturnal space offers a generous sustenance denied to him by the mean flesh of his own mother. It is in the nocturnal body that he takes refuge from the banality of daily life, embodied by his mother and younger brother, whose logic he perceives as existing in opposition to the precision that characterizes his own intelligence, conforming as they do to common sense and 'las normas del día' (p. 84).

The conceited inner voice of the eldest son reflects that of María Chipia, the male twin in *El cuarto mundo*, but while María Chipia had sought to repress his mother's voice, the mother's perspective, as Bernadita Llanos points out, is central to *Los trabajadores*.[33] Both male narrators, however, put forward an authoritative viewpoint which, they claim, is founded on scientific objectivity.[34] The eldest son prides himself on his wisdom and the ingenuity of the battle strategies that he mentally elaborates, which allow him to defeat the male rivals against whom he competes in epic wars and to carry away the maidens who

[32] *The Irigaray Reader*, p. 38.
[33] Llanos, in *Letras y proclamas* (see Llanos), p. 113.
[34] The logic and rationality stressed by María Chipia and the son in *Los trabajadores* are also reflected in the paternal disciplinary power of *Los vigilantes*.

are the plunder to be looted. In spite of his father's absence, he states, his knowledge reflects that of his male ancestry: 'Huérfano de padre, tuve que prescindir de la experiencia de mis antecesores' (p. 72). He thus develops the male rivalry and aggression that, according to Freud, underpin the Oedipus complex and the killing of the primal father, even in the absence of the paternal figure.[35]

The son's imagined battles can be compared to the dreams of the nameless man in the prologue, since both are structured by their epic nature and dominated by the warring actions of male heroes. The narrative authority assumed by the girl over the chronicler of dreams is also reflected in the narrative power that she flaunts over the eldest son in the second section of each act. Her power emanates from her access to the son's latent thoughts and emotions, of which he is frequently oblivious, and from her prescience of the forthcoming tragedy, which allows her to divulge the plot of the novel stealthily before it unfurls.

The eldest son continually underscores his estrangement from his mother and younger brother, emphasizing his self-sufficiency in relation to his family and any ideology of normative power. However, in spite of his attempts to define himself in autonomous terms, he is unable to escape the influence of his primary contact with the maternal body, shuddering when he remembers his aversion to the sick flesh that first nourished him. If we carefully read through the son's authoritative statements, it becomes apparent that his conclusions are based entirely on his relation to his mother, or, more precisely, on his attempts to negate any relation between them. Even when he leaves home, he continues to visit his disdainful mother, since it is only through her that he is able to make sense of his life: 'esas visitas me eran necesarias para recordar por qué debía estar afuera, por qué me era indispensable reconocer que en todas partes me acechaba el odio' (p. 83).

The structure of the mother–son relation thus underpins the son's nocturnal relationship, and his references to 'la noche' collapse into an unknowing euphemism for his mother, as his comments on his devotion to the night make clear: 'La noche me escogió desde el momento de mi nacimiento, aún antes de que se consumara el delito. La noche me escogió para aniquilar la huella de mi padre y borrar de la memoria cualquier rasgo de nobleza de su carácter' (p. 175). His words reflect his mother's claim to name him as the weapon of her vengeance at the moment of his birth, which illustrates how maternal dictates penetrate his unconscious and radically undermine his supposed autonomy. The nocturnal abyss in which the son resides can thus be read in terms of the maternal semiotic, but as in *Los vigilantes*, the mother thwarts the maternal authority that Kristeva has placed in the locus of the semiotic: the *chora*.[36] It is through unconscious semiotic impulses that the mother, in

---

[35] 'The Ego and the Id', p. 32; and *Totem and Taboo*, p. 165.

[36] One of the nocturnal episodes recounted by the son concerns his encounter with a nameless boy who wanders the streets and whose games he describes as marked by rules, repetition, logic and order. Striking similarities exist here with the nature of the son's games

contravention of symbolic law, incites her son's ruthless cruelty towards his father after he meets his half-sister, as the son later comprehends: 'Un padre cruel se merecía la crueldad de su hijo. Ese era el mensaje cifrado que mi madre le había entregado a la noche' (p. 131).

The most momentous instance in the mother–son relationship occurs when the mother urgently whispers the following words to her eldest son as she takes her leave for a distant and undisclosed location: 'Tienes que ir a Concepción, ¿me entiendes?' (p. 86). He is thrown by his mother's instructions, but also entranced by their lack of logic, and subsequently journeys to Concepción. It is here that the son discovers he has been caught in his mother's trap, although he remains ignorant of the tragedy that awaits him: 'Ni siquiera sentía que extrañaba a mi madre y sin embargo cumplía cabalmente sus oficios' (p. 129). As he commences his circular journeys to and from Concepción, his destiny, unbeknownst to him, is watched over by a displaced and deranged oracle, impatiently awaiting the shedding of blood in Concepción. The nameless girl delights in accentuating the son's ignorance of the significance of his journey, which she proclaims is a return to his origin: 'Pero lo que no puedes saber, lo que no quieres saber es que, en realidad, el nombre del lugar te conducirá hasta una trampa porque estás viajando hasta el origen. Hacia tu propio origen' (p. 57). His journey thus constitutes a return to the primal scene of conception, which is subsequently reconceptualized as the scene of his mother's triumph and of his father's defeat; in short, his return to the womb collapses into a scene of death.

It is through the voice of the nameless girl that we learn of the son's chance meeting with his half-sister at a party in Concepción. Ignorant of their shared paternal lineage, he is immediately mesmerized by his half-sister and future lover, gravitating towards her in a manner that fulfils his mother's previous prophecy that he would recognize her as soon as he set eyes on her: 'un cuerpo plagado de señales que mi guagua primera iba a reconocer y a aniquilar' (p. 92). The half-sister succumbs absolutely to the son's advances, ignoring the paternal mandates that haunt her during sexual intercourse and are intoned by the female narrator: 'se ve asaltada por esa madura, repetida, agobiante ordenanza de su padre, pero la aleja y la devuelve hasta la tumba' (p. 109). It is not until the following day that the lovers realize the enormity of their sexual transgression, in a reflection of the moment of *peripeteia* also experienced by Oedipus.[37] The feelings of terror initially experienced by the lovers are swept aside by the intensity of their sexual attraction, which the female narrator links on the son's part to his desire to discover the father he never knew: 'buscas un pedazo de tu padre en el cuerpo que te entrega la muchacha porque cuando intentas

in *Los vigilantes*, which were also located within the realm of the semiotic, illustrating once again how Eltit reworks previous themes and images.

[37] Cuddon describes the Greek term *peripeteia* as 'a reversal of fortune; a fall'. He illustrates the significance of the term in relation to Oedipus' discovery of his filial relation to Jocasta, his wife. Cuddon, pp. 700–1.

escarbar entre tus propios recuerdos nunca lo consigues, no logras aislar a tu padre de tu madre, en tu memoria aparecen siempre juntos' (p. 114).

It is, then, through the body of his half-sister that the son attempts a reconciliation with the paternal body, in an act that inverts Kristeva's argument that a child is reconciled with its mother as an adult through sexual intercourse.[38] As noted in Chapter 2, the fantasy of a father-mother conglomerate united in complete satisfaction has been posited by Kristeva to redress the absence of the mother from symbolic structures. However, although the mother and father in Eltit's novel are symbolically bound together, their unity is based not on complete satisfaction but on the son's inability to distinguish one from the other: 'La noche – ahora lo sé – no es nada más que el doble de mi padre' (p. 177). Through a clear reference to his mother ('la noche'), the son indicates that there is no distinction to be made between symbolic representations of the maternal and the paternal because they are identical: both are in thrall to power, and both use their cultural roles to occlude the violence that underlies their representation.

In his subsequent narrative, the son offers a different account of his moment of *peripeteia*, stating that he is immediately forced to confront the enmity of the spectral paternal figure: 'Por primera vez hube de enfrentarme a mi padre ya muerto y que, no obstante, volvía desde quizás qué mundo sólo para interponerse y mostrar un odio que se había incubado desde mi nacimiento' (p. 131). The origin of his father's hatred is thus the very moment in which he was chosen by his mother to enact her vengeance, which foregrounds the mother as instrumental in fostering the hostility between father and son. The eldest son deplores his father as a dreaded rival to his sexual interests, and perceives their relationship in terms of the imaginary battles that had previously consumed his thoughts, in which the female body represented the booty to be won. Similarly, the half-sister's body now becomes the site of the struggle between father and son. As the son attests: 'Si él se vengaba en ella, yo, claro, no podía sino devolverle su venganza en ella' (p. 131).

It is, states the son, in the abject brutality of his half-sister's female sex that he most directly confronts his father's hatred towards him, but it is also here that he perceives the hostility of the family tribe, made up of his mother and the mother of his half-sister, which denotes the father's sexual monopoly of the women in the primal horde. As the son makes evident, the female sex is overwritten by the superimposition of the phallus onto the female body, and it is his father's male sex that replaces his half-sister's sex as the source of his vehement passion: 'Ah, ese era el legado de mi padre, la herencia radicaba en que el sexo de mi padre era el que daba ímpetu a mi sexo en una escena oscura, amurallada, excediendo a mi madre, burlándola de manera doble en un escenario ambiguo, plagado de jirones' (p. 133).

If this dark, womb-like episode, located in Concepción, is read as the

---

[38] Kristeva's argument was referred to in Chapter 2 in relation to the consummation of the sexual relationship between Juan and Coya in *Por la patria*.

re-enactment of the scene of conception, the father can be seen to portray himself as the sole agent of reproduction, thus erasing the mother from the primal scene. However, the scene described above also suggests father–son incest, which implies that the father attains autonomous symbolic representation by violating the incest taboo, a paternal prohibition that the mother also incites her son to transgress. The actions of both parents thus correspond, since both appropriate their children's bodies to enact their hostility by violating the taboo that they are meant to uphold. If we read the rivalry between father and son as collapsing into a struggle between father and mother, the aim of their struggle, in turn, is to grasp control of the half-sister's body. Since her sex is the site of the superimposed phallus, the aim of the parental struggle is thus analogous to the control of phallic authority.

Caught up in his intense and inappropriate love for his half-sister, the immoderate nature of which reflects Medea's passion for Jason, the son carelessly becomes ensnared in a web of debts, lies and deceit, jolting the reader back into a consumerist, contemporary Chilean context. Like his creditors, the image of his sententious mother unexpectedly appears to demand of him what is rightfully hers. Swelling the turmoil in his life, it is at this point that his half-sister attempts to end their relationship. The son perceives her rejection as incited by his father's cruelty, which spurs his determination to defeat paternal authority through his lover's body. For the first time, the son expresses his desire to bring his father to account for his unpunished acts of adultery and polygamy, a desire that overlaps with his mother's wishes. Indeed, his half-sister's act of betrayal – taking another lover without his knowledge – engulfs the son in the same emotions that marked his mother's life, which in her case were induced by his father's act of betrayal. The son's fury allows his mother, although far away, to foresee that he is ready to act.

As the son travels to Concepción to meet his half-sister for the last time, the first drops of rain for over a year begin to fall, and the bloodthirsty oracle awakens from his enforced rest to witness the imminent bloodshed.[39] Awaiting his half-sister in a shabby room in Concepción, the son slowly begins to foresee the tragedy that awaits them. Under the influence of stimulants, his body is reduced to a mass of jerking, chaotic spasms, but he comprehends that their final tryst symbolizes the definitive battle between him and his spectral father. Through an allusion to the myth of Oedipus, the son accepts that he must erase the horror of what his eyes can no longer bear to witness: 'Se aproxima el instante en que habré de penalizar lo que mis ojos no soportan' (p. 169). However, unlike Oedipus, his violence will not be self-inflicted but will be directed towards the annihilation of his half-sister's body, which he sees as manipulated and corrupted by his father. The son thus aims to usurp his father's place while avoiding the paternal punishment of castration, symbolized by blindness.

---

[39] In the Bible and in Greek tragedy, God and the deities, respectively, were shown to make their power manifest through extreme natural effects, such as drought and floods.

The half-sister's arrival leads to a dialogue that is the first and only instance of direct speech in the novel. Its studied theatricality implies that the words have been over-rehearsed and cited countless times before, and it is only through the use of their first names, Patricio and Mónica, that the son and his half-sister are granted any sense of individuality in their preordained roles. As the son wearily comments, their fate is already sealed by the historical tragedy that they are merely re-enacting, and under his prompting the half-sister details her trysts with her new lover, generating within her half-brother the destructive emotions towards his father that will result in her death: 'No es tu amante, lo sé bien, quien ha venido a condenarte, son tus palabras y tu deliberación, es tu cuerpo banal en el que está inscrita la memoria corporal de mi padre. Es toda su hostilidad la que traes a mi vista. Es su póstuma voluntad de derrumbarme' (p. 184). The thunderous arrival of a tumultuous family quarrel and a flock of crows signal that the time has come for the son to kill his half-sister.[40] Guided by his lucidity and thirst for blood, he murders her after their explosive and final orgasm. As he plunges the knife into her body, the son emphasizes his distance from his murderous yet inevitable actions: 'No soy yo. Es mi cuchillo inevitable el que te sangra y te asesina' (p. 186). That maternal vengeance underscores his fatal act is made clear at the end of his narrative: 'Y allá arriba, entre las vigas, la sombra de mi madre me espía clavada en una cruz digital' (p. 186).

The image of his mother hovering in the beams of the ceiling suggests the immemorial figure of Medea on the palace roof after her act of infanticide, but more striking is the image of the maternal Christ figure.[41] As Masiello notes, 'The gender transformation of the Christ figure along with an electronic image that modernizes the scene of piety and crucifixion moves the static material from its timeless domain and feminizes the final authority.'[42] The image challenges not only biblical representations but also Freud's theory that social organization, moral restrictions and religion originate in the killing of the primal father. Freud argues that murder, according to the law of talion, can only be expiated 'by the sacrifice of another life [...] And if the sacrifice of a life brought about atonement with God the Father, the crime to be expiated can only have been the murder of the father.'[43] As a form of atonement for his murder, states Freud, the primal father is elevated into a god and the patriarchal organization of the family is restored. However, in a gendered inversion of Freudian theory, by placing the maternal body on the cross Eltit suggests that

---

[40] The image of the flock of crows reflects the army of corvine mothers in *Por la patria* (see Chapter 2).

[41] The son makes numerous references to his mother's mortality in the final pages of his narrative, distancing her from the eternal life symbolized by Christ on the cross, but also from the magical and divine attributes associated with Medea. In short, the mother's characteristics and flaws are here portrayed as utterly human.

[42] Masiello, p. 214.

[43] *Totem and Taboo*, p. 179.

the crime to be expiated is the murder of the mother. This, in turn, would lead to the restoration of the matriarchal organization of the family.

So, by elevating the maternal figure onto the cross, Eltit illustrates that the first great act of sacrifice as theorized by Freud is not immutable. However, Eltit also suggests that simply inverting the gender hierarchy of the Freudian myth of origin perpetuates the same structures that underpin patriarchy, indicating that the underlying organization of matriarchy and patriarchy are identical. As with the primal father, atonement with the mother can be achieved only through the sacrifice of a life, that of the half-sister, as the son indicates when he first spies his mother's shadow in the beams of the room: 'esa sombra movediza que me hizo nacer y que pronto se me va a unir, con una sabiduría implacable, sólo para que juntos consumemos la precoz muerte de mi amante' (p. 172). The sacrifice and consummation of the female body, the totem animal and the substitute of the father, may result in the 'at-one-ment' of mother and son, but the enactment of the mother's vengeance essentially mirrors the Freudian primal patricide, since both are founded on the wish to usurp the father's supreme, phallic authority. In short, even by writing the mother into the Oedipal story, subjectivity, agency and the fulfilment of desire continue to be attained through the erasure of the female body.

The mother is thus shown to be complicit in the cyclical and self-perpetuating destruction that serves only to reconstruct the flawed familial and social relations that form the foundation of the patriarchal economy of consumption. In Irigaray's terms, the mother remains as 'the woman who reproduces the social order'.[44] Eltit thus highlights the danger for women of attempting to write themselves into existing symbolic structures. This, she indicates, is not enough, since it leaves intact the current structure of power and merely redistributes power in women's favour. Only by challenging the power relations inscribed in these very structures may true social change occur.

As can be seen, Los trabajadores reworks themes and images that are present in Eltit's earlier novels. The inadequacy of the Oedipus complex in explaining the origins of subjectivity, previously explored by Eltit in Por la patria, is once again foregrounded, although in Los trabajadores it is the construction of masculine, rather than feminine, subjectivity which is examined by Eltit. Another notable difference between this novel and Por la patria is that, while the latter portrays state violence as responsible for the collapse of the myths of family love and of motherhood as a natural and inherent role, in the former it is parental hatred and aggression which devastates family relationships.

Los trabajadores also highlights the repression of maternal desire, a theme that recurs in Eltit's oeuvre. However, in contrast to the transgressive potential inherent in the eruption of the mother's desire in El cuarto mundo, in Los trabajadores the explosion of maternal desire results only in violence and tragedy. Motherhood is portrayed in absolutely suffocating terms and the image

---

[44] 'Women-Mothers, the Silent Substratum of the Social Order', in The Irigaray Reader, pp. 47–52 (p. 47).

of the suppurating umbilical cord that binds the mother to her sons is an image that was also used to depict the abject relationship between Francisca and Sergio in *Vaca sagrada*. The physical toll of motherhood reflects the pain and deterioration that also afflicted the confined mother in *Los vigilantes*. In *Los vigilantes*, however, the nameless son triumphantly seizes control of the maternal body, while in *Los trabajadores* it is the mother who appropriates her son for her own purposes. Journeying to the South is portrayed here as a return to the womb and, as in *Vaca sagrada*, is shown to be deadly.

The novel ends with the Sphinx-like figure of the girl with the mutilated arm. Described as the guardian of 'la entrada del paseo principal' (p. 205) – the central thoroughfare that represents the commercial centre of Santiago – she thus has a role which reflects that of the Sphinx in Greek mythology, who is symbolized as the guardian of territory. Along with the half-sister, the girl with the mutilated arm is the only character in the novel not to partake in consumption, either through the devouring of the totem animal or through her participation in the commercial exchange of goods. As the final words of the novel state, she is 'el legendario enigma' (p. 205), the custodian of an enigmatic knowledge that is inaccessible to us, but which has the power to subvert social norms and myths of origin, both contemporary and archaic. Oedipus may have guessed the riddle of the Sphinx who barred his way into Thebes, but the riddle of the nameless girl is not so easily interpreted or answerable. She cannot be consumed or incorporated, and naming and defining her, Eltit suggests, will result in the appropriation and annihilation of her power of subversion.

Epilogue

To read the novels of Diamela Eltit is to enter a narrative world of crisis in which the most basic precepts and assumptions that we hold of language, culture and society verge on collapse. Her writing emerges from marginal areas where general and universal categories and meanings founder, which prevents the utterance of any totalizing judgements and truths about her work or the marginal world it portrays. While Eltit's novels demand interpretation, these same novels challenge and frequently subvert the power of established interpretative frameworks.

By means of a predominately psychoanalytic approach, my reading of Eltit's novels has focused on the insight that they provide into the possibilities for reinstating the mother and wresting maternal experience from prevailing political and cultural discourses that have appropriated motherhood for their own purposes. Eltit emphasizes throughout her narrative that the representation of the maternal has profound psychic and social consequences, not only for mothers, but also for their children and male–female relations. In her novels, therefore, the textual emphasis on the mother has as its aim the reconceptualization of maternal subjectivity. The maternal body is portrayed as a terrain of semiotic pulses and affects that can and will rupture symbolic structures to open up maternal and feminine subjectivity to a rich variety of interpretations that are potentially empowering for all women, and not just mothers.

The work of Irigaray and Kristeva has productively served to explore some of the themes common to Eltit's novels: the urgent need to redress the absence of the mother from symbolic representations; the semiotic as a privileged means of unsettling symbolic representations; the textual construction of subjectivity; and the necessity of rethinking family relations. In short, their psychoanalytic work has enabled an examination of the repressed and often unconscious maternal terrain inscribed by Eltit in her narrative.

My reading of *Lumpérica* aimed to illustrate how Eltit sheds particular light on the repression of the mother in symbolic representations as a means to disrupt dominant discourse. The occluded maternal body that was shown to underlie linguistic and social structures was incorporated into the novel as a means to allow woman's relationship to the maternal body at the level of the imaginary to be reclaimed. This, in turn, formed the basis of a possible feminine language and subjectivity that did not preclude female specificity and desire. The repression of the desire of and for the mother found in *Lumpérica* was again made evident in *Por la patria*, and was shown to underlie symbolic and political violence. Although the relationship between mother and child is traditionally perceived as a personal experience, in this novel Eltit forcefully collapses the boundary between family and nation to illustrate the highly political nature of Oedipal family structures.

Irigaray's emphasis on the transgressive potential of granting symbolic representation to the mother–daughter relationship aptly framed my reading of *Por la patria*. The rearticulation of the relationship between Coya and her mother not only allowed mother and daughter to be reunited within the paternal Symbolic order that had previously sought to mediate their relationship through violence, but was also the basis of the potential to transform social structures envisioned at the end of the novel. So, while Eltit aims to move beyond the fusion and suffocation that has traditionally encircled the mother–daughter relationship, she can also, like Irigaray, be seen to challenge any definitive separation of mother and daughter. This important point is reworked in *El cuarto mundo*, in which Eltit stresses that depriving the daughter of a relation to origins results in an absence of mutual recognition and love between mother and daughter that prevents the daughter's symbolic self-representation.

El cuarto mundo again makes evident the mother's exclusion from symbolic representation. However, the eruption of the mother's desire forecloses her son's authoritative narrative and permits her daughter to speak, which illustrates the transgressive agency that Eltit inscribes in maternal *jouissance*. As in *Lumpérica*, the self-conscious reflection on the writing process in *El cuarto mundo* reinstates the maternal terrain as the foundation of language and subjectivity, but also explicitly links woman's potential for reproduction with the capacity for cultural production, so transforming the figure of the mother.

The challenge posed to traditional psychoanalytic notions of a pre-Oedipal, unmediated period of attachment between mother and child that is first posited in *Por la patria* is extensively reworked in *El cuarto mundo*. The male foetal narrator of this novel is shown to be always and already performing a script that seeks to uphold paternal law from within the womb. Eltit thus dramatically emphasizes that there is simply no place in current symbolic structures that is not already mediated by paternal law, which illustrates the immense difficulty involved in granting representation to the mother as an autonomous and desiring subject.

Reading *Vaca sagrada* through Kristeva's theory of abjection usefully uncovered the sexual hierarchy in Chilean society, which reduces woman to the abject marker against which male sexual difference is defined. The portrayal of woman's self-identification with horror and abasement in this novel depicts the lasting scar etched on woman's psyche because of her inability to separate from the abject maternal body. However, in contrast to Kristeva, throughout her novels Eltit clearly refutes any possibility of a loving paternal mediator between mother and child because of the violence of the existing paternal order in her society, a clear legacy of military repression.

I perceive *Vaca sagrada* as marking a turning point in Eltit's portrayal of motherhood. While her novels had previously been able to conceive of the maternal body as enacting transgressive linguistic and physical acts that could open up possibilities for social, cultural and symbolic transformation, this novel highlights the inability to move the female body away from the fear and horror displaced onto the mother in phallocentric discourse. The motif of menstrual blood as a symbolic marker of feminine subjectivity is degraded as the novel progresses, since it becomes contaminated by male violence and bloodshed, and is appropriated for male purposes of resistance to the paternal order.

Los vigilantes reworks and intensifies the loss of potential transgression previously embedded in the maternal terrain. Paternal disciplinary power is shown to pervade even the most intimate relationship between mother and child in post-dictatorship society, and childhood is stripped of any innnocence as the precocious hands of the infant son grasp control of the semiotic realm, subjecting his mother to a system of logic and rules that aim to resist paternal norms and dictates, but which ultimately discipline and silence the potential subversion of the mother. However, it is in *Los trabajadores de la muerte* that motherhood is most disturbingly demystified. Eltit draws on the myth of Medea to contest the authorized version of the origins of culture, but while the mother writes herself into the symbolic representations that seek to erase the maternal body from the primal scene, her actions leave intact the patriarchal structures that are founded on the sacrifice of the female body. In a context of globalization and consumerism, the novel emphasizes the urgent need to question the origins of the symbolic constructs that underpin society, which are also shown to be founded on violence and consumption.

Kristeva's theory of the heterogeneous nature of language has been fundamentally important to all of the readings offered here. In Eltit's first three novels, language is portrayed as flowing from the somaticized maternal body, which is the origin of a mother tongue. Kristeva's concept of the maternal semiotic is exemplified in the flow of a richly poetic and often highly ambiguous language, which aims to express an otherwise prohibited return to the rhythms, pleasure and intimacy of the primal relationship. However, as noted in my readings of these novels, Eltit does not posit a nostalgic return to the maternal body outside of social and symbolic confines, but locates the threshold of the realms of the semiotic and the symbolic as the privileged locus for seeking out powerfully different understandings of language and subjectivity.

The liberating potential to unsettle the norms and conventions of the signifying process which had previously been located in the incorporation of the semiotic dissolves from *Vaca sagrada* onwards – that is, in Eltit's novels published during the Transition. As previously noted, the maternal body as the site of resistance and transgression founders, and Eltit's narrative becomes progressively more confined in linguistic, thematic, structural and spatial terms, textually reflecting the increasingly pervasive symbolic and social norms founded on a male sexual hierarchy and the burial of the mother. Notably, it is in Eltit's most recent novels, specifically *Los vigilantes* and *Los trabajadores*, that the central and recurring metaphor of incest is stripped of its previous potential to unite differential categories and inscribe the female child's desire for the mother.

In *Los vigilantes*, incest is once again posited in terms of the recognized taboo of the son's desire for the mother, which leads to the male child's subordination of the mother. In *Los trabajadores*, it is the mother who employs incest as a means to enact her vengeance, sealing her son's emotions in an incestuous cauldron that results in their 'at-one-ment', with tragic consequences.

Throughout this book, Richard's theoretical work has productively situated Eltit's narrative production within the specific and local context. Richard's embrace of the category of the feminine as demarcating a range of oppressed and subversive subject positions can also be found in Eltit's novels, but while Eltit uncovers the multiple discourses of oppression operating in the Latin American context, her narrative also suggests that subsuming the category of sexual difference within other categories of difference is premature and even dangerous in Chilean society. The hierarchy of sexual difference that is upheld in dominant discourses precludes a move away from the primacy of the body and the realm of corporality and experience that underpins sexual difference. Eltit never loses sight of the maternal corporality and experience from which her writing flows, but she does correspond with Richard by conceiving of a feminine writing that it is founded on the interaction of gender categories and the contestation of prevailing social and literary norms, a point made most evident in *El cuarto mundo*.

The plurality of meaning in Eltit's novels is compelling and I have sought to illustrate how it aims to empower readers of her novels, rather than consolidate authorial power. To conclude, my aim has not been to offer any final or totalizing interpretation of Eltit's narrative fiction, but to elucidate one specific and overlooked aspect of her writing. In so doing, I am aware that I have left unexplored other areas of her narrative *oeuvre* which could also be productively analysed to illuminate further an understanding of the processes of critical analysis that underlie Eltit's writing. However, the aim of this book has been to explore the central and informing presence of the maternal body, which simultaneously resists and structures literary and symbolic representations in Eltit's novels.

Bibliography

Águila, Osvaldo, *Propuestas neovanguardistas en la plástica chilena: antecedentes y contexto* (Santiago: CENECA, [n.d.]).

Allende, Isabel, *De amor y de sombra*, 4th edn (Barcelona: Plaza y Janés, 1984).

Anon., 'Editorial', *La Época*, 8 June 1990, p. 6.

Araujo, Helena, *La Scherezada criolla: ensayos sobre escritura femenina latino-americana* (Bogotá: Universidad Nacional de Colombia, 1989).

Arrate, Marina, 'Una novela como radiografía: *Por la patria*' (unpublished master's thesis, Universidad de Concepción, 1992).

Avelar, Idelber, *The Untimely Present: Postdictatorial Latin American Fiction and the Task of Mourning* (Durham and London: Duke University Press, 1999).

Balcells, Fernando, 'Hoy como ayer', *Revista de crítica cultural*, 19 (1999), 40–1.

Barthes, Roland, *S/Z: An Essay*, trans. by Richard Miller (New York: Hill & Wang, 1974).

Baruch, Elaine, and Lucienne Serrano (eds), *Women Analyze Women* (New York: Columbia University Press, 1987).

Bataille, Georges, *Eroticism* (London: Boyars, 1987).

Battersby, Christine, *The Phenomenal Woman: Feminist Metaphysics and the Patterns of Identity* (New York and London: Routledge, 1998).

Beckett, Samuel, *Molloy*, trans. by Samuel Beckett and Patrick Bowles (London: Calder & Boyars, 1966).

Belsey, Catherine, and Jane Moore (eds), *The Feminist Reader* (London: Macmillan, 1989).

Benjamin, Jessica, *The Bonds of Love: Psychoanalysis, Feminism and the Problem of Domination* (New York: Pantheon, 1988).

Berenguer, Carmen, *et al.* (eds), *Escribir en los bordes* (Santiago: Cuarto Propio, 1990).

Bethell, Leslie (ed.), *Chile since Independence* (Cambridge: Cambridge University Press, 1993).

Beverley, John, Michael Aronna and José Oviedo (eds), *The Postmodernism Debate in Latin America* (Durham and London: Duke University Press, 1995).

Bianchi, Soledad, *¿La insoportable levedad … ? Imágenes y textos, postdictadura y modernidad en Chile*, Documento de Trabajo del Centro de Investigaciones Sociales, 21 (Santiago: Universidad Arcis, 1997).

Blanco, Guillermo, 'Las mujeres se interrogan', *Hoy*, 10–16 August 1987, pp. 49–50.

Bombal, María Luisa, *La amortajada* (La Habana: Casa de las Américas, 1969).

—— *La última niebla, El árbol, Las islas nuevas, Lo secreto: Textos completos*, 2nd edn (Santiago: Andrés Bello, 1982).

Braidotti, Rosi, *Nomadic Subjects: Embodiment and Sexual Difference in Contemporary Feminist Theory* (New York: Columbia University Press, 1994).
—— *Patterns of Dissonance* (Cambridge: Polity Press, 1991).
Brito, Eugenia, *Campos minados: literatura post-golpe en Chile*, 2nd edn (Santiago: Cuarto Propio, 1994).
—— 'Desde la mujer a la androginia', *Pluma y pincel* (1985), 42–5.
Brizuela, Natalia, 'Estado y positivismo en el XIX, o los desertores sociales en la narrativa de Diamela Eltit', *Revista Casa de las Américas*, 230 (2003), 113–20.
Brunet, Marta, *Obras completas* (Santiago: Zig-Zag, 1962).
Brunner, José Joaquín, *Cultura e identidad nacional: Chile 1973–1983* (Santiago: FLACSO, 1983).
—— *Cultura y política en la lucha por la democracia* (Santiago: FLACSO, 1984).
Burke, Carolyn, Naomi Schor and Margaret Whitford (eds), *Engaging with Irigaray: Feminist Philosophy and Modern European Thought* (New York: Columbia University Press, 1994).
Butler, Judith, *Antigone's Claim: Kinship Between Life and Death* (New York: Columbia University Press, 2000).
—— *Gender Trouble: Feminism and the Subversion of Identity* (New York and London: Routledge, 1990).
Cánovas, Rodrigo, 'Apuntes sobre la novela *Por la patria* (1986), de Diamela Eltit', *Acta Literaria*, 15 (1990), 147–60.
—— *Novela chilena, nuevas generaciones: El abordaje de los huérfanos* (Santiago: Universidad Católica de Chile, 1997).
Cárdenas, María Teresa, 'Diamela Eltit: otro giro a la literatura', <www.letras.s5. com/eltit080802.htm> [accessed 12 April 2003].
Caro Baroja, Julio, *Inquisición, brujería y criptojudaismo* (Barcelona: Ariel 1970).
Casaula, Eleonora, Edmundo Covarrubias and Diamela Eltit (eds), *Duelo y creatividad* (Santiago: Cuarto Propio, 1990).
Castillo, Debra, *Talking Back. Toward a Latin American Feminist Literary Criticism* (Ithaca: Cornell University Press, 1992).
Castro-Klarén, Sara, Sylvia Molloy and Beatriz Sarlo (eds), *Women's Writing in Latin America: An Anthology* (Boulder: Westview Press, 1991).
Catalán, Carlos and Giselle Munizaga, *Políticas culturales estatales bajo el autoritarismo en Chile* (Santiago: CLACSO, 1986).
Chodorow, Nancy, *The Reproduction of Mothering: Psychoanalysis and the Sociology of Gender* (Berkeley: University of California Press, 1978).
Cixous, Hélène, 'The Laugh of the Medusa', trans. by Keith Cohen and Paula Cohen, *Signs*, 1:4, 875–93.
—— 'Sorties', trans. by Ann Liddle, in *New French Feminisms*, ed. by Elaine Marks and Isabelle de Courtivron (Brighton: Harvester, 1981), p. 91.
Collier, Simon, and William F. Sater, *A History of Chile: 1808–1994* (Cambridge: Cambridge University Press, 1996).
Cooper, Sara E. (ed.), *The Ties That Bind: Questioning Family Dynamics and Family Discourse in Hispanic Literature* (Lanham: University Press of America, 2004).
Craske, Nikki, *Women and Politics in Latin America* (Cambridge: Polity Press, 1999).

Cróquer Pedrón, Eleonora, *El gesto de Antígona o la escritura como responsabilidad (Clarice Lispector, Diamela Eltit y Carmen Boullosa)* (Santiago: Cuarto Propio, 2000).

Cuddon, J. A., *The Penguin Dictionary of Literary Terms and Literary Theory*, 3rd edn. (Harmondsworth: Penguin, 1991).

De la Parra, Marco Antonio, *La mala memoria: historia de Chile contemporáneo*, 4th edn (Santiago: Planeta, 1998).

Docherty, Paul (ed.), *Postmodernism: A Reader* (New York: Harvester Wheatsheaf, 1991).

Domínguez, Nora, 'Diamela Eltit: voces de un erotismo marginal', *Cuadernos hispanoamericanos*, 659 (2005), 25–30.

—— and Carmen Perilli (eds), *Fábulas del género. Sexo y escrituras en América Latina* (Rosario: Beatriz Viterbo, 1998).

Donoso, Claudia, 'Tenemos puesto el espejo para el otro lado', *APSI* (1987), 47–8.

Donoso, José, *El lugar sin límites*, 7th edn (Santiago: Alfaguara, 2000).

—— *El obsceno pájaro de la noche*, 2nd edn (Barcelona: Seix Barral, 1971).

Dopico, Ana María, '*Imbunches* and Other Monsters: Enemy Legends and Underground Histories in José Donoso and Catalina Parra', *Journal of Latin American Cultural Studies*, 10 (2001), 325–51.

Dore, Elizabeth (ed.), *Gender Politics in Latin America* (New York: Monthly Review Press, 1997).

Douglas, Mary, *Purity and Danger: An Analysis of the Concepts of Pollution and Taboo* (London: Routledge and Kegan Paul, 1966).

Drake, P. W., and I. Jaksic (eds), *The Struggle for Democracy in Chile: 1982–1990* (Lincoln: University of Nebraska Press, 1991).

Droguett, Carlos, *Eloy* (Santiago: Universitaria, 1995).

Eagleton, Mary (ed.), *Feminist Literary Theory: A Reader*, 2nd edn (Oxford: Blackwell, 1996).

Edwards Renard, Javier, 'Memorias de la sangre', *El Mercurio*, 16 September 2000, section Revista de Libros, p. 3.

Eltit, Diamela, 'CADA 20 años', *Revista de crítica cultural*, 19 (1999), 34–9.

—— 'Consagradas', in *Salidas de madre*, with foreward by Alejandra Rojas (Santiago: Planeta, 1996), pp. 97–104.

—— *Crónica del sufragio femenino en Chile* (Santiago: SERNAM, 1994).

—— 'Cuerpos nómadas', *Hispamérica*, 75 (1996), 3–16.

—— 'Cultura, poder y frontera', *La Época*, 10 June 1990, section Literatura y Libros, pp. 1–2.

—— *Custody of the Eyes*, trans. by Helen Lane and Ronald Christ (Lumen/Sites Books, 2006).

—— *El cuarto mundo*, 2nd edn (Santiago: Seix Barral, 1996).

—— *El padre mío* (Santiago: Francisco Zegers, 1989).

—— *E. Luminata*, trans. with afterword by Ronald Christ (Santa Fe: Lumen, 1997).

—— *Emergencias: escritos sobre literatura, arte y política*, ed. with prologue by Leonidas Morales T. (Santiago: Planeta/Ariel, 2000).

—— *The Fourth World*, trans. with introduction by Dick Gerdes (Lincoln: University of Nebraska Press, 1995).

—— 'Lengua y barrio: la jerga como política de la disidencia', *Revista de crítica cultural*, 14 (1997), 46–51.

—— 'Los bordes de la letra', *Revista de crítica cultural*, 26 (2003), 36–8.

—— *Los trabajadores de la muerte* (Santiago: Seix Barral, 1998).

—— *Los vigilantes* (Santiago: Sudamericana, 1994).

—— *Lumpérica* (Santiago: Ornitorrinco, 1983).

—— *Lumpérica*, trans. by Florence Olivier and Anne de Waele (Paris: Des Femmes, 1993).

—— 'Lumpérica', *CAL* (1979), 14–15.

—— *Mano de obra* (Santiago: Seix Barral, 2002).

—— 'Palabra de mujer', *Lar: revista de literatura*, 11 (1987), 27–8.

—— *Por la patria*, 2nd edn (Santiago: Cuarto Propio, 1995).

—— *Puño y letra* (Santiago: Seix Barral, 2005).

—— *Quart-Monde*, trans. by Alexandra Carrasco (Paris: Christian Bourgois, 1992).

—— *Sacred Cow*, trans. by Amanda Hopkinson (London: Serpent's Tail, 1995).

—— 'Socavada de sed', *Ruptura*, 6 (1982) [no page numbers].

—— 'Una mirada en los intersticios', *Página Abierta*, 69 (1992).

—— *Vaca sagrada* (Buenos Aires: Planeta, 1991).

—— 'Writing and Resisting', trans. by Alfred MacAdam, *Review: Latin American Literature and Arts*, 49 (1994), 19.

—— and Paz Errázuriz, *El infarto del alma* (Santiago: Francisco Zegers, 1994).

—— and Lotty Rosenfeld, 'Un filme subterráneo', *Ruptura*, 6 (1982), p. 10.

Ercilla y Zúñiga, Alonso de, *La Araucana*, selected and with prologue by Antonio de Undurraga, 4th edn (Buenos Aires: Espasa-Calpe, 1964).

Espinosa, Patricia, 'Las voces del dolor', *La Época*, 2 January 1995, section Literatura y Libros, p. 5.

Euripides, *Medea*, trans. by John Harrison with introduction by P. E. Easterling (Cambridge: Cambridge University Press, 1999).

Faulkner, William, *The Sound and the Fury* (New York: Random House, 1929).

Fiol-Matta, Licia, *A Queer Mother For the Nation: The State and Gabriela Mistral* (Minneapolis and London: University of Minnesota Press, 2002).

Fisher, Jo, *Out of the Shadows* (London: Latin American Bureau, 1993).

Forcinito, Ana, 'Cuerpos, memorias e identidades nómadas: Diamela Eltit y la ciudadanía cyborg sudaca', *Revista de estudios hispánicos*, 37:2 (2003), 271–92.

Foucault, Michel, *The Archaeology of Knowledge* (London: Routledge, 1989).

—— *Discipline and Punish: The Birth of the Prison* (New York: Pantheon, 1977).

—— *The History of Sexuality: An Introduction* (Harmondsworth: Penguin, 1990).

—— *Language, Counter-Memory, Practice: Selected Essays and Interviews*, ed. with introduction by Donald F. Bouchard (Oxford: Blackwell, 1977).

—— *The Order of Things: An Archaeology of the Human Sciences* (London: Tavistock, 1970).

—— 'Politics and the Study of Discourse', *Ideology and Consciousness*, 3 (1978), 7–26.

—— *Power/Knowledge: Selected Interviews and Other Writings*, ed. by Colin Gordon (Brighton: Harvester, 1980).

Foxley, Ana María, 'Diamela Eltit: acoplamiento incestuoso', *Hoy*, 421 (1985), 41.

—— 'Diamela Eltit: me interesa todo aquello que esté a contrapelo del poder', *La Época*, 20 November 1988, section Literatura y Libros, pp. 4–5.

Franceschet, Susan, '"State Feminism" and Women's Movements: The Impact of Chile's Servicio Nacional de la Mujer on Women's Activism', *Latin American Research Review*, 38 (2003), 9–40.

Franco, Jean, *Critical Passions: Selected Essays*, ed. with introduction by Mary Louise Pratt and Kathleen Newman (Durham and London: Duke University Press, 1999).

Freud, Sigmund, 'Beyond the Pleasure Principle', in *The Standard Edition of the Complete Psychological Works of Sigmund Freud*, ed. by James Strachey, vol. 18 (London: Hogarth Press, 1955), pp. 7–64.

—— 'The Ego and the Id', in *The Standard Edition of the Complete Psychological Works of Sigmund Freud*, ed. by James Strachey, vol. 19 (London: Hogarth Press, 1961), pp. 12–66.

—— 'Femininity', in *The Standard Edition of the Complete Psychological Works of Sigmund Freud*, ed. by James Strachey, vol. 22 (London: Hogarth Press, 1964), pp. 112–35.

—— 'The Interpretation of Dreams', in *The Standard Edition of the Complete Psychological Works of Sigmund Freud*, ed. by James Strachey, vol 4. (London: Hogarth Press, 1956).

—— 'Mourning and Melancholia', in *The Standard Edition of the Complete Psychological Works of Sigmund Freud*, ed. by James Strachey, vol. 14 (London: Hogarth Press, 1957), pp. 239–58.

—— *Totem and Taboo: Some Points of Agreement between the Mental Lives of Savages and Neurotics*, authorized trans. by James Strachey (London: Routledge, 2001).

Fuss, Diana, *Identification Papers* (New York and London: Routledge, 1995).

Gallop, Jane, *Feminism and Psychoanalysis: The Daughter's Seduction* (London: Macmillan, 1982).

Garabano, Sandra, '*Vaca Sagrada* de Diamela Eltit: del cuerpo femenino al cuerpo de la historia', *Hispamérica*, 73 (1996), 121–7.

—— and Guillermo García-Corales, 'Diamela Eltit', *Hispamérica*, 62 (1992), 65–75.

García-Corales, Guillermo, 'Silencio y resistencia en *Los vigilantes* de Diamela Eltit', *Monographic Review*, 16 (2000), 368–81.

García Lorca, Federico, *Bodas de sangre*, ed. with introduction by Harry Ramsden (Manchester: Manchester University Press, 1980).

—— *Yerma*, ed. with introduction by Robin Warner (Manchester: Manchester University Press, 1994).

García Márquez, Gabriel, *Cien años de soledad*, 8th edn (Madrid: Cátedra, 1997).

Gligo, Agata, '*El cuarto mundo* de Diamela Eltit', *Mensaje*, 377 (1989), 110–11.

—— '*Lumpérica*: un libro excepcional' *Mensaje*, 343 (1985), 417–18.

—— '*Por la patria* de Diamela Eltit', *Mensaje*, 355 (1986), 524–5.

Gómez B., Andrés, 'Diamela Eltit: "Este país está aturdido"', <www.letras.s5.com/eltit3106.htm> [accessed 12 May 2003].

Gómez, Jaime P., 'La representación de la dictadura en la narrativa de Marta Traba, Isabel Allende, Diamela Eltit y Luisa Valenzuela', *Confluencia*, 12 (1997), 89–99.

González Echevarría, Roberto, *Myth and Archive: A Theory of Latin American Narrative* (Cambridge: Cambridge University Press, 1990).

Grau, Olga (ed.), *Ver desde la mujer* (Santiago: La Morada/Cuarto Propio [n.d.]).

—— et al., *Discurso, género y poder: discursos públicos. Chile 1978–1993* (Santiago: LOM/Arcis, [n.d.])

Green, Mary, 'Dialogue with Diamela Eltit', *Feminist Review. Latin America: History, War and Independence*, 79 (2005), 164–71.

—— 'Diamela Eltit: A Gendered Politics of Writing', *New Readings*, 6 (2000) <www.cardiff.ac.uk/euros/newreadings/volume6/greenm.html> [accessed 13 January 2001].

Grosz, Elizabeth, *Jacques Lacan: A Feminist Introduction* (London and New York: Routledge, 1990).

—— *Sexual Subversions: Three French Feminists* (St Leonards: Allen & Unwin, 1989).

Hines, Donetta, '"Woman" and Chile: in Transition', *Letras femeninas*, 28 (2002), 60–76.

Hirsch, Marianne, *The Mother/Daughter Plot: Narrative, Psychoanalysis, Feminism* (Bloomington and Indianapolis: Indiana University Press, 1989).

Holy Bible, The, authorized King James Version (London: Collins, 1933).

Hornblower, Simon, and Anthony Spawforth (eds), *The Oxford Companion to Classical Civilization* (Oxford: Oxford University Press, 1998).

Hornung, Alfred, and Ernstpeter Ruhe (eds), *Postcolonialism and Autobiography* (Amsterdam and Atlanta: Rodopi, 1998).

Howatson, M. C. (ed.), *The Oxford Companion to Classical Literature*, 2nd edn (Oxford: Oxford University Press, 1992).

Huffer, Lynne, *Maternal Pasts, Feminist Futures* (Cambridge: Cambridge University Press, 1998).

Irigaray, Luce, *An Ethics of Sexual Difference*, trans. by Carolyn Burke and Gillian C. Gill (London: Athlone, 1993).

—— 'And the One Doesn't Stir Without the Other', trans. by Hélène Vivienne Wenzel, *Signs*, 7 (1981), 60–7.

—— *The Irigaray Reader*, ed. with introduction by Margaret Whitford (Oxford: Blackwell, 1991).

—— *je, tu, nous: Toward a Culture of Difference*, trans. by Alison Martin (New York and London: Routledge, 1993).

—— *Key Writings* (London and New York: Continuum, 2004).

—— *Sexes and Genealogies*, trans. by Gillian C. Gill (New York: Columbia University Press, 1993).

—— *Speculum of the Other Woman*, trans. by Gillian C. Gill (Ithaca: Cornell University Press, 1985).

—— *This Sex Which is Not One*, trans. by Catherine Porter with Carolyn Burke (Ithaca: Cornell University Press, 1985).

Iser, Wolfgang, *The Act of Reading: A Theory of Aesthetic Response* (London: Routledge & Kegan Paul, 1978).

Jaksic, Iván, *Andrés Bello: Scholarship and Nation-Building in Nineteenth-Century Latin America* (Cambridge: Cambridge University Press, 2001).

Jaquette, Jane S. (ed.), *The Women's Movement in Latin America* (Boulder: Westview Press, 1994).

Jenckes, Kate, 'The Work of Literature and the Unworking of Community or Writing in Eltit's *Lumpérica*', *The New Centennial Review*, 3:1 (2003), 67–80.

Jones, Anny Brooksbank, and Catherine Davies (eds), *Latin American Women's Writing* (Oxford: Clarendon Press, 1996).

Kadir, Djelal, *The Other Writing: Postcolonial Essays in Latin America's Writing Culture* (W. Lafayette: Purdue University Press, 1993).

Kaempfer, Alvaro, 'Las cartas marcadas: política urbana y convivencia textual en *Los vigilantes* de Diamela Eltit', *Confluencia*, 16:2 (2001), 32–45.

Kaminsky, Amy K., *Reading the Body Politic: Feminist Criticism and Latin American Women Writers* (Minneapolis: University of Minnesota Press, 1999).

Kaplan, E. Ann (ed.), *Feminism and Film* (Oxford: Oxford University Press, 2000).

Kawabata, Yasunari, *House of the Sleeping Beauties and other stories*, trans. by Edward Seidensticker (Tokyo: Kodansha International, 1980).

Kirkwood, Julieta, *Ser política en Chile: los nudos de la sabiduría feminista*, 2nd edn (Santiago: Cuarto Propio, 1990).

Klein, Eva, 'La (auto) representación en ruinas: *Lumpérica*, de Diamela Eltit', *Revista Casa de las Américas*, 230 (2003), 130–5.

Klein, Melanie, *The Psycho-Analysis of Children*, authorized trans. by Alex Strachey (London: Virago, 1989).

Kristeva, Julia, *Black Sun*, trans. by Leon Roudiez (New York: Columbia University Press, 1989).

—— *Desire in Language: A Semiotic Approach to Literature and Art*, ed. by Leon S. Roudiez and trans. by Thomas Gora, Alice Jardine and Leon S. Roudiez (New York: Columbia University Press, 1980).

—— *The Kristeva Reader*, ed. by Toril Moi (New York: Columbia University Press, 1986).

—— *New Maladies of the Soul*, trans. by Ross Guberman (New York: Columbia University Press, 1995).

—— *The Portable Kristeva*, ed. by Kelly Oliver (New York: Columbia University Press, 1997).

—— *Powers of Horror: An Essay on Abjection*, trans. by Leon S. Roudiez (New York: Columbia University Press, 1982).

—— *Revolution in Poetic Language*, trans. by Margaret Waller with introduction by Leon S. Roudiez (New York: Columbia University Press, 1984).

—— *Tales of Love*, trans. by Leon S. Roudiez (New York: Columbia University Press, 1987).

Lacan, Jacques, *Écrits. A Selection*, trans. by Alan Sheridan (London: Tavistock, 1977).

Lagos, María Inés, 'Cuerpo y subjetividad en narraciones de Andrea Maturana, Ana María del Río y Diamela Eltit', *Revista chilena de literatura*, 50 (1997), 97–109.

—— (ed.), *Creación y resistencia: la narrativa de Diamela Eltit, 1983–1998*, Serie Monográfica *Nomadías* (Santiago: Universidad de Chile/Cuarto Propio, 2000).

Laplanche, J., and J. B. Pontalis, *The Language of Psycho-Analysis*, trans. by Donald Nicholson-Smith (London: Karnac Books/The Institute of Psycho-Analysis, 1988).

Larraín, Ana María, 'El cuerpo femenino es un territorio moral', *El Mercurio*, 5 January 1992, section Revista de Libros, pp. 3–5.

—— 'El trabajo es la vida y mi vida', *El Mercurio*, 21 May 1989, section Revista de Libros, pp. 1–5.

Lazzara, Michael J., *Diamela Eltit: Conversaciones en Princeton*, PLAS Cuadernos, 5 (Program in Latin American Studies, Princeton University, 2002).

Lértora, Juan Carlos. (ed.), *Una poética de literatura menor: la narrativa de Diamela Eltit* (Santiago: Cuarto Propio, 1993).

Llanos M., Bernadita, 'Emociones, hablas y fronteras en *Los vigilantes*', *Revista Casa de las Américas*, 230 (2003), 126–9.

—— (ed.), *Letras y proclamas: la estética literaria de Diamela Eltit* (Santiago: Cuarto Propio/Denison University, 2006).

Lüttecke, Janet A., '*El Cuarto Mundo* de Diamela Eltit', *Revista Iberoamericana*, 60 (1994), 1081–8.

McCullers, Carson, *The Ballad of the Sad Café* (Harmondsworth: Penguin, 1974).

McNay, Lois, *Foucault and Feminism: Power, Gender and the Self* (Cambridge: Polity Press, 1992).

Marks, Camilo, 'Diamelismo', *Qué Pasa*, 19–26 October 1998 <www.quepasa.cl/revista/1436/25.html> [accessed 12 July 2003].

—— 'Vigilar & castigar', *APSI*, 494 (1995), 36.

Martínez, Luz Ángela, 'La dimensión espacial en "*Vaca sagrada*" de Diamela Eltit: la urbe narrativa', *Revista chilena de literatura*, 49 (1996), 65–81.

Masiello, Francine, *The Art of Transition: Latin American Culture and Neoliberal Crisis* (Durham and London: Duke University Press, 2001).

Méndez Carrasco, Armando (ed.), *Diccionario coa* (Santiago: Nascimento, 1979).

Mistral, Gabriela, *Tala* (Buenos Aires: Losada, 1998).

—— *Desolación – Ternura – Tala – Lagar*, 9th edn (Mexico: Porrúa, 1999).

Mitchell, Juliet, *Psychoanalysis and Feminism* (New York: Random House, 1974).

Moi, Toril, *Sexual-Textual Politics: Feminist Literary Theory* (London: Methuen, 1985).

Montecino, Sonia, *Madres y huachos: alegorías del mestizaje chileno* (Santiago: Sudamericana, 1991).

Morales T., Leonidas (ed.), *Cartas de petición: Chile 1973–1989* (Santiago: Planeta/Ariel, 2000).

—— (ed.), *Conversaciones con Diamela Eltit* (Santiago: Cuarto Propio, 1998).

—— *La escritura de al lado: géneros referenciales* (Santiago: Cuarto Propio, 2001).

—— *Novela chilena contemporánea: José Donoso y Diamela Eltit* (Santiago: Cuarto Propio, 2004).

Moraña, Mabel, 'Diamela Eltit: el espejo roto', *Inti: revista de literatura hispano-americana*, 55–6 (2002), 161–4.

Moulian, Tomás, *Chile actual: anatomía de un mito*, 19th edn (Santiago: LOM/Arcis, 1998).

Mulvey, Laura, *Visual and Other Pleasures* (London: Macmillan, 1989).

Munizaga, Giselle, *El discurso público de Pinochet: un análisis semiológico* (Santiago: CESOC/CENECA, 1988).

Nelson, Alice A., *Political Bodies: Gender, History, and the Struggle for Narrative Power in Recent Chilean Literature* (Lewisburg: Bucknell University Press, 2002).

Nelson Garner, Shirley, Claire Kahane and Madelon Sprengnether (eds), *The (M)other Tongue: Essays in Feminist Psychoanalytic Interpretation* (Ithaca and London: Cornell University Press, 1985).

Neumann, Erich, *The Great Mother: An Analysis of the Archetype* (London: Routledge & Kegan Paul, 1955).

Neustadt, Robert, *CADA DIA: la creación de un arte social* (Santiago: Cuarto Propio, 2001).

—— *(Con)Fusing Signs and Postmodern Positions. Spanish American Performance, Experimental Writing and the Critique of Political Confusion* (New York and London: Garland, 1999).

—— 'Interrogando los signos: conversando con Diamela Eltit', *Inti: revista de literatura hispanoamericana*, 46–7 (1997), 293–305.

Norat, Gisela, *Marginalities: Diamela Eltit and the Subversion of Mainstream Literature in Chile* (Newark: University of Delaware Press, 2002).

O'Barr, Jean F., Deborah Pope, and Mary Wyer (eds), *Ties That Bind: Essays on Mothering and Patriarchy* (Chicago: University of Chicago Press, 1990).

Olea, Raquel, 'La mujer, un tema social de mercado', *Revista de crítica cultural*, 14 (1997), 74–5.

—— 'La redemocratización; mujer, feminismo y política', *Revista de crítica cultural*, 5 (1992), 30–2.

—— *Lengua víbora. Producciones de lo femenino en la escritura de mujeres chilenas* (Santiago: Cuarto Propio, 1998).

—— and Soledad Fariña (eds), *Una palabra cómplice. Encuentro con Gabriela Mistral* (Santiago: Cuarto Propio/ISIS Internacional, 1990).

—— Olga Grau and Francisca Pérez, *El género en apuros. Discursos públicos: cuarta conferencia mundial de la mujer* (Santiago: LOM/La Morada, 2000).

Olivárez, Carlos (ed.), *Nueva narrativa chilena* (Santiago: LOM, 1997).

Oliver, Kelly, *Reading Kristeva: Unravelling the Double-bind* (Bloomington: Indiana University Press, 1993).

Onions, C. T. (ed.), *The Oxford Dictionary of English Etymology* (Oxford: Clarendon Press, 1966).

Oquendo, Carmen L., 'Yo nunca querría ser una vaca sagrada: entrevista con Diamela Eltit', *Nómada: creación, teoría, crítica*, 2 (1995), 113–17.

Orellana, Carlos (ed.), *Chile en la mira: proposiciones y conjuros para sobrellevar el fin de siglo* (Santiago: Planeta, 1999).

Ortega Eliana, *Lo que se hereda no se hurta: ensayos de crítica literaria feminista* (Santiago: Cuarto Propio, 1996).

Ortega, Julio, 'Resistencia y sujeto femenino: entrevista con Diamela Eltit', *La Torre*, 14 (1990), 229–41.

Oyarzún, Kemy, 'Estudios de género: saberes, políticas, dominios', *Revista de crítica cultural*, 12 (1996), 24–9.

Palestros, Sandra, *Mujeres en movimiento: 1973–1989* (Santiago: FLACSO, 1989).

Parada, Alejandra, 'No tengo que disculparme por pensar', *Cosas*, 285, 16 October 1998, pp. 112–15.

Piña, Juan Andrés, *Conversaciones con la narrativa chilena* (Santiago: Los Andes, 1991).

Pinochet Ugarte, Augusto, *Mensaje a la mujer chilena: texto del discurso* (Santiago: Editorial Nacional Gabriela Mistral, 1976).

Pino-Ojeda, Walescka, *Sobre castas y puentes: conversaciones con Elena Poniatowska, Rosario Ferré y Diamela Eltit* (Santiago: Cuarto Propio, 2000).

Posadas, Claudia, 'Un territorio de zozobra: entrevista con Diamela Eltit', <www. ucm.es/info/especulo/numero25/eltit.html> [accessed 15 January 2004].

Pratt, Mary Louise, 'Overwriting Pinochet: Undoing the Culture of Fear in Chile', *Modern Language Quarterly*, 57 (1996), 151–63.

Radcliffe, Sarah A., and Sallie Westwood (eds), *Viva: Women and Popular Protest in Latin America* (London: Routledge, 1993).

Reid, Anna, 'Disintegration, Dismemberment and Discovery of Identities and Histories: Searching the "gaps" for depositories of alternative memory in the narratives of Diamela Eltit and Carmen Boullosa', *Bulletin of Latin American Research*, 17 (1998), 81–92.

Rich, Adrienne, *Of Woman Born: Motherhood as Experience and Institution* (London: Virago, 1981).

Richard, Nelly (ed.), *Arte en Chile desde 1973. Escena de avanzada y sociedad* (Santiago: FLACSO, 1987).

—— 'Cultura, política y democracia', *Revista de crítica cultural*, 5 (1992), 5–7.

—— 'Feminismo, experiencia y representación', *Revista Iberoamericana*, 62 (1996), 733–44.

—— *La estratificación de los márgenes: sobre arte, cultura y política/s* (Santiago: Francisco Zegers, 1989).

—— *La insubordinación de los signos* (Santiago: Cuarto Propio, 1994).

—— *Margins and Institutions: Art in Chile since 1973*, ed. by Paul Foss and Paul Taylor (Melbourne: Art and Text, 1986).

—— 'La problemática del feminismo en los años de la transición en Chile', <www. globalcult.org.ve/pub/Clacso2/richard.pdf> 227–39 [accessed 12 April 2003].

—— *Masculino/femenino: prácticas de la diferencia y cultura democrática* (Santiago: Francisco Zegers, 1993).

—— 'Reescrituras, sobreimpresiones: las protestas de mujeres en la calle', *Revista de crítica cultural*, 18 (1999), 17–20.

—— *Residuos y metáforas: ensayos de crítica cultural sobre el Chile de la Transición* (Santiago: Cuarto Propio, 1998).

—— 'Revueltas femeninas y transgresiones de símbolos', *Revista de crítica cultural*, 21 (2000), 24–6.

—— 'Síntoma y arabescos', *Revista de crítica cultural*, 10 (1995), 59–60.

—— 'Trama urbana y fugas utópicas', *Revista de crítica cultural*, 19 (1999), 28–33.

Rivera, Anny, *Notas sobre movimiento social y arte en el régimen autoritario (1973–83)* (Santiago: CENECA, 1983).

Rojas, Manuel, *Hijo de ladrón*, 29th edn (Santiago: Zig-Zag, 1998).

Romero, Graciela, 'Diamela Eltit: en la sexualidad la estamos errando', *Paula*, July 1990, pp. 62–3.

Rubin Suleiman, Susan, *Subversive Intent: Gender, Politics and the Avant-Garde* (Cambridge, MA: Harvard University Press, 1990).

Ruddick, Sara, *Maternal Thinking: Towards a Politics of Peace* (Boston: Beacon Press, 1989).

Santos, Susana, 'Diamela Eltit: una ruptura ejemplar', *Feminaria*, 5 (1992), 7–9.

Sarduy, Severo, *Cobra*, trans. by Suzanne Jill Levine (New York: E. P. Dutton, 1975).

Sawicki, Jana, *Disciplining Foucault: Feminism, Power and the Body* (London: Routledge, 1991).

Shakespeare, William, *Macbeth*, ed. by Kenneth Muir (London: Methuen, 1964).

Sommer, Doris, *Foundational Fictions: The National Romances of Latin America* (Berkeley: University of California Press, 1991).

—— *Proceed with Caution, When Engaged with Minority Writing in the Americas* (Cambridge, MA: Harvard University Press, 1999).

Sotomayor, Aurea María, 'Tres caricias: una lectura de Luce Irigaray en la narrativa de Diamela Eltit', *MLN: Modern Language Notes*, 115 (2000), 299–322.

Spivak, Gayatri Chakravorty, 'Can the Subaltern Speak?', in *Colonial Discourse and Postcolonial Theory: A Reader*, ed. by Patrick Williams and Laura Chrisman (London: Harvester Wheatsheaf, 1993), pp. 66–111.

Sprengnether, Madelon, *The Spectral Mother: Freud, Femininity and Psychoanalysis* (Ithaca and London: Cornell University Press, 1990).

Subercaseaux, Bernardo, *La industria editorial y el libro en Chile (1930–1984)*, 2nd edn (Santiago: CENECA, 1984).

—— *Transformaciones de la crítica literaria en Chile: 1960–1982* (Santiago: CENECA, 1983).

Swanson, Philip, *The New Novel in Latin America: Politics and Popular Culture after the Boom* (Manchester: Manchester University Press, 1995).

Swinburn, Daniel, 'Se requieren nuevos imaginarios en torno a lo femenino', <www.letras.s5.com/eltit260702.htm> [accessed 15 January 2004].

Tafra, Silvia, *Diamela Eltit: el rito de pasaje como estrategia textual* (Santiago: RIL, 1998).

Taylor, Diana, *Disappearing Acts: Spectacles of Gender and Nationalism in Argentina's Dirty War* (Durham and London: Duke University Press, 1997).

Tierney-Tello, Mary Beth, *Allegories of Transgression and Transformation: Experimental Fiction by Women Writing Under Dictatorship* (New York: State University of New York Press, 1996).

Unamuno, Miguel de, *Cómo se hace una novela*, ed. by Paul R. Olson (Madrid: Guadarrama, 1977).

Uribe T., Olga, 'Breves anotaciones sobre las estrategias narrativas en *Lumpérica*, *Por la patria* y *El cuarto mundo* de Diamela Eltit', *Hispanic Journal*, 16 (1995), 21–37.

Valdés, Adriana, *Composición de lugar: escritos sobre cultura* (Santiago: Universitaria, 1995).

Valdés, Teresa, *Las mujeres y la dictadura militar en Chile* (Santiago: FLACSO, 1987).

Valente, Ignacio, 'Diamela Eltit: una novela experimental', *El Mercurio*, 25 March 1984, section E, p. 3.

—— 'El cuerpo es un horror y es una gloria', *El Mercurio*, 21 May 1989, section Revista del Libro, pp. 1–4.

—— 'Una novela de masoquismo y sangre: *Vaca Sagrada*', *El Mercurio*, 5 January 1992, section Revista de Libros, p. 4.

Whitford, Margaret, *Luce Irigaray: Philosophy in the Feminine* (London and New York: Routledge, 1991).

Williams, Raymond Leslie (ed.), *The Novel in the Americas* (Niwot: The University Press of Colorado, 1992).

INDEX